Choices in Modern Jewish Thought

Choices in Modern Jewish Thought

A PARTISAN GUIDE

Eugene B. Borowitz

Behrman House, Inc.
West Orange, New Jersey

© Copyright 1983, 1995 by Eugene B. Borowitz
Published by Behrman House, Inc.,
235 Watchung Ave.
West Orange, New Jersey 07052

Cover design by Howard Levy Design
Typeset by AeroType, Inc.

Library of Congress Cataloging in Publication Data

Borowitz, Eugene B.
    Choices in modern Jewish thought : a partisan guide /
Eugene B. Borowitz. — [2nd ed.]
        p.   cm.
    Includes bibliographical references and index.
    ISBN 087441-581-0
    1. Judaism—20th century.   I. Title.
BM565.B67   1995
296.3′09′04—dc20   95-2583
                                                                    CIP

MANUFACTURED IN THE UNITED STATES OF AMERICA

In appreciation of

Sh'ma,

a journal of Jewish responsibility

I wish to pay tribute to three friends, without whom it could not have been founded or maintained in its devotion to the virtues of Jewish pluralism despite our serious differences of opinion on political, social, and religious issues.

SEYMOUR SIEGEL, ל״צז   MICHAEL WYSCHOGROD
                    and, in particular, to
                    ARNOLD JACOB WOLF

Contents

PART IV *The Contemporary Agenda*

PART V *Concluding Reflections*

Preface

In few other periods have so many important, divergent theories of Judaism been proposed as in the twentieth century. This book celebrates the achievement of the thinkers who responded to the unprecedented challenge modernity issued to Jewish faith. Other ages have, without doubt, been intellectually troubled; few have known the depth and range of the difficulties modern Jews confront. Large numbers in our community doubt God's existence, are skeptical about the revelation of the Torah, and cannot believe that the Jewish people has a unique role in human history. Not since Rabbinic Judaism became the accepted standard for Jewish living has so great a proportion of our community been unobservant of the law, ignorant of our heritage, and only mildly discontented with such minimal Jewishness.

Many practical efforts have been made to rectify this situation: better education, the beautification of religious services, group involvement, community organization, and political activism. These set the positive patterns of everyday Jewish life. They produce the facts which we hope will one day be the basis of our place in Jewish history. As the stuff of our Jewish existence, they are reasonably well known, carefully observed, and often commented upon.

The intellectual efforts to respond to our troubling situation, being abstract and academic, remain in the background of Jewish self-consciousness if they are present at all. To many, the last significant Jewish philosophy or theology—I shall use the terms loosely and interchangeably—was produced by Maimonides and his contemporaries. People who hold this view assume that knowing the Jewish intellectual classics of the Middle Ages or the Talmud (from an earlier period) equips one to fashion a philosophy of Judaism that will speak to our situation. They do not appreciate the unique difficulties which modern science and culture raise for all religions and particularly for a minority faith. Yet Philo mastered Hellenistic thought to expound

ix

Judaism to his first-century contemporaries in Alexandria, Saadiah Gaon in the tenth century reacted to the Kalam philosophy of Islam, and Maimonides later utilized the newly rediscovered ideas of Aristotle. These efforts were undertaken to make Judaism intelligible within the context of a particular time and place. Clearly, the responsibility inherent in this chain of Jewish theological tradition did not disappear some centuries ago.

Modern Jews have had an unusually creative group of philosophic pioneers. Though their names are not well known to the masses of Jews, their ideas provided the framework by which modern Jews have thought about their Judaism and, often, the patterns by which they have chosen to live it. To this day the sermons and lectures and magazine articles and popular books that make up the bulk of American Jewish intellectuality derive from six main streams of thought. The thinkers who created these generative systems deserve to be better known. Their ideas deserve the compliment of being directly confronted rather than communicated through the teaching of disciples' disciples, who may no longer know the source of their fervent proclamations. Besides, for those who enjoy good thinking, the conceptual elegance of our great modern philosophers is itself a source of much pleasure. Studying them, even when one disagrees with what they propounded, stimulates one to think more keenly about one's own Judaism. If we desire to transcend them, we must first rise to their level of cultural sophistication and Jewish commitment.

Happily, I have been able to spend much of my life working in the discipline of contemporary Jewish thought. I have had personal contact with five of the thinkers whose work has been significant enough to be discussed at chapter length. I also continue to be involved in the contemporary discussions described in the latter part of this book. I make no claim to be writing here as an objective historian of ideas. My own theological position has inevitably influenced my choice of themes to be analyzed and has determined the criticisms I level. Nonetheless, as I was writing, I tried to distinguish carefully between giving a fair hearing to each thinker and persuading you that my evaluation of each is the proper one. Should you disagree with my personal judgment of the continuing value of these thinkers' works, I trust you will still find my description of their philosophies reasonably accurate.

My position on a number of the issues treated here has not substantially changed over the years. Hence I have felt free to utilize for this book various of my previous writings, which are now out of print, always with careful revision. For permission to do so, I am grateful to the Westminster Press.

Over the years my admiration for Seymour Rossel's editorial and publishing skills have grown, accompanied by a friendship that I prize. He was nice enough to propose that I undertake this project and his sure hand has improved it greatly. I joyfully acknowledge his helpfulness. I am grateful also to Louis Jacobs for his perceptive and generous reading of this manuscript, which enabled me to correct several errors in it. My thanks are also extended to John Simmons for the high sensitivity and fine hand he brought to the final editing of this work.

The process of bringing together the experience of three decades or so has made me freshly conscious of the passage of time and ever more thankful to God who has enabled me, once again, to see a long and demanding project through to completion.

בָּרוּךְ אַתָּה יְיָ. אֱלֹהֵינוּ מֶלֶךְ הָעוֹלָם. אוֹזֵר יִשְׂרָאֵל בִּגְבוּרָה:

"We bless You, *Adonai*, our God, Ruler of the universe, who girds Israel with power."

EUGENE B. BOROWITZ

Preface to the Second Edition

I am grateful for the positive reception this book has received from academic and rabbinic colleagues over the years. It has been a particular joy that even lay readers have found it valuable in pondering their Jewish faith. Time has not stood still in the world of Jewish thought, however, having taken from us several of our luminaries but also enriching us with the burgeoning of two movements, mysticism and feminism, as well as some very thoughtful new writing. I was therefore most grateful to Behrman House for its enthusiastic response to my suggestion that this work undergo revision. I greatly appreciate Ellen Umansky's willingness to do the new chapter on feminist theology (and for her patient waiting as I tried to complete my material), and Joshua Saltzman's most useful critical reading of my new chapters. May God's blessing rest on this enterprise.

E. B. B.

PART I
Setting
the
Context

1

The Challenge of Modernity to Judaism

JEWISH belicf is closcly tied to Jewish history. From ancient times, even as the Bible makes plain, Jewish thought has emanated largely from reflection on the mixed personal and social experience of the Jewish people. Modern Jewish thought is the continuing response to the special problems posed by the emancipation of the Jews from their previously segregated social situation. Our proper point of departure, then, is the historical background that forms the context for modern Jewish thinking.

For purposes of condensation, the development of Jewish religious life before the modern era can be broken into four major stages.

First, the most fundamental phase, was the making of the Covenant. The one God of the universe made an eternal covenant with all humanity, as specified in the story of Noah, but the Bible recounts that humanity remained obdurate and disobedient. So God called one man, Abraham, to be specially loyal to God so that, through him and his descendants, all humankind might one day come to know—that is, to obey—God. In return, God promised to make Abraham's family a mighty nation, to give them a land and to protect them through history. Self, society, and responsibility are thus fundamental elements of Jewish faith. In the Exodus, the Hebrews saw God's Covenant promise spectacularly fulfilled; and at Sinai they received the Torah— the teachings and traditions—which would structure their lives in lioliness, as individuals and as a nation settled in their own land.

Judaism centers on that experience of election, promise, redemption, and mission. Jewish liturgy reviews it every day; the Jewish calendar follows it each year. Believing Jews live in the reality of the Covenant.

The second formative period for the Hebrew spirit occurred on the land. There was settlement, kingdom, the Temple, social division and decline, prophecy, the loss of ten tribes, the conquest of Judah and destruction of the Temple, Exile, and, most startling, there was a return and the Temple was rebuilt. Hebrew saga and legend, law and history, prophecy and wisdom, apocalyptic and story, all found fixed verbal form in this period. The Covenant was amplified by this historic experience and climaxed in the dream of a messianic day when history would be fulfilled in the universal, free service of God.

Jews do not consider the so-called intertestamental literature sacred, yet the era in which it was written constitutes the beginning of the third formative period. Some centuries separate the completion of most of the biblical books from the written teachings of the Rabbis. The Rabbis are the authorities cited in compiling the Mishnah traditions of the first two centuries of the Common Era and the next three centuries of talmudic commentaries on them. The Rabbis, inheritors of the tradition of the Pharisees, framed the Jewish religion as we know it today. Modern Jews read the Bible through their eyes, celebrate and mourn and pray and study in the patterns they created. Thus, when the Second Temple was destroyed, the Rabbis, responding to the event in terms of the Babylonian precedent, created the synagogue style that remembers the Temple but has no sacrifices and whose service any learned Jew may lead. Rabbinic law, *halachah*, intertwines with spiritual teaching, *aggadah*, and together they create an emphasis on democracy and education characteristic of all succeeding Judaism.

In this Rabbinic period, the Jewish people were already scattered across the civilized Western world. This Diaspora (from the Greek word for dispersal) existence of approximately the next 1,400 years had major spiritual consequences, many of them negative. Islam and Christianity debased and degraded Jews. After the First Crusade, European Christians increasingly attacked, robbed, expelled, forcibly converted, and murdered Jews. "Ghetto" and "*shtetl*" are relatively recent terms, and yet they testify to the duration of Jewish segregation. Jews came to see themselves as God's suffering servant in history, and they knew that their defamers, by their very persecution of others, could not be God's chosen. Positively, Jews learned from those cultures that permitted their participation. They began to systematize Judaism in philosophic fashion and developed the speculative mysticism called "*kabbalah*".

After more than a millennium of ostracism and persecution, Jews were astounded when the French Revolution signaled a call for political freedom in Europe, a freedom eventually extended even to Jews. Thus began the modern period of Jewish history. To clarify the nature of the challenges it posed, it is necessary to see the contrast between pre- and post-Emancipation Jewry.

From Pariah to Citizen

The segregated pattern of medieval Jewish existence is justly symbolized by the ghetto. In its standard form, from about the year 1500, the Jewish residential quarter of a city was walled in and its gates were locked from sundown to sunrise. Many scholars think that the imposition of the ghetto may be traced to the Jewish practice of voluntarily living together in close community for protection from the Gentile and for companionship in maintaining the Jewish way of life. Thus, the *shtetl* of Eastern Europe was not created by an imposed physical barrier and the *mellahs* of North Africa were often unwalled. Nonetheless, these Jews, too, lived in isolated and relatively self-contained communities. The image of the locked and guarded ghetto gates of Western Europe poignantly sums up centuries of legislated disabilities among Moslems and Christians alike: the businesses Jews might not enter, the social activities they might not engage in, the hats or badges or other distinguishing marks of Jewishness they were made to wear, the conversionist sermons they were forced to attend, the riots and pogroms to which they were subjected.

When modern Jews read of the conditions under which Jews lived during this period, they visualize an extraordinarily trying existence that makes it all the more surprising that, as far as we can tell, the typical Jew then lived with great integrity of self. In Babylonia, Franco-Germany, or Poland during the Moslem conquests, the Crusades, or the Cossack pogroms, Jews felt no conflict or ambiguity about their identity. Society had a definite place for them as Jews, negative though it was, and they had a countervailing inner certainty that gave Jewishness great worth and deep significance. They knew they were God's own people, chosen for a separate existence and dispersed by God among the nations; God loved them and their people and would ultimately vindicate their suffering for God's sake. Believing Jews possessed an inalienable dignity and lived with high human nobility.

With the European Emancipation of the Jews, beginning about the time of the French Revolution, the lengthy medieval era of the Jews came to an end. Imposed segregation ceased and, to use the symbol once again, the ghetto walls came down. The Jew was admitted into society as an equal and given full rights as a citizen. That, in theory, was what the Emancipation meant.

Yet there are immediate and important qualifications. The Emancipation was not one dramatic event, but a long process, proceeding by fits and starts, and with great regional variation. The United States, having little tradition to defend, gave the Jews freedom almost from the beginning. England, France, the German states, and the Austro-Hungarian Empire were much more liberal than the principalities and nations of Eastern Europe. In Eastern Europe the Emancipation was tediously slow, to the extent, as some have argued, that it hardly took place at all. And in North Africa it was only where the French took over at the beginning of the twentieth century that there was any equality for the Jews. In more backward Moslem countries there was none. Moreover, one can hardly say the emancipatory process has ever, anywhere, been completed. Many Jews still find themselves facing social walls and psychic gates. And Jews in some countries live with a constant sense of threat.

Individual Rights as a Jewish Problem

The revolution in the social status of Jews ended their degradation but ironically also destroyed their sure sense of self. After the disastrous

Catholic-Protestant religious wars, the question of belief was increasingly separated from the political realm and assigned to the area of private activity. The European state began to conceive of itself less as a Christian entity than as a secular one, neutral to the private religions of its citizens and tolerant of all faiths. That is why Jews could properly be allowed to participate in it. By contrast, Jews in feudal times had of necessity been outsiders, for they could not swear the Christian oaths that tied one level of society to another.

In the modern world the only interest that the state, as such, came to have in people's religion was whether it prevented or encouraged them to be loyal citizens. When in 1806, Napoleon, in full imperial grandeur, summoned the Grand Sanhedrin (a council of elders) to speak for the French Jewish community, he wanted assurance that Jewish religious faith, privately held, did not interfere with civic responsibility as publicly enacted. Three of the dozen questions Napoleon placed before the Jewish notables in March 1807 set forth this issue:

> No. 4. In the eyes of Jews, are Frenchmen not of the Jewish religion considered as brothers or strangers?
>
> No. 5. What conduct does Jewish law prescribe toward Frenchmen not of the Jewish religion?
>
> No. 6. Do the Jews born in France and treated by the law as French citizens acknowledge France as their country? Are they bound to defend it? Are they bound to obey the laws and follow the directions of the civil code?

The Sanhedrin had little difficulty (except in the case of one question regarding intermarriage) in giving Napoleon what he wanted. They said, in effect, that Judaism, like Protestantism or Catholicism, is a spur to good citizenship, and being Jewish is, like being Christian, only another way of being personally religious and therefore is a legitimate identity in a modern state.

This transformation of the Jewish position in society that seemed so natural was also the beginning of the divided Jewish self. In a secular nation, rights are given to individuals not groups. In the medieval world, Moslem or Christian, the Jews had a fixed place in society *as a community*. Individual Jews received their right to live in a given locale by virtue of being members of the local Jewish community. If the Jewish community did not acknowledge them, the Gentile society could treat them as outlaws.

Those rationalists who fought for Jewish equality in post-Revolutionary France had no doubt that the rights were to be granted on a personal not a communal basis. In 1789, Mirabeau denounced the idea that Jews or anyone else could be a nation within the French nation. Clermont Tonnere, another great defender of Jewish rights, put the thesis in its classic form: "To the Jews as a nation we must deny everything. To the Jews as individuals we must grant everything." In the secular state, the Jew no longer had to be a member of the Jewish community in order to have a place in things. Rights came by virtue of being a citizen.

Society now taught the Jews that they were basically citizens. They might be Jewish in private, less extensive areas of everyday life if they so wished. The freedom granted was extraordinary but the conditions created a split in the Jewish soul. One had one's modern and one's Jewish lives. How to relate them intellectually emerged as the continuing problem of modern Jewish thought.

Appeal of Modernity; the Problems of Being Jewish

The modern Jew, having been emancipated, could not now easily justify Jewishness on the grounds of the Gentiles' inhumanity. Rather, as Jews took advantage of the opportunities offered by the Emancipation, as they wore the society's clothes, spoke its language, attended its schools, mastered its culture, benefited from its economy, they could not help but be impressed. The *goyim* were not so bad as they once had seemed.

Self-segregation no longer made sense. The emancipated life and Jewish values, it appeared, seemed to fit together very well. Only some such sense of basic affinity explains, on the intellectual level, why Jews everywhere avidly took advantage of the new freedom when it was offered, despite some pockets of resistance to modernity—the Hasidim, for example. Overwhelmingly, Jews sensed that there was something sufficiently worthy about Western civilization to enable them to embrace it fully. Indeed, a new question was raised: If modern culture is so acceptable, why bother being Jewish?

The attractions of modernity were all the more glittering when contrasted to the realities involved in asserting one's Jewishness. It might be permitted, but it alienated one culturally and handicapped one personally. The Jewish religion seemed to smell of the ghetto. Christianity, however, was an active part of Western civilization, endemic to its art, its music, its architecture.

In the early decades of the nineteenth century there was a steady movement of Jews converting to Christianity. It was the impetus of losing such Jews as Heinrich Heine that forced Jewish thinkers to action. Intuitively, they knew that modernity did not imply Christianity. Within a generation or two they made the basic reforms in Jewish education, worship, and general life style that showed how, on a practical level, one could accommodate Jewishness to modern culture. That initial spasm of self-transformation is associated mostly with the Reform Jews of Germany, but Jewish modernity is not the product of any one movement or any single charismatic leader. It is the creative response of an entire community to a new social situation, and—as befits a people of such diversity and individuality—it has taken many forms.

The social adjustments Jews made as a result of their emancipation only exacerbated the basic dilemma of modern Jewish existence. Without these transformations, there would be great difficulty remaining both Jewish and modern. Yet the very act of adaptation acknowledges values in the general culture, thereby making being Jewish at all problematic. As it happened, an even more specialized historical situation appertained for the Jews in America.

Latecomers to Emancipation

For most of American Jewry, emancipation has come only in the last few generations. The great majority are descendants of immigrants from Eastern European countries that never permitted free Jewish integration into their societies. Leaving an essentially segregated, almost medieval, way of life, they came to one of the most technically advanced and democratically organized countries in the world. To be sure, the more emancipated Western Jews, largely from German communities, came by the tens of thousands to these shores in the period from 1840 to 1880. And a minority of the Eastern European Jews who arrived in the United States at the rate of 100,000 and more each year (the war years excepted) until 1924 had been educated in *gymnasia* or at universities, while others had made their way into the world of general literature or politics. Nonetheless, most of these families did not come from emancipated Europe but were, so to speak, fresh from the ghetto.

The immigrant generation before World War I arrived so bound up with Jewish values and emotional patterns that no matter how American their lifestyle became, it was still quite patently Jewish at its roots. Today, looking back at the various forms of humanism or cosmopolitanism that they adopted, we see them less as modern universalists than as secularized Jewish types. Even in radical defiance of Jewish tradition, they somehow showed themselves to be authentically Jewish.

That did not carry over to the second generation, for whom to be a Jew smacked of clinging to the immigrant status they were most eager to leave behind. Young American Jews in the generation before World War II carried out a cultural exodus, fleeing the memories of the ghetto and its mores in a passionate effort to be fully American. They responded to anti-Semitism by seeking invisibility and protective camouflage. They gladly abandoned the Judaism and Jewish style that they felt stigmatized them.

A Community Accepted, Accepts Itself

After World War II, a highly positive attitude toward Jewishness characterized most Jews. Two stages may be seen in the emergence and development of this reversal. First, in the period from 1945 to 1967 expanded freedom made possible a joy in Jewishness that, at its heights, bordered on illusion. Second, in the period from the Israeli Six-Day War in 1967 to the Israeli-Egyptian peace treaty, a series of harsh realities radicalized the Jewish social situation and thus turned Jewish identity from a possible option into an appealing way to live. The earlier, postwar era was characterized by a new sense of Jewish at-homeness in America and a sense that the democracy World War II sought to preserve had begun to function properly. Thus, anti-Semitism faded from the public scene, and such anti-Semites as appeared remained on the fringes of society. Despite their noise, they attracted few followers. Through the mid-1960's, sociologists reported that many young American Jews had never had firsthand contact with anti-Semitism, not even by word of mouth, much less by physical act. At the same time, educationally, economically, and culturally, postwar America welcomed the participation of Jews—and a small-scale miracle took place. The outcasts of a previous era achieved money, status, success, and power to an extent utterly unanticipated in the Jewish community in the late 1930's.

The disproportionate Jewish benefits from the general American economic boom had an ironic side. In the Depression years vocational experts regularly tried to get the Jewish community to abandon its abnormal economic concentration on white-collar and professional occupations. Twenty years later, the new economy demanded the sort of educated, risk-taking, entrepreneurial style that Jewish culture and experience had created. As a result, Jews became one of the wealthiest religio-ethnic groups in the United States. With that came the emergence of Jews in every area of cultural activity. Not only were there more Jewish writers, artists, and professors than ever before, but now they made no secret of their Jewishness—indeed, they often utilized it in their work. By the mid-1960's there was hardly a field where American Jews had not made major contributions and come to positions of leadership.

Being Jewish as an Attractive Life Option

The effect this had on the inner life of the Jew is difficult to over-estimate. Despite Sartre's famous definition of Jewishness as merely a status imposed by society, American Jewry discovered that the non-

Jew no longer served the role of keeping Jews Jewish. In America, one really had a right "even" to be a Jew. This acceptability caused American Jews to see themselves as the first truly free generation of Diaspora Jewry. Some American Jewish thinkers even began to discuss the new freedom as a special peril to Jewish existence. With little anti-Semitism to stand in the way, Jews were free to drift away from the Jewish people. In America, with its pervasive secularity, it was even unnecessary to convert to Christianity to become fully identified with the majority. Already then the increasing rate of intermarriage made the new acceptance of Jews something of a mixed blessing.

The same freedom to give up their Jewishness also made it possible for Jews to choose consciously to be Jewish. That is, rather than being a biological and cultural accident, being Jewish now became a matter of personal decision about how one wanted to live one's life. What began as a fact of birth became an act of existential self-determination. One unexpected result of the new social ease was that noticeable numbers of Jews were positive enough about the emerging American Jewish life style that they were consciously choosing it for themselves. There were not many such newly self-affirming Jews but they were so radical a contrast to the negativeness of Jewish life thirty years before that they were a significant communal phenomenon. And they were the vanguard of the larger number who in the succeeding period made their Jewishness an essential part of their lives.

This process of social acceptance and self-affirmation was so dynamic that it created a special variety of American-Jewish euphoria. Suddenly it seemed as if the community might be entering upon the Golden Age of American Jewry. Much of the shock of what followed and a good deal of the high fearfulness it engendered were the result of these exalted notions American Jews developed about themselves and their place in society.

Rise of Self-Conscious Jewish Ethnicity

Then the time of radicalization began, and the Six-Day War, in both positive and negative ways, dramatically heightened what was at stake in being a Jew. In June 1967, Jewish ethnicity surfaced in a way that no one had ever anticipated. That American Jews had some feeling for the State of Israel was never a question. But no one believed such emotions would prompt significant action or be felt by marginal members of the community. On both accounts, the spontaneous, emotional, activist, nearly universal response of American Jews proved the skeptics wrong. With the Six-Day War began a radical shift in American Jewish self-consciousness. This phenomenon has usually been explained in terms of the hold of the State of Israel on world Jewry and the needs of Jews to assuage their guilt over the Holocaust. After nearly twenty years of exis-tence, the State of Israel had come to mean far more to most Jews than they realized. These feelings were heightened by anxiety that the war might result in a second Holocaust. American Jews in par-ticular were freshly conscious of their indifference to the suffering of European Jews during the 1940's, and the importance of the State of Israel as a positive response to human barbarity. The world-wide attention given to the trial of Adolf Eichmann (1960–1962) brought home the lesson that ordinary people, merely by doing what they are told and by not taking a stand against evil, do the demonic work that degrades humankind. Guilty and caring, American Jews were moved by the crisis of the Six-Day War to act as Jews with a directness and commitment they had never shown before. And in due course, these actions inestimably raised their Jewish self-consciousness.

The Six-Day War precipitated what two decades of sociological shift had brought to readiness. Significant was the new American atti-tude toward ethnicity. With blacks showing the way, various Ameri-can groups had begun vigorously asserting their democratic right to maintain and enhance group identity. This disparagement of the melting-pot theory of cultural assimilation encouraged Jews to be "more Jewish." The Jewish community learned the legitimacy of using political pressure and public campaigns to protect their ethnic inter-ests. Jews now found themselves, for the first time, marching and demonstrating on behalf of the State of Israel, Soviet Jewry, and other causes.

Anti-Semitism Again Becomes a Factor in Identity

This shift in Jewish ethnic self-awareness was made more effective by two negative forces. The first of these was the American Jew's re-awakened sense of anti-Semitism. For most American Jews, anti-Semitism has again become a possibility, perhaps even a threat—something that in the glow of the mid-1960's appeared unthinkable. In the critical period from the closing of the Strait of Tiran to the outbreak of the Six-Day War, the United States government did nothing to forestall the threat to Israel's existence—despite the assurances it had given that it would back freedom of passage through the strait. The State of Israel was left to its own fate, and American Jews felt that they had been abandoned by their own government.

Of course, such aloofness is not anti-Semitism. The move was prompted not by any hatred of the Jews but by calculating American self-interest. Yet in that reckoning, the fate of the Jews was not very important. If necessary, they would—as in the days of the Holocaust—be sacrificed. In the face of such a self-serving diplomacy, American Jews sensed that they, as Jews, were still outsiders to America. This realization was the more traumatic for it came hard upon a period in which American and Jewish interests seemed closely intertwined.

The reaction of the official Christian bodies in those critical days was similarly disheartening. Despite direct appeals, almost no Christian organization spoke out on behalf of the State of Israel. The hopes raised by a decade or more of Christian official pronouncements rejecting anti-Semitism and by the joint work undertaken in many fields of social welfare, particularly civil rights, were shattered. And here one might suspect subterranean prejudice against Jews for stubbornly remaining Jews.

Those wounds could not easily heal in the atmosphere of confrontation that characterized American politics well into the 1970's. With minority groups actively seeking their rights, particularly in the great urban areas, the Jewish middle class found itself increasingly threatened. Particularly as blacks pressured to get a responsive educational program, reparatory job opportunities, and a humane standard of housing, it was often the Jews who stood in the place they were determined to occupy. Worse, there seemed a good likelihood that the established Christian power groups would sacrifice Jewish interests as the cheapest way of keeping blacks from insurrection.

The urban crisis gradually became less frightening but the threats against the State of Israel did not. Until the signing of the Israeli–Egyptian peace treaty, American Jews lived with a constant sense of Jewish vulnerability. The cruelty of terrorism, the international isolation of the State of Israel, American pressures on the Israelis to sacrifice their understanding of their security, the bombings of synagogues in Europe, and the swastika daubings in the United States—all these combined to give a powerful if negative reason for American Jews to think of themselves in terms of their people and its peculiar destiny.

Redressing the Balance Between Judaism and Modernity

As Jewish self-concern stayed high, the passionate modern Jewish concern with Western culture substantially lessened. In this Jews were not alone. They shared the identity crisis that other Americans have undergone. For one, there was the widespread loss of morale, for which the Vietnam War has largely been held to blame; but there have been other causes as well: the dehumanizing effect of population growth and technology; the failure of character in the face of affluence and social permissiveness; the great expectations of American destiny; and the fearful revelations of American venality and violence. In a time of extraordinary human stress there has been no moral force in the culture strong enough to find new insight or provide a sense of noble endurance, much less of human triumph. To the contrary, it is the undeniable reality of a pervasive amorality in individuals and collectives—economic and political alike—that has smashed the old reliable image of America as good and ethical, if often ineffectual; and it has left much of America cynical.

America's failure of national self-confidence had a special effect on Jews. The truth is that for most Jews the American way had become the real faith, the effective Torah, by which they lived. In their amalgam of being Jewish and American, Americanism had become dominant. Now, as American Jewry's operative "faith" collapsed, the possibility of a serious return to one's Jewish roots became more attractive. This rarely involved a total turn from one milieu to the other—it was no migration back to the ghetto. Instead it was the possibility of a new mix of the American and Jewish ways of life. Perhaps the subordination of one's Jewishness was wrong and being Jewish ought to play more of a role in one's life. Some suggested a reversal of the old priorities, making one's Jewishness the foundation of one's existence.

In the 1970's a minority of Jews began actively searching for a new sense of Jewish identity. The movement was largely inchoate but its characteristic social form was the *havurah*, the small face-to-face Jewish group, and its major document, *The Jewish Catalog*, a widely circulated series of volumes that give detailed instructions on how one might fill one's life with Jewish practice and spirit. In a community previously so dedicated to social integration, this was a surprising development. An even more utterly unexpected aspect of it was the effort of some of these Jews to center their Jewishness on personal piety. Belief once more became a matter of Jewish concern. That led a number of searchers to Orthodoxy, while others sought a liberal if recognizably traditional way of living with their Jewish faith. This shift in consciousness is essential in understanding the consequences of the discussion of the Holocaust in Jewish thought.

Beyond Ideology to a Philosophy of Judaism

During the course of these two centuries of emancipation, Jews have responded more in a social than an intellectual fashion. There is a substantial difference between the ideological position of the various Jewish religious movements and what may loosely be called the fully developed philosophies of Judaism. Thus, one may be tempted to try to divide modern Jewish religious thought among Orthodox, Conservative, Reform, and other points of view. Most movements have an ideology, a platform of ideas on which they stand, thus giving their organization some intellectual content. On rare occasions, when a group originates in response to an intellectual plea, it may be highly ideological, as certain Marxist splinter groups or artistic circles have been. Most groups, however, are essentially programmatic in that they appeal to people because of what they suggest to do, or how they suggest to act, in a given situation. If they are to grow and thus extend their ranks, they must appeal to people of different temperaments and concerns. They therefore keep ideological definition to a minimum. This deemphasis on ideology leads to continual identity crises of successful movements as they make desperate efforts to explain what they uniquely stand for while not losing too many adherents in the process. This has been a primary problem in the Zionist movement, but it affects Jewish religious organizations as well.

One intellectual matter does divide Orthodox Jews from non-Orthodox or liberal Jews: God's revelation of the Torah, particularly the revelation of the Oral Law and the belief that there is but one way of amplifying it as exemplified in the recognized Orthodox sages of our day. That is clearly a conceptual issue. Aside from that point, the Orthodox and non-Orthodox communities each split into a number of subgroups which often claim to have a distinctive "philosophy" but which seem to attract their adherents more by their social style than by their intellectual content. Most Jews cannot specify in any detail what their movements stand for theoretically but they are generally quite clear as to what sort of behavior is expected from them.

There is then a considerable gap between the sort of thought one finds in the writings of the ideological leaders of a movement and the sustained intellectual analyses we will be dealing with in this volume. Men like Abraham Geiger of the early Reform movement and Solomon Schechter of the Conservative movement wrote thoughtfully and out of great learning about the nature of Judaism. They did not, however, deal with it in very abstract fashion. In retrospect, they seem unaware of the intellectual problems hidden in their formulations. Perhaps they did not find it fruitful to pursue such questions as: How do we know there is a God? What is the human role in revelation? How is the people of Israel to be defined and its purpose set? When such issues arise in their work, they do not concentrate their intellectual energies on them and seek to give a systematic—that is, a detailed and coherent—account of what they believe and why. There have, however, been Jews who have carried out such an advanced, academically sophisticated analysis of the meaning of Judaism today, and it is with their work that this book is concerned.

Can There Be a Creative Tension Between Judaism and Modernity?

The central issue of modern Jewish thought is set by the situation of emancipation. Being freed brought forth the question, how can one be modern and Jewish? The great movements in modern Jewish life give *practical* answers—that Jews should modernize religious life or revive nationhood. In the one case Jewish observance and in the other Jewish peoplehood are recast in the mold of contemporary social patterns. By contrast, the thinker is concerned with modernity in its *intellectual* manifestations. How can what it means to be a Jew be understood and explained in a convincing fashion, that is, in terms of ideas that carry weight with people today? In America, the challenge may be put more specifically: it is the university. The overwhelming majority of American Jews have had a higher education and their mentality has been shaped by that experience. How does one discuss Judaism with their most thoughtful representatives? The critical issue here is truth, not organizational effectiveness. The presentation of Judaism will be judged by the adequacy of the statement establishing its truth, not by its use in uniting groups for joint action, though a statement of Jewish belief will inevitably have practical consequence for the Jewish people's self-perception and its way of life.

For a thinker, to be modern means to have a system of ideas that have currency in contemporary culture. Finding such a modern way of thinking and determining the way it and Jewish tradition can best be brought into harmony constitute the basic task of the discipline we are examining. Because modern intellectual life in general has been unusually dynamic and many shifts have taken place in it, there have been correspondingly diverse patterns of thought developed among Jewish thinkers. Five substantially different ways of explaining Jewish religious belief have emerged in the past century and a sixth arises from the intellectual issues raised by the Zionist movement and the establishment of the State of Israel. Zionism has seldom advanced beyond the ideological level but the impact of its historical accomplishments and the questions implicit in them have affected all serious Jewish thinkers. Within these six major intellectual options, as might be expected, certain themes recur. A short analysis of these may help to set the varieties of modern Jewish thinking into perspective.

What Should Jews Make of Science, History, Democracy, and Culture?

The first of these is empirical science. The Emancipation brought the Jews from a world of talmudic or medieval Aristotelian assumptions into an era rapidly building on the science of Galileo and Newton. It contradicted classic Judaism on matters of fact, like the age of the earth, or in the likely understanding of nature, like the evolution of humankind, and made the demonstration of God's power by miracle seem mythological. It provided a simpler, more integrated view of the world than Judaism knew, one where mathematically describable patterns, not God's immediate rule, were to be found. Its precision made possible the control of much of nature, and its knowledge opened up the possibilities of creating better ways to live than had ever been imagined. Any modern Jew would have to come to terms with science.

History, in its contemporary critical, inclusive sense, was a particular challenge to emancipated Jews. Their tradition had implied, and most Jews believed, that Jewish life had changed little since biblical times. It seemed natural that an eleventh-century French Jew, Rashi, living in a Christian setting should be the authoritative commentator on the talmudic discussions of the Mishnah edited in a Parthian Zoroastrian setting (early in the sixth century) and that earlier (at the end of the second century) the Mishnah itself should have been compiled by Judah the Prince, who lived under Roman rule in a country many of whose inhabitants were idolaters. By contrast, modern history was determinedly chronological and contextual. It took change to be the basic law of history. It was skeptical, critical of all claims to authority, even in sacred books, unless these could otherwise be substantiated.

As history was applied to classic Judaism, the results were devastating. When examined like any other text of its time, the Torah appears to be a compilation and harmonization of a number of different traditions about Israelite religion and origins. Modern historical analysis shows that Jewish law has changed radically under the impact of economic reality and social situation. Jewish practice also is often seen not to have been as old as most Jews imagined it to be. When set in the context of human history generally, the development of the Jewish people, its religion and institutions, is similar to that of other peoples. For all the problems it creates, this view includes the Jews as part of humankind, a matter of great concern to emancipated Jews. How can today's Judaism not reflect something of that universal sense of history?

Democracy, as it became increasingly effective, held out new opportunities for Jews to determine the social order in which they lived. The ghetto mentality considered the communal arrangements of previous generations fixed almost by divine sanction. The modern political sensibility considers them capable of improvement and invites each citizen to share in bringing about greater common happiness. The Jews had themselves benefited from the new political activism, for they were being emancipated. They were challenged to effectuate their social ideals and their messianic hopes more directly than by performing commandments and waiting for God's saving action. Through politics they might take greater responsibility for achieving their destiny. Any modern description of Judaism would have to deal with the role human beings play in determining and realizing their goals.

Less precisely but often with greater effect, the notion of culture itself challenged the old Jewish sense of the proper dimensions of human existence. Thinkers and writers in general society were concerned with a breadth of human issues that extended far beyond even the vaunted comprehensiveness of rabbinic literature. The social sciences radically changed the common perception of humanhood, and social criticism explored every aspect of contemporary existence. Aesthetically, human creativity was celebrated in ways that went far beyond anything the Jewish community had known. Jews have spent much of the past century catching up with modern standards in fiction, painting, sculpture, musical composition, and the like. The culture also encouraged recreation, play, and enjoying oneself, for it had an intuition of human fulfillment substantially different from that found in the preemancipation Jewish community. Can a modern explication of Judaism avoid this inclusive sense of what it is to be a full human being?

Modernity Implies More Confidence in Humankind, Less in God's Revelation

Above all, the nineteenth-century civilization into which the liberated Jew came centered on the idea of progress, especially that which might be achieved through the use of human reason. Instead of relying on God to save them in this world or compensate them in one yet to come, people felt that they themselves could radically improve things. The impediments were generally either ignorance or thoughtless tradition. Both would be swept away by education and knowledge. What was unknown now would likely soon be discovered through research and analysis. Discoveries concerning disease not only affected people's longevity but gave them added self-confidence that human beings would master the world. The economic expansion of the Western world through much of this period likewise made belief in human creativity the cornerstone of contemporary existence.

Seeing these five strands as major components of what most Jews would take modernity to be, it is clear why Orthodox Judaism has no representative among the creators of major models of modern Jewish thought. By definition, being modern means adopting stands in opposition to the God-given truths of traditional Judaism and the way of life that enshrines them. The Hasidim and the so-called *yeshivah* world reject all such modernity. But another view is taken by the self-consciously modern Orthodox. They may be said to follow the general approach of the great ideologue of nineteenth-century German Orthodoxy, Samson Raphael Hirsch (1808–1888). He interpreted the rabbinic praise of *torah im derekh eretz,* having a worldly occupation while studying Torah, to mean that one can be true to the Torah while adopting the forms of the modern world, those at least that did not contradict Jewish law. The spokesmen of modern Orthodoxy have participated in various contemporary intellectual discussions but have thus far (the works of Joseph Baer Soloveitchik remaining largely unpublished) given us no comprehensive intellectual account of what an Orthodox modern Jewish philosophy might be.

What Liberal Jews Learned from Moses Mendelssohn

For non-Orthodox Jews, the challenge of modernity came to be symbolized by what was seen as the critical failing in the thought of the first notable modern Jew, Moses Mendelssohn (1729–1786). By the middle of the eighteenth century, this slight, ungainly man had made himself one of the most admired thinkers in Germany through his writings on the newly fashionable topic of aesthetics. A self-taught intellectual, he was a follower of the renowned philosopher Leibnitz, but his own restatement of the rationalist position was highly regarded in the pre-Kantian era. His development of a defense of the immortality of the soul, based on that position, was published under the title *Phaedon* and became an international best seller. Thus, some years before the emancipation process was generally under way, Moses Mendelssohn had found a path out of the ghetto and into modern culture.

The anomaly of a Jew being a full participant in the general civilization prompted one of Mendelssohn's critics to address an open letter asking why Mendelssohn had not yet become a Christian. Mendelssohn's response took the form of a small book, *Jerusalem*, in which he expounded his theory of Judaism. He argues that being a Jew is a matter of religion and that the Jewish faith has an unusual character to it. When it comes to beliefs, Judaism is entirely free. It has no dogmas but allows the human mind to search without hindrance for the most comprehensive truth. A Jew has no difficulty in being modern in religious faith, and if the state would only give the Jews true civil freedom, it would find them willing, on their part, to participate fully in society. What keeps the Jews distinctive is the law that God had given them to regulate their behavior. In that respect, Jews are not free to change or modify anything other than in the way their revealed law allows. For Mendelssohn—whose thought is far more subtle and rewarding than these few sentences can indicate—a Jew should be modern in ideas and culture while being observant of the law revealed at Mount Sinai and interpreted by the sages.

Since Mendelssohn was a Leibnitzian rationalist and revelation was still widely accepted in the strongly Lutheran atmosphere of Germany, his answer met the immediate needs that generated modern Jewish thought. In the process, he violated a condition that liberals now find critical. Mendelssohn's system found few intellectual followers, for his position seemed to advocate maintaining two sections in one's mind— one adhered rigidly to the requirements of Jewish law while the other was free to adopt the ideas of modernity. Most of Mendelssohn's contemporaries soon came to believe that his two compartments cannot be so rigidly separated from one another. There are conceptual implications in Jewish practice that clash with the results of free intellectual inquiry. The very notion of a mind divided is even more troublesome for it seems a direct contravention of that sense of unity that is the foundation of religion and rationality alike.

This matter of personal integrity became critical to the liberals. They did not want to be freely human in one part of themselves and constrainedly Jewish in another realm of their existence. They wanted no dividing line between what constituted the modern and the Jewish in the answer they were seeking. It had to be a system, a coherent, interrelated, single pattern of thought. Judaism might be reinterpreted by being seen in a different intellectual light. Doing that would be as legitimate today as it was when the medieval philosophers interpreted Judaism in terms of Neo-Platonism or Aristotelianism. In turn, Judaism was entitled to make its own criticisms of modern thought and resist those elements that were found unacceptable. The precise balance between adjustment and conservation was a problem for each thinker to tackle, although, as will become evident, modern ideas proved so attractive that most of the concessions were made on the Jewish side.

Precursors of Contemporary Discussion

Four thinkers are generally regarded as having made major efforts in the mid-nineteenth century to provide an adequate modern explication of Judaism. Solomon Formstecher (1808–1889) utilized the metaphysics of the spirit developed by Schelling as the basis for his book of 1841, *The Religion of the Spirit*. Samuel Hirsch (1815–1889) did the same with Hegel's thought in his volume of 1842, *The Religious Philosophy of the Spirit*. A thoroughgoing argument against reason in the name of faith was formulated by Solomon Steinheim (1789–1866) in his four-volume work, *Revelation in the Religious System of the Synagogue*. This might on the surface seem an unmodern work but, somewhat like Yehudah Halevi in the Middle Ages, Steinheim used the conceptual apparatus of his time to attack the authority of philosophic rationality and to defend the truths given by revelation. In the end, however, his statement of the major truths of Judaism turns out to be reasonably close to the fundamental liberal assertions of his two more philosophic colleagues. Nachman Krochmal (1785–1840) is the only non-German of the group. The more comprehensive contours of his conception of Judaism have often been attributed to his being a product of the Galician *Haskalah*, the Hebrew-language movement for cultural enlightenment. Krochmal's book, *A Guide for the Perplexed of Our Time*, was published in incomplete form only in 1851, some time after his death. Krochmal's thought is remarkable for seeing the intellectual problem not merely as one of Jewish belief but of the nature of the Jewish people. He interpreted Jewish peoplehood in Hegelian fashion, contending that the Jews are an eternal people because of their identification with the Absolute Spirit that undergirds history. To investigate the spiritual meaning of the different periods of Jewish history, Krochmal undertook a number of pathbreaking investigations into the development of Jewish literature.

None of these works significantly framed the problems or suggested answers, which remain on the agenda of contemporary Jewish discussion. For that we must turn to the intellectual system of Hermann Cohen which, as the last quarter of the nineteenth century began, effectively established the discipline of modern Jewish thought.

PART II
The Six Systematized Positions: Rationalistic Models

2

Neo-Kantianism:
Hermann Cohen

EXTENDED abstract thought is not native to Judaism. The centuries of biblical and talmudic development are essentially free of it. There are traces of argument in the Bible, occasionally even an extended discussion, and the Rabbis use logic to expound the Torah. Nonetheless, these are not the sort of generalization and probing that characterize Greek philosophy or Christian theology. Not until first-century Judaism confronts Hellenistic Greek thought in Alexandria does the first full-scale Jewish philosophy appear—only to be ignored by the normative Jewish community. Were it not for the church's preservation of Philo, there would be no record of Jewish theological reflection until the ninth century, when interaction with Moslem civilization, in which philosophy flourished, produced a steady stream of Jewish philosophical works extending through six centuries. Thus, for over two thousand years, from Moses to Isaac Israeli, Judaism, despite contact with Greek civilization, had little need for philosophic analysis of its faith. Only in the past thousand years, and then only in periods of open cultural intercourse (e.g., in Spain but not in Turkey or Poland), does a self-conscious concern with the intellectual content and character of Jewish identity assert itself.

The emancipation of European Jewry creates that sort of social hybridization more radically than did Alexandria or Spain, for the modern Jew is far more accepted in society today than ever before. The Alexandrian Jew was a monotheist among pagans. The Spanish Jew was tolerated but inferior. The modern Jew is in theory and often in practice a person fully equal to all other persons.

29

Modern Jewish thought is substantially the product of the involvement of Jews with German philosophy. This has something to do with the relative freedom of the Jews of Germany and their sense of self-image in that culture. Then too, German philosophy in the thought of two of its great figures, Immanuel Kant and Georg Friedrich Hegel, set the agenda for much of Western philosophic thinking until well into the twentieth century. The tones of German idealistic philosophy still remain in contemporary Jewish thought in a way that belies the relative marginality of idealism in academic philosophical discussion. Of course, the great Jewish system makers who set the problems and patterns for Jewish religious thought were either German or educated in Germany, the notable exception being Mordecai Kaplan. And, apparently, German idealism appealed to Jews seeking intellectual understanding of their situation in modern society. There is no better way to confront this German-Jewish philosophical synthesis than through the work of Hermann Cohen.

Neo-Kantian Philosopher as Jewish Teacher

The nineteenth century had other distinguished Jewish thinkers, but in Cohen the level of intellectual sophistication and the quality of its application to Judaism reached new and exemplary heights. His work spans the period of Germany's emergence from the Franco-Prussian War of 1870 to World War I, when his definitive book on Judaism appeared posthumously in 1919. In Cohen the era of rationality and social adjustment reached a climax; after him, as much the result of his accomplishment as of a sharp historical turn, a somewhat different set of problems increasingly preoccupies Jewish thinkers.

Born in 1842 and having received his doctorate in 1865, Cohen was eventually invited to the University of Marburg to teach philosophy, which he did from 1876 to 1912. After only three years as a lecturer and despite his Jewishness, he was appointed full professor, a status far more difficult to attain in the German university system than in its American counterpart. Cohen's extraordinary rise to academic eminence was due to his brilliant reconstruction of the Kantian system which, after some decades of eclipse by various forms of Hegelianism, he and other philosophers now returned to prominence. Cohen's own solution to the problems of the Kantian philosophy was so telling it became one of the three great patterns of Neo-Kantianism that now emerged, the so-called Marburg school version, and it brought him and his university international renown.

This work was purely secular and academic. It had no inner relationship to the fact of Cohen's Jewish birth or to his early Jewish education. (His father was a cantor and his good Jewish background was extended by his spending some time at the Jewish Theological Seminary in Breslau.) His unique interpretation of Judaism cannot be understood except in terms of his general philosophic system. Moreover, had Cohen not succeeded in the general culture, his exposition of Judaism might never have received the Jewish acceptance it did.

Cohen's technical work, resolving the paradoxes inherent in Kantianism, is not directly relevant here. Yet a word must be said about it insofar as it made possible his new philosophy of Judaism.

The Philosophical World Cohen Inherited

The Kantian revolution in philosophy may be described, with gross oversimplification, as a response to the skeptical questions raised by the thought of David Hume. This Scottish thinker had inquired about how we truly know what we claim to know about nature and reality. For example, scientists regularly speak in terms of cause and effect but one never actually sees a cause or hears an effect; one sees only a sequence of events. Our senses tell us that one thing follows another with regularity; our conclusion that this effect was produced by that cause is our mental way of describing what occurred. Since it isn't a conclusion produced by the senses themselves, it cannot claim comparable certainty. Why, then, do we rely so steadfastly on what our minds tell us?

Kant said that Hume's skeptical questions awakened him from "dogmatic slumber" about how we know what we know. Kant accepted

Hume's problem as legitimate and, in responding to it, he rethought all the major problems of philosophy in a way that has affected almost all subsequent philosophers.

Kant proposed resolving the issue of the certainty of our knowledge, particularly that of science, by conceding that we cannot know what the world-itself really is like.* All we can know is how rational people would properly think about it. We best learn this by analyzing the necessary patterns a mature human mind utilizes. Kant thus shifted the focus of philosophy. Previous thinkers had assumed that what the mind had said about reality was, in fact, true of reality-itself. Kant agreed with Hume that we could no longer identify our thoughts with reality-itself. But since we could know what proper thinking would now be and therefore what true ideas are, Kant concentrated his philosophic efforts on how the mind would reason about the world-itself.

For Kant, the sophisticated intellect operated in three related but disparate realms: science, ethics, and aesthetics. These are all characterized by our applying a rational structure to them. For example, in the realm of science our efforts are directed not just to the collection of facts but to their interpretation. We want to move beyond the data to an abstraction about the data. Scientific thinking is most fully carried out when we can speak of a given area in terms of a broad generalization, that is, in terms of a universal law. The best human reason is characterized by that sort of thinking and it was Kant's genius to show how such rational patterning operated not only in science but in ethics and aesthetics as well.

The skeptical concession that grounded Kant's philosophy destroyed the possibility of proofs for the existence of God that had characterized the philosophy of religion since medieval times. Kant forthrightly acknowledged this, insisting that the arguments of the human mind say only what people correctly *think*, not what is actually "out there" in reality-itself. Kant also went on to create a new way of

---

*"World-itself," "reality-itself," and other similar terms are used here to indicate the Kantian effort to analyze the faculties of reason and perception while acknowledging that apprehension of things-in-themselves (*noumena*) is impossible. By these *ersatz* terms, I am trying to avoid the intricacies of technical philosophy while providing the reader with some critically needed orientation.

intellectually validating religion. He argued that ethical experience gives us unique insight into the reality that transcends humankind, and reasonable people, on the basis of the certainty of rational ethics, would believe in God, freedom of the will, immortality of the soul, and such classic religious doctrines. This way of thinking about religion, which starts from human experience and *then* seeks to establish God's reality, is the opposite of traditional religion, that was based on the idea of God giving people knowledge or revelation. The liberal approach to religion is based on this procedure.

Reconstructing Kantian Philosophy

Kant's philosophy did not vigorously survive the early decades of the nineteenth century. Kant had overlooked a basic problem: *If all we can truly know is how the mind operates, how can we assert that there is a world-itself to which our ideas reasonably correspond? All we know for certain is how we think.* That problem, in various forms, produced many systems of German idealism, that is, many intellectual structures of thought that tried to show how the ideas of the human mind produce our sense of reality. The absolute idealism of Georg Friedrich Hegel ingeniously equated fundamental reality with mind. But as the second half of the nineteenth century moved on, the suggestion was made, most notably in the work of Friedrich Nietzsche, that the old enterprise of rational philosophy had now come to an end and a radically new beginning to human thought, with perhaps wildly different contents, was now in order. The call to revive Kant came about in this situation and was soon successfully answered by Hermann Cohen, who had begun his philosophic work with studies of Plato.

Cohen argued that Kant had not been sufficiently rational in explaining even how the scientific mind operated. Kant had distinguished between raw sense data and the necessary categories of human thought like cause and effect or space and time, which give structure to sense perceptions. Cohen argued that even our sense data themselves are the process of the mind's creative, structuring power.

There are no "raw" data, for by themselves being "data" they have already been shaped by our minds. For Cohen, reason, in this activist sense, is the basis of all knowing. We therefore need to understand the process by which science operates as a continual creative effort by the mind to construct a rational reality out of what confronts it. The realm of "what confronts it" cannot be defined or explained. In-itself, it is simply not within the reach of "knowledge." But we may accurately describe it as "the problem-over-against-us." Using our minds, we create problems to solve and work out patterns of understanding what we have encountered. We resolve some of our questions in new and more comprehensive rational structures. Doing this increases our knowledge but also, as it turns out, our sense of what remains unknown. Cohen's model for this sort of thinking is mathematical, the differential calculus, in which, by continual finite operations, extended to infinity, we come to know a technically limitless sum. Human knowing, then, is a process, going on endlessly, ever enlarging its scope and, as new concepts fit into the growing system, demonstrating its validity. Cohen's philosophy analyzes the patterns that the mind necessarily uses in this dynamic process.

Cohen maintained the Kantian distinction separating the three different areas in which the human mind operates: science (which Cohen identified with mathematics and thus often called, in his special sense, "logic"), ethics, and aesthetics. He presented his own constructive statement concerning each area. In his last years, after his retirement from Marburg in 1912 and a move to Berlin, where he taught at the *Lehranstalt für die Wissenschaft des Judentums*, the seminary for liberal rabbis, he paid special attention to the place of religion in his system.

Cohen's Emphases in Philosophical Ethics

To a great extent Cohen's view of religion grew out of his passionate concern with ethics. Cohen continues the Kantian description of the rational character of ethics, that is, that an ethic must be universal and take the form of law. Any imperative to act that is limited to given classes or races could not be ethical, and nothing could be a moral imperative unless one's sense of what is right could make it a rule for all people in a similar situation.

Cohen extended this line of thought in a social direction. Face to face relations might lead on to social responsibility but a properly universal ethics, in Cohen's view, must be essentially social and take into its purview the whole of humankind. Every ethical act ultimately aims at the moral interrelationship of all people. We may begin with our own society but we cannot be content until there is global justice and understanding. Ethics, like science, is a dynamic, infinite enterprise. Each opportunity to act awakens a new moral challenge, one we cannot be relieved of because we were ethical in our last few deeds. And each act of goodness can be fulfilled only when we reach out and embrace all people in it. As is the case with scientific knowledge, our efforts to realize the good never accomplish the ideal, which, with each achievement, still seems to be as far away. Being ethical, like striving to know, is a permanent activity of the rational person.

While Cohen's conscience is directed to all humankind, he sees a special ethical role for governments in the accomplishment of a united humanity. States properly come into being when they express the will of their citizens. Since action on the basis of one's free choice is the heart of ethics, democracy is a major means of realizing our social ethical responsibility. Cohen did not mean his ideal of the state to be identified with any real state, for that would mean it was fully ethical and beyond improvement. Like individuals, nations must continuously seek to improve themselves.

Cohen himself had no difficulty applying his philosophical standard to the political situation of his day. He accepted that aspect of the Marxist analysis of society that showed the many ways in which the powerful exploited those dependent on them and then trained them to accept their degraded status as right for them. He considered democratic socialism the logical outcome of his ethical theory and publicly espoused that position despite its unpopularity and the special difficulties it caused for a Jew.

A *Rational Argument for God*

Cohen's ethical position led him, in a way different from that of Kant, to the need of an idea of God. Two forms of this argument have been noted in his work that may, in the end, be one. Initially, Cohen's system as it develops from science to ethics suddenly manifests a basic incoherence. One cannot claim to be ethical because one has been thinking about ethical problems or mentally analyzing the nature of moral decisions. The imperatives of ethics need to be acted out in the real world. But the world that science discloses to us seems alien to ethical striving. Nature is ruled by laws that determine what will happen. In ethics, the moral law confronts one with a duty that one is free to do or not do—and the ethical decision is found in the consequent response of the free will. The world that science discloses is indifferent to values like good and evil but goes its unconcerned, relentless way. Ethics is, by definition, the realm of what we know to be good and of what ought to be done even, if necessary, in the face of whatever contrary forces confront us. For a thoroughgoing rationalist like Cohen, this contradiction between the natural and ethical realms is philosophically intolerable.

In order to maintain its rationality, the system now requires an idea that will allow the two modes of rationality their distinctiveness yet bring them into relation with one another. Turning science into a free realm like ethics, or ethics into a determined order like science, would destroy the form of rational thinking characterizing each area. Hence the new idea cannot be identical with the basic idea of either science or ethics. It must be the ground of each realm so as to be fully related to it but it must not be limited to it. It must also transcend them both so as not to be the same as either of them. It must be more comprehensive than either of them so that it may bind them into a greater unity. That idea will give us an integrated world that we may be confident will permit ethics to be lived out in the realm of nature. The classic term for such a grounding, transcendent, comprehensive, integrating idea is "God." As Cohen sees things, a rational person requires an idea of God to harmonize a properly embracing world view.

Cohen, of course, is not talking about the world-itself, for he does not see how any rational person can hope to do that. His God is not a being or an existent reality of some sort. Things, for Cohen, are far less important and, so to speak, less real than are true ideas, that is, ones that are required by a rationally elaborated system. God is the most significant "thing" Cohen can imagine, for God is precisely the idea that is at the basis of his entire intellectual system, integrating it into the unity that makes it properly rational.

Realizing the Ethical Task

The other line to Cohen's affirmation of God may be traced by way of the infinity of the ethical task. If people believed morality could never reach its goal, that belief might generate despair and abandonment of ethical striving. There is something about the imperative to do the good that makes people believe it will eventually be accomplished. But that again involves us with nature. For the ethical task to continue infinitely to its ideal completion, there must be some guarantee that nature and humankind continue without an end. Yet the scientific view of the world includes the law of entropy, which states that the world is running down to randomness. This contradiction in the system is again resolved by the idea of God, which now is understood to guarantee the infinite duration of nature and humanity, thus making possible the continuity of ethical striving.

The Kantian pattern of beginning with the certainty of ethics and then building on that to explain belief in God is evident in both these lines of reasoning. Cohen extended this liberal approach to religion in a consistent manner and suggested that all modern thought about God should follow a method he called "correlation." One should not make statements about God that are not correlated with some assertion about humankind. As against traditional religion, which knew about God from God's own revealed words, or traditional philosophy, which taught that human ideas could give one understanding of Divinity-in-itself, liberals know that human thinking is at the root of every assertion about God. At the same time, one cannot properly speak about human beings without also saying something parallel about God, for humankind is situated in an integrated world-view of which God is the most fundamental idea. Cohen's sense of God is humanistic, or, equally, his humanism is religious. And of course, with ethics the critical aspect of being human, the theory of correlation lends additional activism to Cohen's philosophy.

The ethical task will be accomplished only in that ideal time religion has called the coming of the Messiah. In Cohen's construction the Messiah cannot be one person who rather miraculously creates the peaceful and just world order. For him, such thinking remains mythological. He rather sees humankind gradually becoming more ethical and extending the range and depth of moral relationships through its own natural efforts. The messianic time itself, as a reality, never actually occurs. If it did, instead of being the fulfillment of human existence, it would be its negation for it would bring to an end our singular human task—that is, being ethical. Messianism remains our most exalted human ideal, one that we are continually approaching by our good deeds but that remains infinitely distant.

Though specifically biblical terminology has been used to describe Cohen's vision of human destiny, it must be emphasized that all this is part of his academic philosophy, not the explication of a sectarian religious doctrine. As a secular thinker dealing with purely intellectual matters, Cohen found a rational need for concepts like God and messianism.

Is Religion of Reason Philosophical or Religious?

Cohen termed his understanding of science, ethics, and aesthetics integrated by an overarching concept of God, *religion of reason*. He meant that any rational person needs a God-idea to bring together a coherent world-view and thus would be involved in its ethical and religious consequences. Cohen originally meant the term "religion of reason" as another of the ideals that are so significant a feature of his system (and that make him part of the idealist stream of philosophy). In that case, no actual religion will be the same as the philosophically defined religion of reason but the latter serves as a criterion and a goal for the former. In Cohen's later years, when he gave special attention to religion and then to Judaism, there seems to have been some wavering on the issue of identifying religion of reason with a historic religion.

The beginnings of this problem are to be found in his book of 1915, *The Concept of Religion in the System of Philosophy*. The title might be read to say that Cohen, having expounded his philosophy in previous years, now intended to show how religion fit into it. If so, religion is thoroughly subordinate to a philosophic idea of God and to ethics. It has no independent intellectual status and thereby could require only what philosophic reason mandated. One might say that for the fully rational person religion had been superseded by God-grounded ethics (an implication quickly picked up by later generations of Jews who heard of Cohen's teachings at second or third hand). Cohen himself had long insisted that religions were still a practical necessity. Most people were far from fully rational and the great faiths communicated religion of reason to them in a form in which they could accept it. It also was valuable for motivating them to live the ethical life. The fervor it generated was a major factor in helping people overcome the many lesser impulses in their lives and the many social and natural difficulties that hindered their moral growth.

These instrumental justifications of religion were supplemented in the 1915 volume by an argument that religion has a unique sphere of competence. Philosophy, by dealing with universals, necessarily slights the individual. Religion, despite proper concern with its community, is based on the single self. It speaks to one's particular situation in a way that no general philosophical system can. Specifically, religion deals with the problem of sin and the rectification of sin in a way philosophy cannot. Reason can elaborate the need to do the good, or the failure to use reason which leads to doing evil, or the consequent importance of being rational in the next situation. Still, there is the actual history of moral failure, a serious concern to any sensitive human being. Religion speaks to this human situation by teaching of a God who forgives sin. It declares that God not only "wants" the good but equally "wants" people, once they have sinned, to atone. God is "ready" to be reconciled to all people who repent. This doctrine remains humanly active. God's forgiveness is not magically obtained but is the result of a free human return to God, in contrition and with the resolve to improve. Religion, not philosophy, by imparting the faith that human repentance is accepted, teaches us how to face guilt without lessening our moral responsibility.

Is Judaism "the" Religion of Reason?

This theory of religion seems an extension of Cohen's previous thought, not a break with it. There the matter might have rested had it not been for Cohen's next book, his extended interpretation of Judaism. In his earliest years as a university lecturer, Cohen wrote almost nothing about Judaism. In 1880, he published his first significant essay on a Jewish theme, responding to a vicious anti-Semitic essay by Heinrich von Treitschke. That esteemed German historian alleged that the Jews were an utterly unassimilable tribe, being thoroughly alien to the spirit of the German nation. From then on, and most notably after 1890, Cohen wrote many papers on various aspects of Judaism, interpreted from his philosophic position. Not until his retirement to Berlin did he write a full-scale exposition of his understanding of Judaism.

The book began as a series of lectures to students at the Lehranstalt. Cohen died before having fully prepared them for publication but since, as was the custom, they were fully written out, this task did not prove to be an unmanageable one. The work was entrusted to the brilliant young philosopher Franz Rosenzweig and it appeared in 1919. Rosenzweig and others seeking a new path in philosophy were impressed that Cohen's lectures showed a passionate identification of Judaism with religion of reason. They felt this demonstrated that Cohen had finally come to recognize the inadequacy of a strictly intellectual approach to existence. They argued that the shift from pure philosophy implicit in the 1915 study of religion had been as good as completed in the new book. Now religion, specifically Judaism, broke the domination of philosophy and came into its own. As a result Rosenzweig gave the book the title *The Religion of Reason Out of the Sources of Judaism*.

If that interpretation is correct—and it certainly indicates the direction Rosenzweig himself was taking—then the carefully integrated rationalism of the Cohenian system had been shattered. Once a nonrational factor is introduced into so tightly logical a system, it cannot assert its ideas to be required by reason. At any point one might refer to belief or some other such nonrational and nondiscussable ground. And one might introduce almost any doctrine into a religion that was more than rational. Many of Cohen's students thought he was fully aware of that problem. In their reading, his last work does not justify the judgment that Cohen had now turned his interest from the *ideal* of religion of reason to *actual* religion. When the second edition of the book emerged, they removed the article "the" from the title so as to make certain the reference to "religion of reason" is not too specific. The English translation follows that version and calls the book only *Religion of Reason Out of the Sources of Judaism*.

The Essence of Cohen's Judaism

Regardless of what historians may yet determine concerning the development of Cohen's thought, the major outlines of his interpretation of Judaism are unmistakable from his essays as well as his posthumous book. Cohen came to Judaism with a sure knowledge of the truth about the human situation, namely, religion of reason. The Jews of biblical times, like all human beings, had been in search of truth. In that pre-philosophic time they sought it and expressed what they found in ways that mixed reason with less dependable aspects of the human consciousness. In Jewish literature, most notably the Bible but also the rabbinic literature, one finds the expression of the Jewish national spirit. This is particularly significant because Cohen, stressing the universal quality of truth, believes that a group's spiritual search is more valuable than that of an individual. He therefore studies classic Jewish texts—more precisely, he selects and cites texts—that show the Jewish people's intuitive recognition of the Neo-Kantian truths about God and ethics. His general program is to indicate how religion of reason may be found in the sources of Judaism—exactly as announced in the title of the book.

This may be put in condensed form. The central thread of Jewish national consciousness is ethical monotheism, a concept of the unity of God grounding moral responsibility. When one looks for this theme in ancient Jewish writings, one cannot help but be astonished at its omnipresence. Prophetic literature brings it most clearly to the surface, and Cohen's exegesis, demonstrating that the prophets anticipated philosophic religion, is extended and impressive. Cohen identified prophetic Judaism with the highest spiritual insight of the Jewish people and with ethical monotheism.

Uncovering Religion of Reason in Judaism

Cohen and his numerous followers showed the hermeneutic riches that resulted from a search for ethical monotheism in Jewish sources. Thus, for Cohen the biblical fight against idolatry is not a mere rejection of inadequate, pagan forms of religion. It conceals a major Jewish intuition about the proper relation of Deity to the world. In idolatry, God can be identified with some aspect of nature. That identification destroys God's transcendence and robs the concept of God of its power to command. For if God can be identified with what is, we may deduce that it ought not be changed. A passivity to the world sets in as when one says, "What can you do? That's just the way things are."

The biblical polemic against idolatry is at its root a fight against making God so imminent that God cannot effectively command us, that is, ground the realm of ethics. When the Bible and the Talmud refer to God as "king" or "high in the heavens," they are not making anthropomorphic or spatial comments. They are symbolically trying to give proper transcendence to our concept of God. When God is understood to stand logically on another level than humankind, God has a right to set its proper standards and serve as the ideal for its development.

Cohen considers it simplistic to think of monotheism as primarily a rejection of polytheism. Of course, having many gods would not allow for an integrated concept of nature and ethics. However, the unity of God is asserted in religion of reason not as a mere mathematical statement about God but as a qualitative one. Monotheism fundamentally proclaims God's uniqueness. God is not to be identified with nature, for that would destroy ethics; or with ethics, for that would destroy science. God's oneness says that God is, logically, on a level where nothing else is. God is unique in being prior to all else. Thus what follows in the system is subordinate to God ("commanded").

As a result, Cohen is as antagonistic to pantheism as he is to polytheism because pantheism's identification of God with the world similarly negates Cohen's sort of ethics. Spinoza is his chief target here and he considers that philosopher's famous usage, "God or nature," a contradiction of reason and a rejection of Judaism. Spinoza did write about ethics, but the passivity and resignation that he necessarily considers to be the highest good contrast radically with Cohen's activism and messianic aspiration.

Cohen's Justification of Jewish Observance

Similarly enlightening results come from searching for religion of reason in Jewish practice. In the popular mind Yom Kippur may be considered a day of fasting and prayer undertaken to persuade God to forgive people as the new year begins. Under Cohen's probing it turns into the great reaffirmation of human moral freedom. The heart of the liturgy that day is a call for repentance, an act whose great power is celebrated in the afternoon reading of the book of Jonah. That is not a story about a whale but the astonishing tale in which the honest return to God of the evil citizens of Nineveh, hated enemies of the Jews, is accepted, and thus their punishment is averted. Yom Kippur is not a series of magical rites that bring God to cleanse humankind of its sins. Rather, it calls people to use their freedom to improve themselves. For sins against others, the law mandates an effort at restitution as the prerequisite to repentance being accepted. Even for sins against God, people begin their return by gaining insight into the evil they have done, feeling sorry for it and confessing their regret to God. But it is the resolution not to commit the sin again, a return to one's self as a moral agent, that completes our responsibility. What the holy day comes to proclaim is that if we accept our ethical responsibilities—the day's confessions do not include ritual matters—God will find us acceptable despite what we may have done in the past. Without some such assurance we might be so weighed down with guilt we could not face each moment's new obligations. Our past would destroy our future. Repentance comes to restore the future to us and thus Yom Kippur makes the coming year literally new in possibility for us. As the book of Deuteronomy says, God sets before us life and death and asks us to choose life.

Similarly Cohen sees the Sabbath as an ethical institution unique in human creativity. As contrasted with Babylonian days on which no work was done for fear of the gods, the Sabbath is devoted to rest, worship, and study. It testifies to the uniqueness of human rationality for it occurs not as a result of any natural phenomenon but in response to the human ability to count the days. It also exemplifies human freedom. People, by an act of will, cease work and devote themselves to other activities. Nothing else in nature could carry out so creative an act. The required activities of the day direct people to their rational capacities through devotion to God, to study and to personal refreshment. The crown of this observance is the insistence that the day of rest be extended not only to one's family but also to one's slaves and the aliens resident in the community. Not even the powerless and the outsider are excluded from the class of the truly human, but the concept of a universal human community is given nuclear recognition.

The Appeal of the Cohenian Approach to Judaism

Since Cohen believes religion has a significant function in human life, he argues that we ought to keep all the observances of our faith that sensitize and empower us to be ethical. By this standard he provides modern Jewry with an answer to one of its most important questions: Which acts must we still do and which may we change and still remain authentic Jews in the modern world?

For Cohen, ethical monotheism, as the truth about our world, is permanent. All the practices that inculcate or express it may not be given up. The many activities in which the Jewish religion indirectly substantiates that truth are also desirable and should be retained. But any law or custom that violates our understanding of religion of reason must be revised, for it represents a faulty sense of truth.

This line of reasoning was well known in early nineteenth-century liberal thought. Cohen gave it much more compelling utterance and thereby made his understanding of Judaism highly attractive to many Jews. Seeking to modernize themselves, they sought the assurance that in avidly devoting themselves to the general culture they were not denying Judaism. Cohen's understanding of ethical responsibility, particularly in its social ramifications, gave rational justification to their dimly sensed judgment. Cohen's philosophy turned the focus of Judaism from the Jewish people itself, particularly as developed in the ghetto period, to humankind as a whole. His teaching encouraged the integration of Jews into their society as a primary religious duty.

Cohen's theory also performed another major intellectual service. It clarified why Jews who sought to be modern should not become Christians, an enticing option for many in those days. If religion of reason is the criterion by which actual faiths are to be evaluated, Judaism is superior to Christianity. It does not center on miracles like the virgin birth, the incarnation, the resurrection, and the ascension, and its religious practice does not contain sacraments, human acts in which God is actually involved. Judaism is also more consistently monotheistic for it has no notion of a man being God or God's unity simultaneously being a trinity. It is far more directly ethical for it places its stress on acts, not on faith, and it directs them by law, not by appealing to an amorphous sentiment like love. Cohen did not invent these themes. They were common to previous Jewish writers, but in Cohen's towering exposition of religion of reason they seemed to many Jews particularly persuasive.

The Place of Cohen in Subsequent Jewish Thought

Directly or indirectly, Cohen's influence has dominated American Jewish thinking through most of the twentieth century. Practically speaking, it has shaped the way most Jews understand Judaism. They have largely received their ideas about it from their rabbis, who in turn received it from their teachers at rabbinical school. Until relatively recently, almost all scholars who wanted a doctorate in Judaica went to Germany, which meant studying in a milieu in which Cohen's understanding of Judaism was the common way of discussing it. Generations of rabbis were taught to think of Judaism in terms of its rationality and ethics. However, Cohen himself was rarely studied. Only in 1971 did the first translation of some of Cohen's Jewish essays appear. An English rendering of *Religion of Reason* was published a year later. Thus, though Judaism as ethical monotheism is probably the standard religious ideology of American Jews, the powerful intellectual structure that stood behind it has been largely forgotten.

Cohen's influence remains in the model he set for succeeding Jewish thinkers. He did not justify Judaism on a parochial basis, demonstrating only to the faithful what they were already fairly well convinced of. He clarified a standard of truth that any person of intellect might debate and challenge. He spoke in terms of a full range of humanistic knowledge and on a high academic level. He was fully conscious of the intellectual problems of his time and gave them a bold solution. He was a learned, loyal Jew but he did not hesitate to think fearlessly about how Judaism in the modern age needed to change in belief and practice. He gave leadership to his people and defended them against their maligners. Since Cohen, serious Jewish thinkers have been measured by his standard.

Criticizing Cohen's Views of God and Practice

The great success of Cohen highlighted what succeeding thinkers have also seen as his major failings. On every level of Jewish affirmation—God, Torah, and Israel—critics have found fault with his teachings, often claiming that history itself has validated their objections.

Cohen's God is an idea. In the way that philosophical idealists might use the term, God is therefore "real." But most Jews are not philosophers and even fewer are so rigidly idealistic as to think that the most real thing there could be is a true thought. The abyss between the committed philosopher and the rest of us yawns wide at this point. Cohen was devoted to ideas and they often roused his passions to the heights we see reflected in his writings. In response to critics who chided him for suggesting that people might actually love an idea of God, Cohen wrote, "How can one love anything save an idea? For even in the love of the senses one loves only the idealized person, only the idea of the person."

The matter should also be considered on a practical level. Many Jews accepted the watered down version of Cohen's ethical monotheism that they were taught because it required them only to have an *idea* of God. That freed them from establishing a personal relationship with God. All they needed to do was to utilize a God-concept as the organizing principle of their view of the world. That done, the idea-God could be respectfully ignored as one turned to the ethical tasks of human existence. Subsequent thinkers who agreed with Cohen in most other matters often felt compelled to revise Cohen's God-idea. Leo Baeck is the outstanding example of a thinker who sought to make a rational God-idea "more real." Mordecai Kaplan's rationalism results from describing God in a different philosophic mode.

Cohen's justification of Jewish practice evoked a more ambivalent response. In claiming that universal ethics is the core of Jewish duty, Cohen elucidated a theme that was not often explicit in classic Jewish texts but that spoke to the conscience of modern Jews and legitimized their participation in an emancipated society. Cohen's high estimate of ethics in Judaism remains the conviction of most modern Jews. But the implications of Cohen's theory for the rest of Jewish observance caused major difficulties.

Cohen knows ethics to be commanded as a simple rational matter. No other Jewish duty has such compelling power, though study might come close. All other religious activities are not required, only desirable. Cohen can authorize them only on an instrumental basis. That is, though they are not *necessary*, rituals, celebrations, and such are often *helpful* in bringing us to a proper ethical level. Most human beings do not live by their ideas. They need religious activities to bring them to a higher spiritual state than they could achieve on their own. This fact makes the other than directly ethical acts valuable—but does not make them mandatory or even very important. They are at best useful, but that also means they may be evaluated in terms of how effectively they carry out their function. Should daily prayer or observance of the Shavuot festival on a Wednesday not prove particularly conducive to ethical living, one may dispense with it. Many American Jews have used that point as an excuse to give up much of Jewish duty except for ethics. To them traditional Jewish practice seems an inefficient means to the ethical life. Politics, therapy, the arts, recreation all suggest themselves as leading more directly to it—so they become the new "Jewish" commandments.

Cohen's Troublesome Attitude Toward the Jewish People

Perhaps Cohen might have redeemed this situation by a strong doctrine concerning the Jewish people and its place in Judaism but that would have been inconsistent with his ethical universalism. He rigidly interpretated Judaism as a religion. The Jewish people's only legitimacy derived from its devotion to its idea of God and its resulting messianic ethics. Cohen scorned duties based on membership in a racial or national group. That derived commandment from mere biology or history, thus irrationally confusing science or continuity with ethics. Cohen was therefore a vigorous anti-Zionist. He dismissed, as unworthy of rational beings with a universal outlook, the calls for a return to the land and a revival of the national tongue. Jewish nationalism particularly distressed him, for he believed the Jewish people had a mission to instruct humankind in the notion of ethical monotheism.

In his final book he had tried to explain why, though any rational mind should come to religion of reason, the Jewish people were still needed in history. He argued that the Jews were the first people to break through to this understanding of the relationship between God and humankind. Then, in an uncharacteristic shift of logic, he insisted that this primacy in time had given them a permanent and special status in history. The statement is so odd for Cohen that it deserves citation.

> I do not assert that Judaism alone is the religion of reason. I try to understand how other monotheistic religions also have their fruitful share in the religion of reason, although in regard to *primary origin* this share cannot be compared with that of Judaism. This primary origin constitutes the priority of Judaism, and this priority also holds for its share in the religion of reason. For the primary origin is the distinctive mark of creative reason . . . which produces a pure pattern. Primary origin bears the marks of purity. And *purity* in creativity is the characteristic of reason.

The argument has seemed to critical readers a shift from logical priority to historical precedence, a movement from idea to experience normally not allowed by Cohen.

Cohen believed the Jewish people now existed to keep the ideal of ethical monotheism alive in history and to disseminate it to all humankind. He could not grieve over the destruction of the Temple and the consequent dispersion of the Jews, for they were the necessary means by which the people of Israel progressed from a particular national existence to universal human service. As an ethical, not an ethnic, duty, ethical monotheism rightfully claimed the allegiance of all Jews to their people. Zionism, by contrast, rejected the universal ties of humankind by calling on Jews to leave the countries in which they found themselves and move to the one land where the nation might fulfill itself. Nothing could be more antithetical to Cohen's position than classic nationalist Zionism.

Two painful, additional themes occur in Cohen's Jewish writings that must be mentioned. Cohen believes that suffering is the price Jews must pay to carry out their messianic role in history. He writes feelingly about the pain Jews have had to bear in the past and he does not advocate seeking out persecution. There is a nobility to his call to Jews to be ready to face any hardship in order to bring the message of ethical monotheism to humanity. But it must be said that he seems fundamentally acquiescent and uncomplaining about the pain others bring to the Jews and his God-idea in no way mitigates this burden of suffering. Cohen obviously had an exalted sense of duty; he also died some decades before the Holocaust. The contemporary reader would almost certainly agree with Richard L. Rubenstein that if the chosen people doctrine required us to accept the Holocaust as our Jewish due, an ethical person would give it up.

Even more disturbing is Cohen's judgment about the German nation. He identified its spirit with the highest ideals of humanity and argued that all Jews faithful to Judaism ought to be its admirers. During World War I he wrote two pamphlets equating the German and Jewish ideals and calling on world Jewry to support the German cause. In philosophy one ought not let a mistaken historical judgment invalidate an otherwise compelling system of thought. In this case the error is so blatant and the consequences so tragic that one can hardly help doubt the rigid universalism he so enthusiastically espoused.

Evaluating Cohen from an Altered Historical Context

Most of Cohen's attitudes toward the Jewish people seem problematic today. They seem to us utterly unrealistic, but we come to them with sixty years or so of experience which include the Holocaust, the founding of the State of Israel, and a general decline of confidence in the moral quality of Western civilization. (Only with temerity should a scholar today assert that what the European or American academic mind considers rational is universally true for all humankind, on whatever continent or in any circumstance.) In Cohen's day, Jews were concerned primarily with achieving full human status, not with deepening their Jewishness. Many Jews were still observant and well educated. They often lived in communities whose traditions went back centuries. And there were always anti-Semites to reinforce their Jewish identity. Their primary Jewish question was the authenticity of general human activity. Cohen answered their need convincingly. But to a generation secure in its humanness but concerned about Jewish particularity, Cohen seems a problematic guide.

When, however, inquiring Jews ask about universal issues, Cohen's thought once again becomes relevant. He remains a challenge to anyone who would assert that Judaism is essentially particularistic and mandates only a grudging participation in the affairs of humankind. Cohen made universal ethics the center of modern Judaism. Anyone who would make Jewish duty radically folk-oriented must contend with his sense of the Jew as primarily a person of broad ranging conscience.

Reviving his philosophic defense of this position would be difficult today. The Neo-Kantian understanding of reason has largely been rejected by contemporary philosophers, so one would need to do for Cohen what he did for Kant. A view that considers people to be fundamentally rational, and rationality inevitably ethical, seems intolerably optimistic. Yet Cohen's teaching about Jewish humanitarianism bespeaks a central religious intuition of modern Jewry. It knew leaving the ghetto was the right thing to do and, despite its disappointments in Emancipation, it is not going back there. If emotionalism and thoughtlessness continue to grow in the Western world, if moral permissiveness continues to foster selfishness and violence, Cohen's plea for rationality and ethics will increasingly seem self-evident and necessary. And any interpretation of Judaism that concerns itself mainly with the Jewish people and its practices will show itself false to the lasting universal message that he disclosed was implicit in our tradition.

3

Religious Consciousness: Leo Baeck

ONE MIGHT fruitfully study twentieth-century Jewish religious thought by asking how its leaders sought to overcome the nineteenth-century identification of Judaism with ethics. The virtues of that stand were so great that it could not readily be swept aside. By emphasizing a well-accepted modern truth, the primacy of ethics, it simultaneously validated Jewish participation in general society, invigorated the practice of much of Jewish law, and explained the superiority of Judaism to Christianity. Most Jews still consider Judaism a uniquely ethical religion. Even the traditionally minded largely retain the liberal notion that the first among many Jewish duties is moral behavior to all people. They are somehow personally offended when a Jew who is meticulous about ritual observance is publicly demonstrated to have acted unethically.

As the twentieth century moved on, Jewish thinkers were increasingly troubled by the liberalism derived from Hermann Cohen. It led to the easy inference that everything in Judaism other than ethics—belief in God, devotion to the Jewish people, the rich way of life mandated by the Torah—might almost be eliminated, or, at least, considered secondary. The issue is not so much the primacy of ethics but their sufficiency. The premise may be put positively: an authentic Jewish existence is more than ethical though ethics are central to it. But what constitutes the more-than-ethical aspects of being a Jew?

53

How are they to be validated so that they speak of the modern Jew with something like the authority of the moral law? These and corollary questions continue to be at the heart of debates on the nature of Jewish identity and obligation. We begin our pursuit of this theme— Hermann Cohen being the classic case of the equation of Jewish faith and ethical existence—with Leo Baeck's effort to modify rather than break with the rationalist interpretation of Judaism.

Harnack's Antagonist and Emulator

Cohen had foreseen that the intellectual most likely to carry on his work was Leo Baeck. At the turn of the century Baeck won wide and almost instant recognition with the appearance of his book, *The Essence of Judaism*. The German Jewish community recognized that the previously unheralded young rabbi of the provincial town Oppeln had a unique gift for epitomizing and justifying his faith. Though he drew heavily on the ideas current in German Jewry and particularly on the Jewish thought of Hermann Cohen, Baeck already showed originality in his philosophy of Judaism.

Baeck's work was stimulated by the extraordinary reception given Adolf von Harnack's volume of 1900, *The Essence of Christianity* (entitled in translation *What Is Christianity?*) and has often been seen as a Jewish response to Harnack—which in part it is. Baeck never mentions Harnack in his work, yet the continual comparison of his Judaism to Harnack's Christianity is obvious. For Harnack, Christianity is centered on one man and his teaching. By contrast, Judaism knows no single, dominating figure but rather a continuous succession of teachers on whom Jewish history centers. Christianity, according to Harnack, suffered a major dislocation of its pristine faith. This dislocation was healed by the Protestant Reformation, a healing now renewed in Protestant liberalism. Judaism, Baeck contended, demonstrates an essential continuity of teaching expressed in different forms over the ages but remaining essentially true to itself. While the fundamental message of the Church is a love for all people that stems from being loved by God, Judaism preaches a more stringent social ethical relationship to God in which the deed rather than the heart is central.

Baeck borrowed more than a title from Harnack when he called his book *The Essence of Judaism*. He took over Harnack's claim that the thinker could expose the underlying, permanent truth of a religion. As religious liberals, both men believed in religious change. They therefore had the responsibility of clarifying what remained true in their faith today as in the past, despite all the apparent reforms of ideas and practice. Harnack did this by applying to Christianity some of the ideas of the philosopher of history Wilhelm Dilthey. That sage had suggested that one could understand a historical period or great work only if one brought to it a certain measure of empathy. Scholars were, of course, tied to their own time and place but, knowing this, they might imaginatively enter another moment in history. The subjectivity this might unleash was to be kept in check by a deep personal immersion in the primary sources of the era.

Harnack was the ideal German historian to carry out this project in relation to Christianity. He had an awesome mastery of the sources of Christianity. During his long life he published hundreds of detailed philological studies and a number of major books. In the lectures that were published as his *Essence* he put aside his historical researches momentarily to let the data speak through him. Having steeped himself so thoroughly in the history of Christianity, he could hope that its eternal truth would attain utterance in his description of it.

Baeck borrowed Harnack's method and applied it to Judaism. Unlike Cohen the philosopher, Baeck did not begin his work by establishing rational categories with which to explain Judaism. He spoke more as a historian, in that special sense of German, idealist history in which the researcher is concerned less with specifying just what happened or why it happened than with what it meant as a manifestation of the human spirit. While Baeck served all his life as a community rabbi, he was uncommonly scholarly. His special competence was *midrash*, a discipline that allowed him to range freely through the history of Jewish ideas. By his interest in mystic texts, for example, Baeck was one of the precursors of Gershom Scholem.

Baeck was free not only of a philosophical system as he approached the texts, but also of the traditional theologian's insistence that they were God's revelation. For Baeck the validity of Judaism did not rest on a unique event at Sinai, but rather on the truth of the central ideas that the Jewish people had maintained over the ages. Baeck maintained this intuitive-historical stance toward the interpretation of Judaism in all his writings.

Rationalism Alone Cannot Adequately Explain Judaism

In terms of result there is not much to separate the rabbi-historian Leo Baeck from the philosopher of Judaism, Hermann Cohen, because Baeck found ethical monotheism to be the essence of Judaism. Baeck, however, departed from Cohen in basing his exposition of Judaism not only on our sense of the ethical but on religious consciousness as well. To some extent, that shift from rigorous rationalism may be found in the first edition of *The Essence of Judaism*, but it dominates the greatly expanded and revised second edition which appeared in 1922. By then the major supports of Baeck's intellectual structure were firmly set, and in the seven subsequent editions there are only minor alterations.

For all his new premise, Baeck did not abandon or modify the Neo-Kantian insistence on the primacy of ethics. He wrote:

> From the very beginning of the real, the prophetic, religion of Israel, its cardinal factor was the moral law. Judaism is not merely ethical, but *ethics constitute its principle, its essence*. Monotheism came into being as a result of the realization of the absolute character of the moral law. [Italics in original.]

Much still sounds like Cohen. But Baeck adds a sentence that hints at the move to another dimension: "The moral consciousnesses teaches about God." The word "consciousness" is highly significant to Baeck. It points to a different realm of experience from the scientific-ethical rationalism to which philosophy is limited by the Neo-Kantians. It echoes Friedrich Schleiermacher's interpretation of religion as a unique human experience. For Schleiermacher, religious consciousness is quite distinct from the sort of practical reason that Kant identified with morality. It is the feeling people have within them, naturally and properly, of absolute dependence, that is, on God. Such a consciousness is distinct from rationality, for properly understood it is far more fundamental to human existence than is reasoning. In this mid-nineteenth-century theory, Schleiermacher pioneered the idea that religion was to be understood and validated as a matter of inner experience rather than of reason.

Baeck takes great pains to differentiate his approach from that of Schleiermacher—which is good reason to think he was not oblivious of his debt. Baeck may also have been influenced by Rudolf Otto's book, *The Idea of the Holy*. Appearing in 1917 to wide acclaim, Otto's study gave new vigor to the notion of religion arising from a unique level of consciousness. Otto sought to make Schleiermacher's somewhat diffuse identification of the religious consciousness much more precise. Religious consciousness, he argued, was a direct perception of the numinous, characterized by deep feelings of awe and fascination—our sixth empirical sense, so to speak. What surely influenced Baeck in his effort to move beyond Cohenian rationality was the new intellectual acceptance Otto had won for the idea of religion based on personal experience. Baeck could speak without hesitation of our consciousness of mystery as the deepest root of our religiosity. But Baeck rejected Otto's theory as inadequate to Judaism for it did not make ethics a primary ingredient of the holy. To Baeck as to Cohen, the two were inseparable.

Baeck's addition of this new principle of religious consciousness shatters the philosophic integrity of the Neo-Kantian argument. Cohen's carefully integrated system is fully dependent upon "pure" knowledge, "pure" will, "pure" feelings. These are defined as utterly rational, in need of no validation other than thought itself. Once that purity is broken, once an element beyond Kantian rationality can be decisive, the entire system falls. From the rationalistic philosopher's perspective, such thought ceases to be rational and hence becomes intellectually worthless. For Baeck to expound Judaism, even partially, in terms of special religious consciousness is tantamount to repudiating the chief virtue of Cohen's work. But by 1922 Cohen was dead.

Baeck surely realized that he had made a major methodological departure, but he was a rabbi in concern as in profession, and his primary interest was in the quality of the religious life produced by a philosophy of Judaism. Cohen's Neo-Kantian exposition had established the centrality of God in human existence but did so in terms of God as an idea or a concept. Cohen's God is the logical ground of our world view who integrates the divergent aspects of our rational activity into a coherent system. Such a God, Baeck felt, is too abstract to elicit piety and hardly provides a reason for expanding ethics into a broader pattern of religious observance. Of course, for an idealist philosopher there is no reality greater than that of a systematically required rational idea; certainly there is no more important idea in Cohen's system than the idea of God. Nonetheless, to the devout, there remains an unbearable distance between what philosophy says God is and what the religious life discloses. Whether in response to the yearning for personal contact with the deepest level of reality—a widespread phenomenon after World War I—or whether in simple reassertion of traditional Jewish piety, Baeck, by utilizing the notion of religious consciousness, now introduced the felt, subjective aspect of religion into his explanation of Judaism.

The Consequences of Having Two Major Premises

Baeck's exposition of the essence of Judaism is worked out in terms of two major motifs, human ethics and religious consciousness. As a direct result, he develops most of his ideas in a dialectical fashion, balancing one notion against another that moves in a somewhat different direction. For instance, one of his central ideas is that human beings have an elemental sense of being created (somewhat like Schleiermacher's sense of absolute dependence) and yet also know they are most true to themselves when they are creators, which is when they act ethically (an activism that is radically different from Schleiermacher's sense of religion). Such interplay of exposition in terms of ethics and religious consciousness is characteristic of Baeck's thought, though not all of the polarities he develops stem so directly from this basic dichotomy in human religiosity.

Baeck's unique, nonphilosophic approach to human piety appears in his treatment of the ground of ethics. He situates this not in our rationality but in the mystery that a religious consciousness senses behind the creation. Both Kant and Cohen knew the philosophic desirability of extending ethics beyond its specific content. In Kant, ethics lead on to the practical knowledge that there is a God who guarantees moral fulfillment. In Cohen, the idea of God guarantees that the infinite moral task will have infinite reality in which to work itself out.

Those philosophic assertions pale beside the personal certainty of devout believers. They know that the commandments concern them individually, that they derive from what is most real in the universe, that failure to do them properly induces guilt, and that a day will come when righteousness will visibly triumph on earth. Religious certainty is incalculably richer than the rational assertions of philosophy. Religious experience testifies to what lies beyond the ethical, to the God who is more than the idea implied by ethics but is the One who has the right to issue imperatives and make them categorical. Reason cannot reach such a God.

For Baeck, ethics without this mysterious grounding in God is mere moralism. For Judaism, there can be no ethics that does not stem from such a living God who establishes relationships with humankind. With the rejection of a living God, Baeck contends, the rejection of ethics cannot be long delayed. Such has been the gloomy truth of modern history.

However, to glorify human feelings and allow them to determine the content of the religious life is dangerous, producing an anethical religion of self-concern or utter inwardness. Or, directed outward, such emotions might easily produce fanaticism or superstition. Having often suffered from human irrationality, Judaism knows better than to base itself on unbridled feeling. Its religious consciousness, Baeck insists, receives authentic expression only in ethical acts. When it

threatens to emerge in any other guise, it must be rejected as tempta-
tion. However, when feeling is channeled into the ethical realm, it
brings power and strength to the ethical, receiving in turn the secure
guidance it needs if our humanity is not to be perverted.

This dialectical tension between religious consciousness and ethics
is Baeck's unique intellectual creation. In its assertion, Baeck broke
with the Neo-Kantian, philosophic understanding of Judaism. In actuality, Baeck was more concerned to dissociate himself from Schleiermacher's sense of religion as absolute dependence. Baeck found this
concept intolerable because it renders human beings ethically inert
and so destroys our dignity. Practically, too, by Baeck's time German
Romanticism had made clear its great potential for viciousness, not
least by its close link with a growing anti-Semitism. Schleiermacher
would have despised such an extension of his thought, but thinking
about these matters decades later, Baeck could not fail to be concerned about the danger of abandoning oneself to one's emotions.
Baeck's debt to Cohen and the Kantian stream in German Jewish
thought is most evident at this point. Because of their teaching, he
insisted on containing religious experience within the structure of
ethical command, even while defining it ultimately in romantic, not
rational, terms.

God, Personally Sensed but Ethically Demanding

Baeck's exposition of Judaism remains typically liberal. It says much
more about human beings, their ethical sense, and their consciousness
of the Divine than it says about who God is and what, if anything, God
does—but that humankind on which he focuses is spoken of in terms
of its full range of consciousness. As opposed to Cohen, Baeck argues
that the *idea* of God has little more religious value than any other pure
idea. Our certainty that God is real comes not from our rational
demonstration that God is the First Cause or the One who orders
nature. We find it rather in what has happened to our lives, in the inner
consistency, the moral power, and the sense of meaning and direction

we now have gained. We know that our lives must be lived in response to a question put to us from beyond the mystery we sense at the heart of existence.

Can we say, then, that Judaism affirms a personal God? Of that, Baeck insists, nothing can be said today and nothing was said in classic Judaism. God is not to be understood as a God of qualities or about whom dogmas may be stated. Judaism has no dogmas, no explicit statements about God's reality that all Jews must accept. However, Judaism knows that since people are conscious of God as one close and responsive to us, one who penetrates our innermost depths, "God is therefore understood personally and regarded as personal." This is typical of Baeck's use of religious consciousness to reclaim aspects of traditional Jewish piety that were inaccessible to the Neo-Kantians.

Baeck naturally balances this emphasis on personalism with ethical rigor. Intimate talk about God engenders an anthropomorphism that believers can take seriously. This destroys God's transcendence, thereby vitiating the authority by which the ethical comes to us as a categorical demand. The medieval philosophers waged a protracted battle against this misunderstanding. They succeeded but only by turning God into an abstraction that denied the innermost reality of religious experience. Judaism overcame that danger by asserting a fundamental paradox about God: the exalted, transcendent God is nonetheless the present, personal God. Nothing stands between each individual and God—God is that close—but the very same God remains the God of the infinite heights and depths of creation. The ethical and the devotional are simultaneously affirmed in Judaism.

The sensitivity with which Baeck uses these two interpretive devices is well illustrated in his treatment of God's wrath or jealousy. Baeck feels we cannot reject these biblical terms simply because they are anthropopathisms, for then we would also have to give up such meaningful symbolic expressions for God as "Father." Encountering such disturbing language, we need to investigate what aspects of the religious consciousness are being articulated. God's anger is a way of expressing our sense that ethics must be uncompromising. Genuine morality always involves a protest against, and resistance to, indecency. It will not have any intercourse with evil. Every trace of unrighteousness implies a denial of

God and a perversion of human dignity. Immorality brings one into a realm without meaning, value, or ultimate reality. Against the Bible's admonition, we leave life and choose death. There is no compromise with evil or tolerance of it. God's jealousy powerfully symbolizes this aspect of the belief that God is one.

Baeck's Theory of Evil

Baeck is similarly categorical in his theory of evil. The source of evil is the misuse of human freedom. That people are fully free to do the good is an essential Jewish teaching—as well as the necessary premise of any serious ethics. So people are responsible when they do evil, even as they are praiseworthy when they do the good. Nothing may be allowed to impinge on this primary human need to be ethical or on the human capacity to act ethically. Baeck is relentlessly polemical in his arguments against the Christian doctrine of original sin. He insists that it utterly misreads human nature and that its promulgation provides people with an easy excuse for not summoning their moral power and doing the good.

Similarly, when people have done evil, their doing so does not destroy their fundamental ethical freedom. They can change their way and make themselves again acceptable to God. The Rabbis termed this action *teshuvah*, "repentance." In Baeck's modern, ethical reworking of the doctrine, we are always responsible for what we do, even for turning from our sin and reestablishing our relationship with God. For good or for evil, the power is utterly ours.

Baeck set forth his theory of evil in the 1920's. His passionate commitment to ethical existence and his corollary emphasis on human responsibility form the essential basis for understanding his response to the Holocaust.

Baeck was the only major modern Jewish theologian to enter and survive Hitler's death camps. When Hitler came to power, Baeck was the leading liberal rabbi of Berlin and such a significant figure in the German Jewish community that he was named president of its representative organization. The dignity that he brought to a justly proud community about to undergo a tragedy unlike anything perpetrated by a civilized nation—and how can one compare this to what uncivilized people did in their barbarity?—has been movingly described by survivors of that period. Despite many opportunities to leave the country permanently, including several official trips abroad, he chose to stay with his people. In January 1943, he was sent to a concentration camp. His demeanor there; his concern for others; his efforts to keep them human by teaching them, from memory, the great humanistic classics; his refusal to be less than ethical, or to let the Nazis make him less than human, made him one of the heroic figures of an impossible situation. By error, chance, the sacrifice of others; by his spirit and the grace of Providence, the seventy-year-old rabbi survived Theresienstadt.

He went to London in July 1945, and in the years that followed, until his death in 1956, he continued writing and lecturing. Despite his experience, he did not feel that the Holocaust had changed anything he believed, and he did not see it requiring him to rewrite what he had said so powerfully in an earlier, happy time. Evil was the result of free human choice and God dignified us by not interfering with our freedom to determine what we would do. The Nazis had been more ruthless, more effective, more barbaric than other great evil-doers. Yet, they had not fundamentally changed the problem of evil. Certainly they taught nothing new about God, though perhaps they had shown something new about the human capacity for, or will to do, evil. Even that drew no comment from Baeck. Perhaps having taken the power to do good so seriously, he had known all along how destructive the choice of evil could be.

The Continuity of Baeck's Thought After the Holocaust

Baeck published one book after the Holocaust, *Dieses Volk: Jüdische Existenz* (in the English translation, *This People Israel: The Meaning of Jewish Existence*). Much of its first part had been written before his internment and while he was in Theresienstadt. Part two was the product of the early post–World War II years. Its concerns seem already enunciated in "Theology and History," an essay he published in 1932 in the face of the increasing rejection of rationalism in Protestant theology and the alarming growth of Nazism.

"Theology and History" states the need for a theology of Judaism to be new in its particularity but not in its essence. Baeck warns against importing into Judaism the new methods of particularistic terminology of recent Christian theology, the Biblicism of Karl Barth or the existentialism of Rudolf Bultmann or Paul Tillich. He sees these as distorting any description of Judaism. Instead, he urges a continued use of the science of Judaism with its critical, rational approach to the Jewish past. In the present situation, however, it needs to be utilized for the purpose of clarifying the continuing validity of Judaism. The historic continuity of the essence of Judaism is the one firm basis for Jewish theology.

What had changed for Baeck was not the method of doing theology, which still follows Dilthey, but only the focus of concern. He now proposed to elucidate the particularity, that is, the distinctive characteristics of the Jewish experience, but he still meant to explain them in terms of the universal truth of human ethics and religious consciousness.

This People Israel is the fulfillment of that program. His new interests are given by the full title. Where once he wrote about Judaism, here he is concerned with the Jewish people. Before, he searched for the essence. Now it is existence that matters. Yet for all the concern with Jewish history and even the Land of Israel, Baeck does not break with his former way of thinking. He explains and justifies Jewish particularity in terms of its relation to the essence of Judaism, which remains a generally available human truth, ethical monotheism. Baeck had not given up his universal-oriented ethical approach for an existentialist, particularist approach to Judaism. *This People Israel* is only an extension of what he had written in *The Essence of Judaism* a quarter of a century before. He gives the Holocaust less than one page of attention and the slightly larger treatment of the State of Israel is substantially taken up by two prophetically insightful questions: How will Israelis get along with Arabs? And will nationalism or religion be fundamental to the state? Baeck believed that the theory of the Jewish people he had given in *The Essence of Judaism* remained correct. All he needed to do in the later book was give it more ample statement and apply it to the people's actual history.

Baeck's attitude toward the Jewish people and Jewish law should be understood in the context of his analysis of Judaism's essence as a universal human truth. Only in the final pages of *The Essence of Judaism* did he treat the particularistic doctrine of Judaism in some detail. Clearly, he was not unconcerned with Jewish sources and what they had to say about the people of Israel or its practices. He continually cites the Jewish classics—the Bible, the prayer book, the Rabbis—making many an often quoted phrase refract a new light. He does so to carry out an ethical transvaluation of their meaning and disclose their hidden, universal message. Baeck studies the Jewish tradition to prove that the general human apprehension of ethics, extended to its religious depth, has been the creative force in Judaism.

Truth, for Baeck, remains universal. Whatever is true about Judaism must be true for all human beings. Baeck does not believe the Jews had a revelation no other people had or could have had. He does not think anything their religious consciousness intuited and expressed in their people's way of life was unavailable to all other peoples. This being the case, Baeck is forced to confront rationalism's continuing challenge to all forms of particularism: If truth is generally available, why is your view of it, your people's particular sense of it, and your group's way of living it worthy of special devotion? The question is particularly poignant to Jews, for being a Jew not only carries with it many responsibilities, but it involves the heavy burdens of minority existence extended to the point of potential special suffering.

Baeck's Understanding of the Jewish People

Baeck's particular mix of universalism and particularism emerges clearly in his treatment of the traditional Jewish doctrine of God's having chosen this people "from among all peoples." In Baeck's system, religious consciousness allows us to conceive God through our sense of the mysterious depth to human createdness. This is not a sufficient philosophic basis for saying God acts in history. Rather, since God's relationship with people has a universal ethical structure, any notion of chosenness as preference is precluded. The God of Baeck's ethical monotheism must be equally available to all, a concept known to traditional Judaism. Baeck goes further. His God cannot be particularly related to any one people—a negation of the classic Jewish doctrine that the universal God has a special people. What, then, constitutes Jewish "chosenness" for Baeck?

The universally available idea of ethical monotheism came to the Hebrews as it might to any people. In their case alone it became decisive for their self-perception as a people. They applied the universal demands of ethical monotheism to their folk life and staked their ethnic existence on their religious insight. Remaining faithful to their vision despite periods of infidelity, they became conscious of themselves as set apart from other peoples. They felt themselves uniquely pledged to God and historically identified with the idea of ethical monotheism. They thus became a people with a mission. They survived as a people not only for their own sake, but so that humankind might come to know and serve the one God. In this knowledge they found the strength to endure their suffering over the millennia.

Baeck does not assert Jewish particularity in terms of Judaism's essential content, which is universal, but only in the historic actuality of its appropriation and continuing expression. The Jews are "chosen" because they chose to devote themselves to God. They were confronted, as all people are, with God's command to be human, but they alone made that behest the foundation of their ethnic life. As this became their deepest consciousness of themselves, they called themselves God's chosen people. Again, Baeck's two principles balance out. What ethical theory had made improbable, the coordinate theory of religious consciousness has now explained.

Baeck's Polemic Against Christianity

Jewish particularity has existential rather than mere historical validity only if it can be argued that no other community carries the idea of ethical monotheism through history. In *The Essence of Judaism*, Baeck identified two types of religion—world-affirming and world-rejecting. He considers Judaism the classic example of the former type and he calls it a religion of ethical optimism. He does not deny that there are ethical teachings in the world-rejecting religions, of which Buddhism is the prototype, but their essential stance toward life is withdrawal. Buddhist ethics gains its objectives by eliminating human desire and thereby reducing contentiousness. However, its adherents no longer care deeply about anything. Their detachment keeps them from being passionate about righteousness or outraged by immorality.

Christianity seems to share Judaism's faith about God and ethics. But Baeck insists that Christian self-consciousness differs radically from its Jewish counterpart. He developed this thesis extensively in the essay "Romantic Religion," published first in 1922 and later somewhat expanded.

Baeck also employs the typological method to identify two varieties of religious experience. "Classic" religion is positive, activist, outgoing, social, ethical, deed-oriented, rational, masculine. "Romantic" religion is passive in the face of reality, individualistic, self-centered, inward, concerned with faith and its content, confirming itself in feelings, emphasizing grace. It has a feminine cast.

Pure types exist only in thought but history knows outstanding representatives of these possibilities. Judaism is closest to the classic type while Christianity is the finest example of romantic religion. Baeck ranges through the breadth of Christian history, Catholic as well as Protestant, to exhibit its nonrational, ethics-subordinating features. Since these are fundamental to Christianity as a religion, in principle it cannot hope to become a more activist, ethical faith by accepting liberal ideas. Judaism, by contrast, was always essentially the religion of world-transforming ethical monotheism, so its modernization is only the fulfillment of its classic stance. Baeck insists that he is making no value judgments in this essay but only describing the two faiths. But to anyone who cares about religion of reason, the message is clear.

Subjectivity is the problem of all typologies, and Baeck's argument is no exception. Why there are just two types, why these are romantic and classic, why Judaism and Christianity are the chief representatives, why

all the countervailing evidence in both religions is ignored—none of
these issues is examined; none of Baeck's premises is explained. Each
is a mere assertion. Baeck speaks of Judaism in liberalistic terms as an
ethical, rational faith. He contrasts this modern, German reinterpretation of Judaism with traditionalistic Protestantism and Catholicism.
Baeck was so fully committed to this method that he believed his
statement of the essence of Judaism to be objectively visible, not a
highly subjective reading. But what he and Harnack, in the self-
assurance of their humanistic, scientific approach to the interpretation of history, took as self-evident now appears as self-justification
masquerading as science. Baeck's argument for Jewish uniqueness says
more about Baeck's love for his tradition than it does about reality. As a
consequence, his resolution of the problem of Jewish particularity is
seriously compromised.

The Jewish Role in History

Baeck drew a uniquely activist conclusion regarding the Jewish mission to humankind. Exemplification, the classic Jewish strategy, is not
enough for him. He believes modern Jews should undertake a cam-
paign of proselytization. Though Jews in medieval times did not seek
converts and seemed rather to discourage them, he argues that this
stance was largely the result of external pressures. While in talmudic
times the Rabbis occasionally protest against proselytes, the overwhelming majority of their statements are positive. Baeck reads that
history as saying that when the Jews were free, they proselytized.
Therefore, he feels that today, in all dignity and faithfulness to their
belief, they should do so again.

Baeck occasionally takes this line of reasoning one critical step
further. He declares that the idea of ethical monotheism cannot now
be detached from Israel. Significant spiritual notions become part of
human reality by being borne by specific peoples or cultures. Other
groups may come to know the meaning of ethical monotheism but the
Jews alone, having identified themselves with it, are responsible for its

fate in history. Since human beings are prone to relapse into paganism, the people of Israel's task is not short-term. Stubborn endurance is a Jewish ethical imperative; for a Jew, to exist is a commandment.

Typically, Baeck balances this realistic depiction of the world with Jewish optimism. Israel's service will not be in vain. Humanity can reach a time when it fulfills the command addressed to it. This messianic faith enabled Israel to survive over the centuries. The Jewish people now stands in history as a witness not only to the truth of messianism but to the efficacy of hope. A despairing humankind needs Israel to remind it that human ethical striving need not be defeated. Baeck devotes *This People Israel* to showing how the different stages of Jewish history contributed to this continuing Jewish service.

Jewish Law, a Means to the Universal End

This line of reasoning logically leads to Baeck's theory of Jewish law. Jewish law enables the people of Israel to carry on through history in devotion to its faith. The distinction between commandment and law is critical here.

Baeck normally uses the word "commandment" only for that which comes from God, namely ethical behests. People may come to know the ethical better or express it more fully but it is not subject to human will or imagination. Baeck uses the term "law" to refer to a broader realm of obligation, one whose precepts are legislated by people, essentially for their own purposes. Law therefore is subject to human evaluation and revision. Jewish law makes its most immediate claim upon Jews insofar as it states or leads to ethics, that is, to "commandment." In any tension between commandment and Jewish law, ethics has priority since it is the essence of Judaism.

Baeck is liberal. He favors change in the "law" to allow "commandment" to become more evident. Yet in all other cases, Baeck advocates our keeping Jewish law, for it carries out another function. It helps the Jewish people survive history, keeping the people together and faithful through time and despite place. Though widely dispersed, in dissimilar climates, under differing economic systems or disparate political orders, the law keeps them one Jewish people, dedicated to their universal mission. It also separates them from the paganism of humankind and enjoins a community life of warmth and beauty which is the most effective antidote to anti-Semitism. If the law served only a social function it would have no compelling power. However, its high ethical content keeps Israel not only alive as a people but loyal to its task.

How Satisfying Is Baeck's Reworking of Rationalism?

Baeck's thought may very well represent the last of the great Jewish universalist intellectual systems. At the moment it seems unlikely to have any significant successor. Thoughtful Jews today regularly call for a Judaism that emphasizes particularism, specifically, a rich appreciation of Jewish peoplehood and a strong sense of ritual observance. If Jewish authenticity now requires such particularity, universally grounded Jewish theologies have been unable to provide it. Baeck's thought demonstrates this failing.

Though he went beyond Neo-Kantianism to create a system with a personally felt relationship to God, he remained in the world of philosophical idealism he had inherited. By grounding the essence of Judaism in universals, he left open a series of almost unanswerable questions regarding Jewish particularity. If ethical monotheism can be known by any person of religious consciousness, why does one need Judaism? If this universal truth is reasonably clear today, why chance distorting it by particularizing it? And, most dangerous and probing of all, if the essence of Judaism is available in direct, intellectual form, are we not ethically required to spare future generations of Jews the possible suffering entailed in perpetuating our people?

These questions arise directly out of Baeck's idealism: in his thought, the people, Israel, exists for the sake of its idea, ethical monotheism. If so, Baeck has made it possible to argue, particularly after the Holocaust, that one should choose a less dangerous instrument to accomplish the same end. Baeck might respond that the Holocaust proves how far from ethical existence even supposedly civilized people are. If anything, it demonstrates the supreme importance of the Jewish people continuing its humanizing mission.

Baeck's actual intellectual response to this argument, however, seems alien to his system. A Hegelian could argue, with some consistency, that an idea requires a people to carry it through history, but such an assertion cannot be made on the basis of ethics or religious consciousness, which all people possess. Baeck's assertion that the Jewish people has become inextricably tied to the idea of ethical monotheism seems hardly credible when we recall the Kantian origins of this concept. At the very least it seems odd that a Gentile German philosopher and his successors were able to clarify what is asserted to be "the essence of Judaism." If ethical monotheism can be recognized by all rationally competent and religiously attuned people, on what basis can one argue that the idea cannot survive without the Jewish people?

Jews Today and in Baeck's Vision

Baeck's notion that the Jews exist for their religious truth leads to added complications. As with Cohen, his universalism prevents him from seeing significant value in Jewish ethnicity, though unlike the philosopher, he can see considerable instrumental worth in it. Thus, where Cohen was resolutely anti-Zionist, Baeck is only a non-Zionist. Baeck found virtue in whatever unites the Jewish people so long as it also contributes to their worldwide mission. So he appreciated and participated in the effort to resettle Palestine and to bring Jews there in escape from Hitler. There was a kind of Zionism for which he had little or no sympathy. He saw no point in ethnic activities for their own sake and opposed secular, nationalistic interpretations of Judaism. After his rescue from Theresienstadt he did not settle in Jerusalem but lived in London. The choice was not merely a matter of personal convenience. Like so much else of Baeck's life, it was symbolic and consistent with his philosophy.

The critique of Baeck's particularism can also be extended to his theory of Jewish practice. Assuming that the Jewish people is the bearer of ethical monotheism in history, why must Jews go beyond doing the good and believing in God? Is not all the rest of Jewish observance formality? If we are ethical and loyal to our people, why must we seriously attend to a lunar calendar, Semitic celebrations, and Hebraic liturgy? Although they might enrich our lives and solidify the Jewish people, they are also a special burden. By contrast, our society has many groups working for ethical ends. Membership in them is particularly appealing when they also consciously attempt to overcome the divisions between groups.

On a practical level the challenge is put this way: Isn't it enough to be a good Jew if one is ethical and believes in one God? In a day when so many ethical demands compete for proper attention, most people are quite satisfied if they can manage to live the simplest life, to do the essence. They are only too willing to abandon activities that are not essential though they might be useful, particularly when these are burdensome and require a special effort. And this competition for time and energy tells much of the story of modern liberal Judaism.

Baeck's system might have spoken to the needs of a generation so solidly Jewish that its universalization was no threat to its Jewishness. Our community is in another situation. We are substantially integrated into the general culture. An interpretation of Judaism that speaks mainly of our relation to humanity and gives little emphasis to our distinctiveness avoids the major problem of contemporary Jewish existence.

The broadest intellectual criticism is that Baeck never explains how religious consciousness and ethical understanding are bound together. Why does inner experience need to be limited in action to what the ethical can allow? Why must the ethical command rest on a mysterious ground? One cannot claim their balance is self-evident or even rational for, in substantial measure, they contradict one another. Philosophically these limits go against the teachings of the intellectual schools that created these concepts. In response, Baeck might argue that he is not a philosopher. He is only describing in modern terms the unity Judaism envisioned and taught through the ages. This brings critics to their most penetrating question: Just how does Baeck know this? What is the methodology by which he ascertains the essence of

Judaism? What are the criteria by which he knows what is unessential and secondary? Why has apparently contradictory material been ignored? Surely his proposal, for all its persuasiveness, differs from the self-understanding of the Jewish tradition. No Jew before the nineteenth century talked about Judaism or its essence, no classic Jewish book mentions "ethical monotheism." Jews now doing so have a substantial burden of proof if they are to convince skeptics that their doctrine is authentically Jewish rather than a modern idea read back into the Jewish tradition.

Yet there is lasting greatness to Baeck's thought. In the face of the great philosophical accomplishments of Cohen, Baeck reasserted the right of religion to speak to the heart. Rationalism greatly appealed to modern Jews. It served to validate their participation in modern culture and their rejection of conversion to Christianity. For many Jews, reason alone was an adequate way of bringing modernity and Judaism into harmony. But not for Leo Baeck. While granting the virtues of the Neo-Kantian interpretation of Judaism, he dared to extend its scope and, in so doing, to make the religious life more substantial. He introduced the notion of personal experience into modern Jewish thought and insisted that personal spirituality was part of the essence of Judaism.

While his theories of the Jewish people and Jewish law have been seriously challenged, it is hard to imagine any contemporary Jewish thinker arguing that religious consciousness is peripheral to authentic Jewish being.

4

Nationalism: The Zionist Interpretation of Judaism

THREE events play critical roles in shaping modern Jewish thought. The Emancipation sets its context, the Holocaust remains its major unresolved theological issue, and the State of Israel by its success implicitly poses the questions of what constitutes authentic Jewish existence. One may say without qualification that nothing in contemporary Jewish life—and perhaps nothing in the last two millennia—has given rise to more Jewish pride and elicited more support than the State of Israel.

The Israeli accomplishments have been so varied that they command world Jewry's admiration. Israelis have created a modern economy, reclaimed land, absorbed refugees, provided for social welfare, operated a government, fought wars, projected a humane image of the Jews, created an Hebraic culture, remained a democracy and, in the face of terror, contumely, threats, and isolation, indomitably pursue a decent life for themselves and their children—all this in stark contrast to the callousness and barbarity that has characterized twentieth-century politics generally. Moreover, the State of Israel has largely been the product of refugees rescued from Hitler's death camps, or later from Arab countries. That people so maltreated by their enemies, ignored by most of humanity, and neglected in their time of trial even by their own people would now reassert their humanity, reaffirm their ethnic identity, and reenter history as a political entity is awesome.

Since Israel did not exist until well into the twentieth century, an analysis of its place in modern Jewish thought must begin with the thinking of the Zionist movement, out of which the state arose. Compared with the other systems that we are considering, Zionist thought was heavily ideological; it was not a systematic, academic search for the truth. No single Zionist thinker produced a coherent, theoretical justification of Zionism as an intellectual response to the meeting of Judaism and modernity. Nevertheless, Zionism had a lasting historical impact and positive influence upon Jewish life.

What If the Jews Are a Nation?

Zionism put forward a revolutionary premise: the Jews are a nationality. Or, to put this in European usage: the Jews are a nation. To Americans the term "nation" carries political overtones that imply that Jews are not wholeheartedly loyal to the countries in which they reside. Such an imputation of double loyalty, or worse, of a primary loyalty elsewhere, would be abhorrent to almost all American Jews. Some years back, the term "nationality" allayed such fears, for many immigrant groups remained attached to their national homelands while being loyal Americans. Today, when we are more accustomed to speaking of the diversity of America's ethnic groups, the radicalism of the original Zionist thesis would be lost if it were to be stated: the Jews are an ethnic group. The Zionists wanted to say far more. They were determined to rethink Jewish life and duty in strictly political terms.

In many countries, most notably in the lands of Eastern Europe with its dense Jewish population, the citizenry often comprised many national groups. Each folk might have certain rights, perhaps even receiving government support for the maintenance of certain of its national institutions and cultural activities. But with the spread of the ideology of nationalism in the nineteenth century, groups united by land and language often strove to achieve political independence as well. Italy is the classic case of such nationalism; and Zionism is the Jewish version of this nineteenth-century idea. It may also be called the characteristic Eastern European response to modernity. Just as Western Jews, living in religiously pluralistic nations, modernized by equating Judaism with religion, so Eastern European Jews equated Judaism with nationality and thus freed themselves to create an emancipated Jewish way of life.

Land, Statehood, and Nationality

The Jews were united by languages, culture, history, and the problem of anti-Semitism. But Jewish nationality had one obvious difference from that of other European groups: the Jews did not live on their ancestral land.

In its earliest stages, Zionist Jewish nationality was occasionally thought to be separable from the Land of Israel. In his revolutionary pamphlet, *The Jewish State*, Theodor Herzl, who initiated the modern Zionist movement, said that the problem of the Jews was national and required a political solution. When such a solution was offered by the British in 1903 in the form of a proposal that Uganda become the national homeland for the Jews, Herzl was prepared to accept. For him, "the Jewish state" need not be on the Jewish land; there was need for an immediate homeland to answer the pressing problem of anti-Semitism. Indeed, for some decades thereafter a Jewish territorialist movement existed, nationalistic but willing to accept any country for Jewish settlement. Simon Dubnow, author of a ten-volume history of the Jewish people, similarly envisaged a distinction between Jewish nationality and territory. In his theory, one great accomplishment of the Jewish people was its evolution beyond geographic fixation. The Jews were the first cosmopolitan nationality, a model for the future of humankind. Most Zionists rejected such universalizing conceptions, considering it unthinkable that the Jewish state could be established anywhere but on the Land of Israel, *eretz yisrael.*

For a long time, Zionists did not always equate Jewish nation-hood with political independence. The program adopted in Basle at the First Zionist Congress in 1897 said only, "The aim of Zionism is to create for the Jewish people a home in Palestine secured by public law." It was conceivable that, as in Europe, national existence might be possible within the sovereignty of some other political power. When the 1917 Balfour Declaration publicly committed the British government to work for "the establishment in Palestine of a national home for the Jewish people," many Zionists thought that the movement had completed its work. Not until the 1942 Biltmore Program was adopted by a specially called conference did any but a minority of Zionists say that Jewish nationalism required a sovereign Jewish state.

David Ben-Gurion, who was responsible for the Biltmore statement, applied this understanding in deciding on the name of the new state established in 1948. Many had thought it would be called Judea, a continuation of the name of the last Jewish commonwealth. Ben-Gurion preferred the name Israel, *yisrael* (the declaration of independence also calls it the "State of Israel," *medinat yisrael*), since he wanted the name of the political entity to be identical with the name of the people. In Ben-Gurion's Jewish nationalism, political sovereignty was a fulfillment of national existence.

Can Jews Rely Upon the Emancipation?

Three intellectually significant notions were contained in the assertion that the Jews were a nation. The first was the proposition that the Emancipation was a tragedy, not a godsend, for the Jewish people. This negative assessment resulted from a shifted perspective. The Emancipation might be a boon to the individual Jew, but to the Jewish people, in terms of its culture and its community life, it was a disaster. Being Jewish was reduced to religious activity; the folk as such played no formal role in the social structure. The results in the West were already obvious: by the second liberated generation, emancipated Jews no longer shared a Jewish tongue as their primary language, and Jewish styles were being shed for those of the surrounding people. Even in Eastern Europe, where the Haskalah (enlightenment) movement had hoped to make Jewish culture attractive by active involvement with the world, this loss of folk vitality was evident. The Haskalah ideal was "Be a man abroad and a Jew at home," a prescription that unwittingly indicated how marginal and internal Jewish life would have to become in any society whose ethos was created by non-Jews.

Paralleling this Jewish assimilation was the emergence of a new type of anti-Semitism. What had been essentially religious was now secularized. Jews were hated as unassimilable outsiders, perhaps even as national enemies. When race theories emerged toward the end of the nineteenth century, anti-Semitism took on pseudo-scientific, biological hypotheses, thereby fatefully making Jews different in their very life stuff. This prejudice could not be met by the liberal Jewish strategies of education or assimilation for the more the Jews made their way into the society the more they provoked the host nation's anger at their intrusion. Some Zionists, like Vladimir Jabotinsky, carried this theory through to its logical conclusion, arguing not only that European Jewish life could not long continue but that a major calamity awaited Jews who did not immigrate to the Land of Israel. Most Zionists considered Jabotinsky an alarmist and his position extreme. They persisted in this naivete well after the Jews were already in the Nazi ghettos.

Ending Anti-Semitism Through Zionism

Almost all Zionists agreed that only the establishment of a Jewish national homeland would solve the problems of Jewish life and anti-Semitism. With Jews in their homeland, a proper Jewish national life and culture might be revived. In an influential pamphlet written in 1882, Leo Pinsker suggested to Russian Jews that the cause of anti-Semitism was the lack of a clear social status. The establishment of a

Jewish state would provide a national Jewish identity, thereby ending anti-Semitism.

Herzl's analysis placed the blame for "the Jewish problem" on Jewish population density and consequent economic competition with the indigenous citizenry of Eastern Europe. Zionism would remedy anti-Semitism by moving large numbers of Jews to the Jewish state.

Clearly, both Herzl and Pinsker, like many of the early Zionists, believed that overcoming anti-Semitism was a primary purpose for Zionism. In retrospect, this part of their program was doomed to ironic failure. Not only has anti-Semitism remained alive since the establishment of Israel, but some have argued that political opposition to the state has given new form and focus to the old prejudice.

For Jews living in the post-Hitler era, it is difficult to comprehend why there should have been Jewish opposition to Zionism, why positive Jews opposed the effort to establish a Jewish state. One clue lies in the way in which Zionism opposed the adaptation strategy being utilized by the majority of Europe's Jews. The overwhelming number of Jews wishing to modernize either moved to countries where there was a greater degree of democracy or tried to adjust to their societies. The migrants, at great personal cost, based their hopes on the practicality of social integration. By rejecting the Zionist thesis that Emancipation was a fraud, they committed themselves to one of their major life decisions. In the Zionist arguments that true safety was possible only in a Jewish state, they perceived a threat to their claim that they could be wholehearted citizens of their adopted nations.

Nor was this true only for Jews who had immigrated to Western Europe. Those who came to America found a congenial ideology in the melting pot theory. Integration was the ideal for minorities, and emphasizing one's ethnic existence put one's Americanism in doubt. The Reform Jews were the leaders of anti-Zionist opposition, for they had pioneered the ideal of Jewish integration into the general society. Classic Reform Judaism considered the Jews a purely religious group whose central teaching was ethical monotheism and who continued as a separate entity because they had a mission to teach this universal doctrine to all humankind. This theology was already under heavy attack when Hitler's intentions began to become clear. Disclosures of the horrors of the Holocaust and the establishment of the State of Israel effectively put an end to it, though the vestiges of this point of view remain preserved in the American Council for Judaism.

Politics as the New Means of Salvation

The fears of many Jews in regard to Zionism were further exacerbated by the method the Zionists adopted to accomplish their goal. This method, political activism—or, in philosophic terms, human self-assertion—constitutes the second major intellectual theme in Jewish nationalism. Herzl was not the first to advocate a Jewish state. His genius lay in projecting it as an open, collective effort to be carried out by the World Zionist Organization he created. The Zionist Congresses, with their worldwide representations, were utterly unprecedented in Jewish life. Such public political exposure immediately offended Western Jews who had been declaring for a century that they were a religious group. They were sufficiently outraged to prevent Herzl from holding the first Congress at Munich, where it had been originally scheduled; he had to shift its site to Basle.

Political action was the heart of Herzl's program, but more than that, it was the first manifestation that the Jews were a nation. It was also a direct challenge to inherited Jewish belief. It was traditionally held that God was responsible for the return of Jews to their land and the reestablishment of Jewish hegemony there. God would send the King Messiah to accomplish this only when God was ready to do so. Until then, Jews must wait patiently and not try to "force the coming of the End Time." (The notion of doing so by political action did not exist before the transformation of world politics in the nineteenth century.) This comparatively passive attitude to redemption was somewhat relieved by an activist strand in Jewish faith. There was a steady stream of would-be Messiahs in post-biblical Jewish history, and the Lurianic *kabbalah* of the sixteenth century had radically reversed the rabbinic teaching, putting the power of achieving

Israel's redemption into the hands of the mystic adepts. In a complex way, this change made possible the worldwide Jewish response to the last great false Messiah, Shabbetai Tzevi (1626–1676). His ultimate conversion to Islam, particularly after having messianically introduced certain changes into Jewish religious practice, provoked a major reaction on the part of the rabbinate. Messianic activism was thoroughly rejected—the Hasidim transforming it substantially into a subjective goal—and taking the initiative to change Jewish practice was resolutely opposed. This mood of resignedly accepting the Jews' fate was reinforced by the economic and social deprivation in which most Jews lived.

Orthodox Tensions with Zionism

Zionism began as a self-conscious rejection of Orthodox Judaism and its passivity. For much of the nineteenth century, writers reviving the Hebrew language as a literary medium had savagely criticized the life style of traditional Jews. They attacked its superstition, parochialism, worldly ignorance, and dogmatism. They accused the rabbinate of fostering and supporting these retrogressive elements of Judaism and contrasted them disparagingly to the love of nature, the appreciation of the body, the pleasure in human emotion, and the outreach to all humankind that characterized the modern spirit. Much of that negativism carried over particularly into Eastern European Zionism, where, as was often the case, it was influenced by the Marxist analysis of society with its view of religion as a reactionary force.

The Zionists defined the Jews as a nation in order to destroy the exclusive authority of the rabbinate to say what a good Jew was. Jews who wanted to be religious would surely not be prevented from being so, but those who wished to adopt much of Western civilization might do so in good Jewish conscience so long as they remained loyal to the nation. Specifically, the Zionists ridiculed the notion that Jews should accept their suffering as God's punishment or trial and wait for the King Messiah to redeem them when they were perfectly capable of taking action to improve their immediate welfare. Leo Pinsker entitled his pamphlet of 1882 *Auto-Emancipation*. Jews need not wait for some other people to free them as a nation; they could take responsibility upon themselves. The title may also have referred to God, for the Jews need no longer wait in utter dependence on God to grant them freedom.

The accommodation of Orthodoxy to Zionism was well under way before World War I and a party reconciling traditional Jewish belief with Zionism, *Mizrahi*, soon became a significant minority faction within the World Zionist Organization. Not all Orthodox Jews were convinced the two positions could be reconciled, of course. In 1912, when the World Zionist Organization decided to undertake educational and cultural activities, a group of Orthodox leaders withdrew from the Organization and established the *Agudat Israel* in opposition to secularist Zionism. Their party in the State of Israel has occasionally participated in government coalitions, but they reject the notion that the State of Israel can be Jewish if it remains steadfastly secular. Some smaller groups, notably the *Neturei Karta* and the Satmarer Hasidim, consider the establishment of a pre-messianic Jewish government on the Holy Land an act of heresy.

Turning Religion Into National Culture

This brings the third intellectual theme of Zionist nationalism into sharp relief. Because of their ideology, the Zionists wanted to secularize Jewish life. Classic Zionism was strongly anti-religious and anti-clerical. In addition to the positions already mentioned, most Zionists equated modernity with the death of God and the end of religion. A self-confident humankind, taking history into its own hands and trusting in science to provide it with a reliable world view, had no need for religious faith, laws, or institutions.

The Zionists set about secularizing Judaism. The "holy tongue," Hebrew, became the language of everyday speech. "Redeeming the land" became the purchase of real estate. The Psalmist's cry, "Who can retell the mighty acts of God!" became the Zionist song (now associated with Hanukkah) "Who can retell the mighty acts of Israel!" The mystic credo, "Israel, the Holy One, Blessed be He, and the Torah are one" likewise became a song—omitting God. The examples could easily be multiplied, for the strategy largely succeeded. Much to the surprise of many American visitors who think of Judaism primarily in religious terms, the State of Israel remains substantially secular and most of its Jewish citizens have a nationalistic interpretation of Jewishness.

The three theoretical issues—the rejection of the Emancipation, the reliance on political activism, and the secularization of Jewish life—form the background for those questions that have been more openly debated by Jewish thinkers.

Do Most Jews Live in Exile?

The first group of such issues has to do with the rigidity with which Jewish nationalism should be defined. Chief of these is the argument over whether Jews living outside the Land of Israel are in Exile, *galut*, or only in Diaspora, the *tefutzot*. The difference seems at first linguistic, but major consequences for Jewish life follow on the choice of term. "Diaspora" is a Greek word meaning "scattered" and already in Roman times the knowledge that Jews were widely dispersed made the term useful. Some peoples do have their nationals scattered in many countries. Saying they are in dispersion is merely descriptive and attaches no judgment. But "exile" is an evaluative term. The Bible authors use it with very strong negative connotations. If the Land itself is holy and given to the people of Israel by God as part of the Covenant, to be put off the land is a terrible punishment, religiously as well as nationally.

The Rabbis maintain and extend this attitude. They call other lands religiously impure, rule that residence on the Land and ownership of it have special legal priority, describe Jewish life elsewhere as hazardous, and depict Israel's Exile not merely as a local, national-religious matter but as a cosmic tragedy, for now God too is in Exile. With the increase in suffering by Jews in the Middle Ages, the term's negative significance intensified; "Exile" implied that the degradation of the Jews had a metaphysical root that only the coming of the Messiah could correct.

Mainstream Zionists rejected all the religious connotations of the term "Exile" and politicized it. The Jewish people was in Exile as long as it did not have its own state; individual Jews are in Exile until they come to live on the Land of Israel, particularly now that a Jewish state has been established there. "Exile" therefore is also a geographic term. Stepping out of the borders of the State of Israel, a Jew is in Exile; a step the other way and a Jew has left the Exile—an important part of the revised concept of redemption. The Zionists retained all the negative connotations of the term "Exile," secularizing them now into a judgment on the deterioration of Jewish life and the persistence of anti-Semitism outside the land of Israel.

How Many Centers Does World Jewry Have?

Several corollary questions emerge from this distinction. What is the destiny of Jewish life away from the Land of Israel? And how important a Jewish duty is immigration, *aliyah*, to the Land of Israel? If Jews abroad are only in Diaspora, some environments may make possible their continued existence as Jews. If they are in Exile, their Jewishness will not long continue. Similarly, Jews in the Diaspora may choose Jewish fulfillment through *aliyah* or be satisfied by the Jewish life off the Land. If they are in Exile and immigration to the Land is practical, a loyal Jew must make it one of life's highest priorities. An interesting variant of these issues has been proposed by existentialist theoreticians. Utilizing the concept of general human alienation, they have argued for Exile as a condition of the self as well as of the Jewish people. Redemption therefore cannot be complete until the human self is restored to wholeness. Political action will not suffice because

God is necessarily involved in completing human finitude. More surprisingly, the existentialist view depicts even Jews residing in the Land of Israel as in *galut*, until God's redeeming work is accomplished.

A parallel issue is the relation of the State of Israel to world Jewry. The pledge that qualifies one as a Zionist able to vote for delegates to a World Zionist Congress affirms the "centrality" of the State of Israel in Jewish life. As befits organizational language, the term "centrality" is broadly inclusive. Descriptively, it indicates the unique intensity Jews bring to Israeli affairs, thus embracing almost all Jews. In Zionist ideology it implies that nothing in Jewish life should take priority over the State of Israel's concerns. Thus, the World Zionist Organization Department of Education wants all Jewish school curricula to center around the State of Israel. If the Jews are a nation, what could be more important? Moreover, the doctrine of centrality has strong political overtones, suggesting that the State of Israel should lead all of world Jewry, democratically but with unique authority. At the extreme, it means that Jews off the Land have no right to criticize the State of Israel. Some Zionists find that illogical. They argue that if the State of Israel fulfills world Jewry's nationality, Jews everywhere have a stake in the manner in which it translates the Jewish heritage into social reality.

The Special Demands Jews Make of Jews

What should be the character of Jewish nationhood? Are the Jews a nation "like all other nations"? Or is there some special character to Jewish life that must be maintained lest Israelis no longer be authentically Jewish? In many respects the Zionists aimed to make modern Jews a normal nation. They attributed many Jewish problems to abnormalities in Jewish existence—for example, the absence of a laboring class or farmers. Zionism attempted to restore Jewish normalcy economically, culturally, and spiritually. For years the hero of the Zionist movement was the *halutz*, the pioneer who settled on the land. Contrast the artistic image of the Jew as a bearded, pale, frail, old man bent over a book, with the common expectation that the Israeli will be youthful, tanned, and vigorous, perhaps a soldier. A transformation has taken place, to the joy of most Jews.

Normalcy also implies that the Jews do not have to be better than anyone else. Politically, why should the Israelis be judged by uncommonly high moral standards while their antagonists are excused for practicing realpolitik? Yet would world Jewry be satisfied if the State of Israel conducted itself with the normal cynicism of governments? Would Jews everywhere passionately identify with it, if the State of Israel operated at about the level of the other Middle Eastern states?

Ahad Ha-Am: Zionism as Elitism

One early Zionist theoretician asked and responded to these questions. His answers endeared him to Diaspora Zionists. Ahad Ha-Am—the pen name of Asher Ginzberg (1856–1927)—was reared in a traditional family in Russia, educated himself in modern culture, and became a leader in the Hebrew literary renaissance of the turn of the century. As an editor and writer he is credited with having developed the modern Hebrew prose style. Though many of his essays were prompted by events in the Jewish world in the three decades before World War I, they are distinguished by a philosophic cast of mind not common among other Zionist writers.

Ahad Ha-Am thought science had refuted religion. Unlike other Zionists, he substituted a high appreciation of the human spirit and a humanistic sense of nationhood for the old belief in God and revelation. His "*cultural Zionism*" contained several major priorities.

Ahad Ha-Am rejects as unscientific any supernational motive for the continuation of the Jewish nation. Rather he points out that every people naturally wants to survive. A national will-to-live continues unabated in most Jews despite the misery of discrimination and the excitement of emancipation. By projecting a program leading to a revived Jewish folk life, Zionism could summon these latent national energies. Jews could abandon their unbelievable and unrealistic appeals to God's command or a Jewish mission to humankind as reasons for Jewish continuity.

At its best, every nation produces a culture of many dimensions. Jews are dissatisfied with the present state of Jewish life because of the poverty of Jewish culture. In the ghetto-*shtetl* period it had atrophied, retaining only a narrow religious focus. The fully developed arts of the general society, by contrast, have rendered irresistible the Emancipation's promise of full cultural self-expression. As long as Jewish culture remains unreconstructed, sensitive Jews will defect to the non-Jewish world. Zionism should draw on the extraordinarily variegated resources of the Jewish heritage to create a rich literary and artistic life. The positive response to the Hebrew literary revival proves that given a humanistic Zionism, Jews will once again make the good of the Jewish people the highest aim of their lives.

The People of Spirit Need a Spiritual Center

Ahad Ha-Am carried this concept one critical step forward. He offered a secular theory of the special character of the Jewish spirit. His intellectual resource was folk psychology, the academic predecessor of sociology. It sought to understand peoples as if they were persons. As individuals have certain talents, so do ethnic groups, and these produce their particular civilization. The Jews, Ahad Ha-Am proclaimed, had a genius for high culture centered on ethics. He not only identified this with the prophets' teaching, as the German Jewish liberals had done, but with Moses' leadership and talmudic law as well. The regeneration of the Jewish people, then, was a qualitative matter and could be accomplished only through cultural work of high creativity and ethical sensitivity. Ahad Ha-Am was a self-conscious elitist. For him Jewish culture was synonymous with the best in the human spirit. In that humanistic sense he considered Zionism a spiritual endeavor.

He conceived of the revived Jewish state as the people's "spiritual center." Only by returning to its homeland could the Jewish people reconstitute its culture in its own terms and express its natural genius. The spiritual products of the resettlement would reflect an authentic Jewish ethos that could be communicated to Jews all over the world.

Local circumstances might permit them only a truncated Jewish existence, but, strengthened by the culture they received from the Jewish spiritual center, they could continue living as Jews. For Ahad Ha-Am, the word "spirit" has a fully secular, not a religious meaning.

Determining the Priorities of a Jewish State

Ahad Ha-Am tried to get the Zionist movement to implement his vision. Giving priority to culture, not political assurances or a changed Jewish economic profile, he resolutely opposed mass migration to Palestine. He was less interested in having Jewish farmers than in creating the cultural conditions that would keep them from becoming peasants. He proposed restricting immigration to those whose spiritual preparation was complete. These notions brought him and his followers into sharp conflict with the Zionist leadership, which gave priority first to political tasks and second to migration and settlement. None of the practical Zionist accomplishments satisfied him for he envisioned the movement rebuilding the spirit of the Jewish nation by reviving its culture. For him, nationalism and humanism were indivisible.

In unforgettable fashion, Ahad Ha-Am insisted on the proper quality of a Jewish state. The bare rudiments of national existence—being on one's land, speaking one's language, perhaps having political sovereignty—were not enough. A nation had to be true to its history and folk genius. He connected the Jews with superior human achievement and insisted that the national revival should settle for nothing less.

The Fate of Those Who Call for Quality

Ahad Ha-Am's ideas have been much beloved by Zionists who do not propose to make *aliyah*, for he propounds a theory of Diaspora rather than Exile. He does not advocate life outside the homeland, but he expects it to continue and believes a national spiritual center can keep it vital. Though immigration is a major Zionist responsibility, Ahad Ha-Am places greater weight on involvement with Hebrew culture. He is the spiritual father of American Jewry's efforts to benefit from Israeli art, literature, and music.

He has markedly less influence in the State of Israel, though the Israelis' intense concern for culture may in part be traced to him. Because of the State of Israel's constant struggle to survive, political realities have taken precedence over the Zionist aim of reviving Jewish life everywhere. Something of Ahad Ha-Am's fate also befell the three other notable theoreticians who sought to introduce an element of quality into Jewish nationalist theory. All were religious thinkers. Aharon David Gordon (1856–1922) had a spiritual appreciation of the life-power invigorating nature and created a quasi-mystical doctrine of the importance of a nation working its soil in nonexploitive, socialistic relationships. Rabbi Abraham Isaac Kook (1865–1935), the chief Ashkenazi rabbi of Palestine for the last twenty-one years of his life, had an all-encompassing mystical vision of the universe and the central role of the Jewish people in it, for which return to the Holy Land as a nation was a prerequisite. Rav Kook's combination of Orthodoxy and Zionism was unusual because of its mystical grounding and the sympathy he showed the mainline Zionists despite their determined secularity. The third such thinker was Martin Buber, and his Zionist philosophy will emerge from the general discussion of his thought given later in this book (see Chapter 7). Of the three, his thought had the fewest followers.

Zionism as a Reversal of Judaism in Exile

Some Zionists criticized Ahad Ha-Am and his followers as continuing *galut* ideals of proper Jewishness. Instead, they advocated a radical turn from the values of European Judaism. These thinkers were too extreme to have their philosophies widely adopted, yet their vigorous advocacy of nationalism influenced Zionist ideology more than did the cultural elitism of Ahad Ha-Am. Joseph Hayyim Brenner (1881–1921) is often considered the foremost exponent of the theory of *shelilat hagalut*, the negation of Jewish life in the Exile. He had almost nothing good to say about the Jewish experience since the days of an independent Jewish existence on the Land. He considered *galut*-culture valueless for it reflects the servile status of its creators. Its religion largely denies the elemental, natural forces of human life. Contemporary Jews in Exile hardly constituted a living people, having allowed their national will to degenerate to a resignation he considered more animal than human. The Emancipation, which supposedly civilized Jews, only showed their capacity for mimicry and their willingness to deny their own identity in the futile dream of social acceptance. Such hope as Brenner had in Zionism required it to transform radically the Jewish spirit from what Exile had made of it over the centuries.

Micah Joseph Berdichevsky (1865-1921) similarly decried the *galut* and excoriated what he saw as its perversion of the true Jewish spirit. He drew intellectual inspiration from Friedrich Nietzsche's call for a radical human change, for a "transvaluation of all values." In his many literary works Berdichevsky sought to expose the hidden vitality of the pristine Jewish spirit. This he found in the Jew's relation to the life forces animating nature and the human body. He read the Bible as an effort to repress this natural Judaism in favor of a false Judaism of spirituality. In his anthology of talmudic legends, he featured those that showed the passional, mythic underside of Jewish life. Against the usual glorification of intellectuality and piety, Berdichevsky stressed the virtue of physical development and military prowess. He considered Jewish universalism the major intellectual reason for the continuation of the Exile and therefore wanted to end "Judaism" so that the Jewish nation might be redeemed by return to its soil.

In Defense of Jewish National Normality

The most extreme position with regard to Jewish nationalism was probably that of Jacob Klatzkin (1882-1948). Where the two previous thinkers were essentially literary figures, Klatzkin was essentially a philosopher. His theory of nationalism is elegantly simple. A nation is defined by having a common land and language; all other factors of national life may be desirable but they are not essential. Klatzkin was no opponent of Jewish culture and by his many literary efforts sought to promote it. But unlike Ahad Ha-Am, he considered Jewish culture an embellishment of national existence, not one of its distinguishing characteristics. Only what gave any nation individuality, its land and language, separated Jews from other people, in their case the Land of Israel and Hebrew.

Klatzkin was an uncompromising advocate of *shelilat hagalut*. For nearly two millennia the Jews had been in Exile and suffered from its deleterious effects. Until the Emancipation, persecution kept them alive. They had managed to survive as a nation by the self-destructive strategy of restricting Jewish life to religious bounds. The Emancipation now doomed that tactic. As persecution declines into mere social antipathy and religion grows ever more unbelievable, the Jews in Exile will die out. Immigration is the central Jewish duty of our time; Zionism and *aliyah* are as good as identical.

Once settled on their land and speaking their own tongue, the Jews may create whatever they wish, or nothing much, and still be authentically Jewish. They will have fulfilled the definition of nationhood and their Jewishness ought not to be judged in any other terms. Klatzkin, though himself a highly sophisticated intellectual, provided Zionism with its most thoughtful statement of the Jewish State's right to mediocrity or worse.

All these issues and others—most notably that of a proper relation to the Arabs in Palestine—were on the agenda of concerned Jews by the early 1920's. Since that time, Zionist philosophy stood still, almost certainly because most Jews cared little about theorizing while the lives of Jews or the survival of the State of Israel was at stake.

When Do I Listen to My People?

Despite the emergencies that world Jewry has faced, the past decade or so has witnessed the slow surfacing of a previously subterranean issue, one that often is at stake in discussions between Israelis and American Jews. When does ethnic or national loyalty properly impose duty upon an individual? Zionism asserts that the nation may rightly make great claims upon its members, for example, immigration to the State of Israel. What if the demands of the nation conflict with one's conscientious judgment of what one ought to do?

For example, the abstract issue of corporate authority has disturbed Americans with particular power ever since the Vietnam War. The U.S. government demanded that citizens risk their lives in what many found to be a senseless or even evil conflict. Many Americans concluded that one ought to give up one's nationality if it substantially contradicted one's mature sense of personal responsibility. The American psyche remains scarred by that experience. And the presumption of the past is now reversed: if collectives do not serve individuals' needs, why should individuals be expected to respond to them?

Or, in terms of our discussion, why should being a Jew mandate making *aliyah* or building one's Diaspora life around Israeli culture? Either would be good for the Jewish people but each also conflicts radically with the life goals of most American Jews. As a result, Orthodox Jews comprise the overwhelming majority of American immigrants to the State of Israel. Their religious belief motivates *aliyah*. If Zionism remains secular, how can one justify giving priority to one's group rather than to one's autonomy?

A common Israeli response has been to sound the classic Zionist theme, the prevalence of anti-Semitism in the Exile. Espousing *shelilat hagalut*, many Israelis argue that anti-Semitism will inevitably destroy Jewish life overseas. The United States may be unusual but it is no exception to the law of modern Jewish life. Anti-Semitism remains persistent and virulent in America—and these Israelis are sensitive to every incident of it. One has a simple moral duty to go where one can live in safety and without apology. Since one must be a Jew, one ought to do so most positively, by participating in the vibrant life created by Jews living in self-determination on their ancestral soil.

American Jews have not been convinced by such arguments. Theoretically, they evade the issue of individual versus corporate authority. Practically, they argue that "America is different." This claim inevitably precipitates a debate comparing European nations to America and German anti-Semitism to that in America. The quality-of-life argument is also hotly disputed. For all its Jewish virtues, the State of Israel faces a collective anti-Semitism of world nations and very often has more people leaving it than come to settle there from the United States.

Making the Case for Liquidating the Exile

Since Ahad Ha-Am's day, most Zionist writers have piously described only the movement's accomplishments. But, as the State entered its fourth decade, Israeli-American disputes were raised to a new level by the sophisticated statements of two writers who had long since made *aliyah*. Their candor about the realities of existence in the State of Israel was remarkable.

In *Letters to an American Jewish Friend*, Hillel Halkin offers a major restatement of *shelilat hagalut*. A former American, Halkin understands and forcefully rebuts arguments for a meaningful Jewish life in the United States. He does not deny that many projects once considered visionary—like university chairs of Jewish studies—have become reality. In the long run, he claims, such accomplishments mean little. Despite talk of pluralism, America demands that its various ethnic groups largely assimilate to the national ethos. He ruthlessly reminds American Jewish optimists of the rising rate of intermarriage and the community's endemic ignorance and apathy. Its current resurgence of Jewish ethnicity is a response to the State of Israel's emergencies, not an indigenous Jewish folk passion. Most important, religious belief will not long survive a secularized world. Already most American synagogue affiliation masks a deepening agnosticism and hypocrisy.

Refreshingly, Halkin makes no counterclaim that life in the State of Israel is humanly satisfying or Jewishly exalting. He concedes that one's Zionist ideals make the tawdriness and discomfort of everyday Israeli life rather unbearable. Israeli culture is mostly a second-rate imitation of international styles and the Hebrew language itself is undergoing adulteration in its polyglot social situation. With hostile neighbors and poor demographic prospects, the very survival of the State is thrown in doubt. Why then should Jews come to the State of Israel? Because it is the last, best hope for the Jewish people. Committed Jews can find no better way of expressing their Jewishness. Halkin is self-critical enough to admit that such commitment to one's people must be called a matter of faith, a secular one to be sure. He does not explain why any nation deserves a devotion entailing such self-sacrifice. But neither he nor any other secular Zionist has given an intellectual response to this critical question.

Arnold Eisen has presented a contemporary validation of Zionism in his book *Galut* (Exile). He argues that exile is the fundamental theme of Judaism and the desire for home its dialectical partner. After studying these historically, he elucidates how our homecoming, the State of Israel, has given them unique form. Too realistic an observer and too idealistic a Jew to find Israel the long-hoped-for "home," he identifies exile with being human anywhere. Thus his nationalism is too "metaphysical" (i.e., religious) for *galut* to be purely political and Israel to be its "redemption." Yet his Zionist honesty prevents his being seduced by the attractions of living as a Jew elsewhere and denying the pain of it as *galut*. Jewish alienation today arises from affirming nationalism when politics has become suspect and from professing religion when secularity reigns.

Eisen's sophisticated analysis does not explain what still powers Jewish identity—Exile indeed.

Zionism at Heart Must Be Religious

In *The Zionist Revolution*, Harold Fisch approached Zionism from a radically different perspective. A British immigrant, Fisch concentrates his argument on the Israeli's special suffering. Terrorism makes suffering a part of daily existence and wars inflict it *en masse*—this for a people still wounded by the Holocaust. How does one explain the devotion and heroism with which Israelis have faced up to their pain?

Why does this nation exert a passionate will to live despite the sacrifices demanded of it? The secular theories of Jewish nationalism professed by most Israelis are utterly incompetent to motivate such dedication. The Israelis' insistence on doing their Jewish duty regardless of its human cost can have only one basis, though they are unconscious of it or hide from it. They are responding to a Transcendent Reality that has laid its claims upon them. At its core, Fisch argues, Zionism has always been an act of faith. Once this had to be masked in secular form. Now, when the long-range, maximum devotion of Jews is needed for its fulfillment, secularity can no longer serve to motivate Zionism. The faith that moves Zionists must be exposed in its true depth. Belief in God and God's Covenant relationship with the Jewish people makes maintaining the State of Israel the chief collective duty of all Jews.

Interestingly, Fisch's deeply felt and cogently argued position gathers some strength from the Israeli courts. In two widely publicized cases—the Brother Daniel and Binyamin Shalit cases—the Israeli Supreme Court denied that a complete separation could be made between the Jewish religion and ethnic Jewish identity. In the first case, the Court ruled against both Zionist theory and traditional Jewish law. It said that the Israeli government should respect the common Jewish opinion that a Jew who has converted to Christianity is no longer part of the community. Hence an apostate has no right to immigrate to the State of Israel under the law of Jewish return. In the second case, a furor resulted from a decision that the Shalit child might be registered on the Israeli population rolls as Jewish in nationality but of no religion. The government then promulgated a regulation that, unless a Jew converts to another faith, the religious registration will be "Jewish." Taken together, these cases made it apparent that Jewish nationalism contained more religious content than its secularistic ideology had heretofore conceded.

Fisch's own argument is fully Orthodox. His faith that God gave this Land to the Jews as the Torah teaches is absolute. He denies Arabs the rights not only to Samaria and Judea (the West Bank), but to Eastern Palestine (Jordan). Faith here resolves the issue of motivation and sacrifice. We suffer and act for God's sake. What remains in contention is the sort of faith modern Jews can accept, and particularly the role of human conscience in it.

Happily, these controversial issues arise in the context of the State of Israel's extraordinary human and Jewish accomplishments. In a few generations, the Zionist movement revolutionized the Jewish community. It made the tone and quality of Jewish life immeasurably better as the twenty-first century nears than anyone dreamed when the twentieth century began. Largely for good, then, the questions raised by Zionism remain high on the contemporary Jewish intellectual agenda.

5

Naturalism:
Mordecai Kaplan

IF PHILOSOPHY is the child of leisure, 1934 would seem a strange year for the appearance of the first major American philosophy of Judaism. The United States was deep in crisis, and so was Jewish life. The economic depression had shattered morale, provoked hostility, and suffused the country with an anger born of frustration. Every stress was felt with special force in the American Jewish community. Anti-Semitism was an open, publicly approved, well-supported movement.

Much of American Jewry fled its Jewish identity. Participating in Jewish life kept one an alien, while investing one's energies in democracy enabled one to gain from a system that rewarded talent impartially.

Into this disheartening scene came a message of Jewish hope. With the publication of *Judaism as a Civilization*, Mordecai Kaplan emerged as the intellectual focus of the generation. He had not been unknown before the book appeared. For many years he had taught at the Jewish Theological Seminary of America, influencing scores of men entering the burgeoning Conservative rabbinate or being trained as educators in its Teachers' Institute. He also exerted great influence on Jewish social workers because of his efforts to transform the settlement house into what became the Jewish center. Now, maturing as a thinker, he challenged American Jewry with a full-scale analysis of its situation.

Mordecai Kaplan's continuing response to crisis in Jewish life was to redefine Judaism and thus to redirect Jewish activity. Kaplan proposed

99

to articulate a social philosophy for the Jewish community. He was a rationalist, yet he differed from the German rationalists by focusing not on the autonomous, thinking individual but on the Jewish people. Zionist theory influenced him greatly. He agreed that one cannot usefully speak of individual Jewish identity without talking about the corporate nature of the Jews.

The Two Premises of Kaplan's Philosophy

In Kaplan's eyes, contemporary Judaism's difficulties arise from the upheaval that has affected all Western peoples and religions in modern times. Two terms epitomize it: "nationalism" and "naturalism." Both are used quite broadly.

"Nationalism" means more than the nineteenth-century ideal by which ethnic groups sought political self-assertion, that is, to become a state. For Kaplan it encompasses the entire process by which monarchy gave way to democracy. The concept of society as divinely ordered—and hence unchangeable—gave way to that of a secular state founded on a social contract. Everyone, therefore, was entitled to equal rights in it. Nationalism brought the Jews emancipation, the end of ghetto existence both physically and spiritually. After centuries of segregation, full participation in the life of their country entailed a radical change in their accustomed way of life and their manner of thinking about it.

Kaplan uses the term "naturalism" to identify the way people in secular states think about the world. At the simplest, naturalism is the rejection of supernaturalism. Moderns limit their thought to this world and structure it in terms of the natural order. They consider the scientific approach to reality, including human beings and society, the most reliable method of ascertaining truth. As a consequence, naturalistic religious thinking focuses on people and their welfare rather than on God or God's purposes. Modernity involves a radical shift from theocentrism to anthropocentrism and Kaplan often employs the term "humanism" in this people-focused but not God-denying sense.

Theological humanism revolutionizes the classic religious emphases on supernatural revelation, miracles, and otherworldly salvation. Not just God's word, but God too, must now be found in, not above, the natural order; miracles are dismissed as unscientific; and this world, the only one human beings can know, must be the place in which they seek salvation.

Change Ensures Survival

Most moderns live by these views, though some are unconscious of that fact. Kaplan therefore has no patience with religious leaders who timidly still use the old religious terms. Their very evasion of definition or philosophy indicates that they no longer hold a traditional faith. A truly contemporary understanding of Judaism must be naturalistic so as to be coherent with our modern world view. Liberal Jewish thought has proved that change has always been part of Jewish life. Kaplan also agrees that the unconscious evolution of the past is inadequate to the dramatic change brought about by the Emancipation. Judaism needs to be rethought in terms of the philosophy implicit in modern science. In turn, the reconstruction of Jewish group life must be based on the scientific study of social development. Sociology thus becomes the critical science for Kaplan's interpretation of Judaism. He explicitly cites Durkheim—from whom much of his social orientation is taken—in affirming that religion must now receive its function and character from scientific observation.

Religion cannot be dispensed with. It significantly supplements nationalism and naturalism. The nation has purposes other than the well-being of its citizens. Particularly when the state has failed to serve persons but has demanded instead that they serve its needs, religion can rise in prophetic judgment against it. Religion's mystical element can also usefully complement naturalistic thinking. Applied rigidly, naturalism reduces the universe to an amoral mechanism, thereby negating human freedom and undercutting human aspiration. Religion, without reverting to supernaturalism, can evoke an awareness of the mystery of existence and the reality of spiritual values, thereby assuring people that the universe supports human striving. Personal and social progress are unthinkable without some form of religious life.

This brief statement of Kaplan's basic intent demonstrates that Kaplan's rationalism has it limits. He is not as skeptical of reason's claims as was Leo Baeck. Kaplan appears to have undiluted trust in the adequacy of human rationality and thus in humankind's potential. Yet in rejecting the strict naturalism that denies God's existence and human freedom, he appeals to religious intuition. Why one should accept such unscientific premises is unclear, unless one does so for their usefulness. But how can one scientifically know what is good for people before these premises are accepted? The circularity of the reasoning hints that Kaplan retains something of a reliance on faith.

The Social Scientific View of Religious Groups

What do the social sciences teach us about religion and peoples? An open examiner cannot help being impressed by the universality of religion in human society. In primitive or high cultures, or in societies that are animistic, polytheistic, or imagistic, religion is found wherever there are records of human existence. Modern thinkers need not proclaim there are gods who impose themselves upon people or attribute religion to the clever manipulations of priests or capitalists. Its source is human need.

We have a natural urge to self-fulfillment, to utilize our capacities fully. Life itself cannot be the highest value for there are ideals without which we would rather die. The good life is a continual quest for self-realization and self-expression; religion is the human institution that helps us to achieve it. And as our need for such consummation is universal, so is our need for religion. For us the accomplishment of the basic human striving for fulfillment is "salvation." In a naturalistic, this-worldly era, that old religious term cannot mean getting to

heaven. It must be freed from all such mythical notions and reinterpreted to refer to self-actualization in this world.

Though human beings are individuals and religion is social, the two
are inseparably joined, for salvation must be communal as well as
personal. How can individuals be serene when they live in a wretched
world? Conversely, no society can claim to have reached its goal as long
as its individual members are frustrated and unhappy.

Much of the present-day confusion over religion arises here. We
moderns will sometimes admit that aspects of our life are as socially
determined as they are personal. Yet we often insist that religion
is a strictly private matter. Emile Durkheim, the first great modern
sociologist, had argued that individuals do not create religions. Rather,
their personal needs and desires are given shape and expression
by their culture. A people is prior to its religion. One first shares
its way of life and consequently shares in its religion. Kaplan was
overwhelmed by Durkheim's insight. He called the social reorien-
tation of the origins of religion the "Copernican turning point"
in his thinking. He followed its implications rigorously. Where traditional Judaism spoke of God giving the Torah, thereby constituting the people of Israel, Kaplan argued that the Jewish folk
created its culture, Torah, including its religion, climaxed by its idea
of God.

What fundamentally differentiates religions is not their theological
content so much as their social elaboration. Since science views the
universe as an integrated whole, there can be but one God and one
ethics. Religious truth is as universal as the operation of human
reason. Some peoples have not yet attained the level of monotheistic,
ethical religion. That is a historical accident or social lag, not an
indication that reality is not equally available to everyone. Each folk
clothes the universal content of religion with the garb of its unique
symbolism. As a result of its ethnic experience it has come to revere
certain people, events, places, books, and acts. These are its *sancta*, its
channels of reverence. Through them a people expresses individu-
alistically the religious feelings common to all humankind. Religions
have different *sancta* because the articulation of human reverence
necessarily takes particular form. Ethical monotheism, by contrast, is

as common to humanity as is the human nature on which religion is ultimately based.

A social emphasis pervades Kaplan's philosophy. He has a passionate commitment to folk existence. Since a civilization can survive many generations, its death can be compared only to the death of an individual. Similarly, Kaplan can conceive of all religions one day having the same theology and ethics. He denies that this would mean the end of separate peoples, for they are an enduring feature of human existence.

Defining Judaism as a Civilization

Following the theories of the renowned sociologist Sumner, Kaplan boldly identifies Judaism as the Jewish people's civilization. Religion is not its only or even dominant content. A civilization is the organic unity of the people and its land, its language, its literature, its mores, its folkways, its laws, its sanctions, its arts, its religion—in sum, the social forms through which a folk expresses itself. Previous liberal Jewish thinkers erred by identifying Judaism in church-like terms. Kaplan's ethnic perspective leads to a far broader conception of the rebuilding of Jewish life. Following the usage of the social pragmatists of the 1930's, Kaplan called his theory Jewish Reconstructionism. Its creative implications emerge from a consideration of its uncommonly far-ranging component aspects.

A people generally comes into being by virtue of living in a certain territory. Its land then becomes a critical factor in the development of its civilization. The Jews are no exception to this pattern. The Torah speaks continually of the importance of the Land of Israel to the Jewish people and of the life it must create because of the Land. When the Jews were dispersed, they prayed for a return to their Land and celebrated festivals based on its agricultural cycle. An other-worldly religion might be able to dispense with its tie to a specific country. Judaism, as the civilization of a people, cannot.

Kaplan can now make a strong case for the identity of Judaism and Zionism. A civilization as contrasted to a religion requires a place where it can be fully lived and only its homeland will do. Were Kaplan's social philosophy a simple nationalism, land and language would take precedence over culture and only *aliyah*, immigration, would be the preeminent Jewish duty. Kaplan's theory of peoples and their culture does not require him to "negate the Exile" but allows him to hope for a positive Jewish existence in the Diaspora. Like Ahad Ha-Am, Kaplan argues that once the folk center has been established, Jews elsewhere will benefit from its civilization, thereby perpetuating their Jewishness.

With a land goes a language. Hebrew never died as the Jewish tongue *par excellence*. Of all the ancient languages that modern national movements have sought to resuscitate, it alone is truly alive. Worldwide Jewish civilization is increasingly united by it. On this score, too, Kaplan's teaching is in full accord with Zionism.

Once Judaism is seen as the civilization of the Jewish people, the arts, too, have a significant place in it. Religious interpreters of Judaism have been puzzled by Jewish folk songs and dances. Secular theoreticians have been embarrassed by the largely ritual concern of Jewish art and poetry. Both sorts of thinkers fail to grasp the breadth of Jewish self-expression. To the contrary, Kaplan argued, everyone should have been shocked at the lack of Jewish artistic expression in the 1930's or its limit to ritual activities.

Social habits form the bulk of a civilization. Jewish life possesses abundant folkways, ranging from ethical customs to honored recipes. In pre-modern days the major folk acts were authorized as religious duties. They were *mitzvot*, "commandments (given by God)." For modern Jews with their this-worldly orientation, the term *mitzvot* can only be a metaphor, testifying that these acts arouse or articulate a Jewish religious mood. We are far more likely to perform *mitzvot* when they are freed from any connection with a commanding God and seen instead as our ethnic ways to self-fulfillment and folk-survival. This humanistic view of "commandments" has the added advantages of allowing them to be changed as needed or created as seems fitting. In a democratic society, Jewish law must be the community's participatory legislation of its standards. The folk creates "law" as another facet of its civilization; against tradition, the law is not the criterion or creator of the people. Kaplan is that liberal in his reinterpretation of Judaism.

Any group is obligated to manifest high ethical standards. When it does not reflect these universal values, individuals lose their humanity and the group, its rationale. The glory of Judaism has been its exemplary ethical concern, personal and communal as well. Nothing less will do today. Here too Kaplan follows Ahad Ha-Am. He is so committed to ethics that he limits the right of a people to develop its civilization as it sees fit only by this ethical consideration.

The People Takes Precedence Over All Else

If modern Jews are to live as a full-scale civilization they require an appropriate pattern of community organization. Kaplan suggests creating an American version of the European Jewish community structure, the *kehillah*. Abroad, it was an autonomous, governmentally authorized body. Here it might be a voluntary association of all Jews and Jewish institutions committed to the people's survival. All Jews should have their basic loyalty to the community. It, in turn, should be responsible for meeting the diverse needs of Jews in the community. Thus, congregations should no longer be independent entities, as if religion were not another part of Jewish civilization. In Kaplan's "organic community," they would be maintained for the groups desiring them. Rabbis, too, would be retained by the community to serve its various religious needs.

A fully integrated organizational structure makes the Jewish people itself, not any single facet of its culture, the focus of Jewish loyalty. Operating democratically, the organic community would develop our modern Jewish equivalent of law. With the people legislating for themselves, the living relationship between the folk and the law would be reestablished. This would bridge the present-day gap between the rigidity of the traditional requirements and the permissiveness of modern Jewish living.

The secret of Jewish survival has now become clear. The Jews continue from generation to generation not as bearers of an idea of God or because they have a mission (à la Cohen and Baeck). Kaplan does not conceive of the "essence" of Judaism as an idea. He is not that sort of rationalist. Judaism's essence is its social base, its ethnicity. The Jews survive because they are a people. Jewish culture changes; the Jewish folk endures. Peoplehood has provided Jewish identity over the centuries; if properly understood and reinvigorated, it will do so today. Kaplan is certain that the Jewish people can survive the present age of transition. Its civilization may adopt many of the ideas of the surrounding society, but as long as it remains a healthy, self-affirming people it will express them in an authentic Jewish civilizational form. Kaplan therefore dedicated himself to "reconstruct" Jewish peoplehood.

Religion has thus far been omitted from this discussion of Kaplan's theory only to emphasize how radically he had departed from traditional and liberal philosophies of Judaism. Kaplan does not deny the central role of religious belief and practice in Jewish life over the centuries. He is determined, however, to put them into proper sociological perspective.

As Durkheim demonstrated, all civilizations have a religion at their core. It integrates the people's way of life. It gives cosmic authority to the values it cherishes. It empowers the institutions and laws that effectuate these goals in people's everyday lives. The religion also inspires and motivates individuals to strive for these ends. Religion, while only one element in a civilization's variegated activities, is the most important of them, "the first among equals." For Kaplan, Judaism must be a *religious* civilization. He did not substantially alter that position during the next forty years in which he continued to write.

Kaplan's Response to the Changing Social Mood

Since Kaplan wrote his magnum opus, the intellectual climate of Western civilization has lost much of its previous reliance on science and human reason, and something of a turn to religion has been under way. One might have expected this changed evaluation of modernity to cause a major readjustment in Kaplan's thought. Instead, he was among the sharpest critics of the synagogue-focused Judaism of the 1950's and 1960's. He envisaged this trend stemming from a need to belong to a Jewish community, not as an outcome of any deeply held belief. As religion it would not go very deep until there was a naturalistic reconstruction of Jewish theology. As an expression of solidarity with the Jewish people it was ineffective because it used the church instead of folk civilization as its model.

Kaplan also rejected the effort by some Jewish thinkers to substitute existentialism for naturalism as the philosophic context for modern Jewish thought. Kaplan criticized the surrender of rationalism, damning it as a weary society's typical "failure of nerve." For the moment, human beings have lost faith in themselves and their capacities. Thus naturalism, which is founded on that faith, has seemed less appealing than nonrational philosophies. Kaplan has no doubt this mood will pass and naturalism will once again be the handmaid of modernity.

The Zionist aspect of his 1934 social perspective could not help requiring serious reconsideration after the State of Israel's establishment. Its subsequent growth and development posed many problems for Kaplan's understanding of Zionism as a civilizing force. His continuing power as a thinker was evident in his willingness to confront these issues. Mostly, Kaplan was disappointed by the Israeli refusal to reorient Diaspora Jewish life to a full range of cultural self-expression. Kaplan believed Zionism must serve the welfare of the Jewish people and not essentially seek world Jewry's support of the State of Israel. To insist that the movement focus on *aliyah* or preparation for it vitiates Zionism's greater possibilities and ruins the morale of Jews who will not immigrate. Kaplan has gone so far as to suggest making clear that the State of Israel is not properly described as a "nation." There is, rather, an Israeli state, while world Jewry is an international people, rooted in the Land of Israel but with branches everywhere.

Kaplan's criticism went even further. If Zionism seeks to enrich the life of the Jewish people, then reconstructing Judaism is a problem for Jews within the State of Israel as well as for the Jews of the Diaspora. Despite the advantages of land, language, and Jewish social context Israelis too need a properly balanced Jewish religious civilization.

Responses to Kaplan's Program

Time has not dealt kindly with Kaplan's organizing program for American Jewry. No organic communities have been established or are likely to be in a society where congregational affiliation and independence remain the general norm. However, with a static or declining Jewish population having great difficulty financing independent Jewish programs in the 1980's, some greater pooling of local resources seemed indicated. Should the economic pressure intensify, Kaplan's proposal for organic communities might yet come into its own.

Kaplan's social theory has likewise had shifting fortunes. In the middle decades of the century, America assimilated its immigrant communities and became pluralistic, primarily in religion—the famous "Catholic, Protestant and Jew" that often adorns even the inauguration of American presidents. With economic expansion benefiting almost everyone, the American dream displaced the older concern for one's ethnic roots. In the 1970's a radical shift of mood took place. The once pervasive confidence in democracy was shattered and a resurgence of ethnic interest took place. Among Jews this attitude was heightened by the perils of the State of Israel and by the occasional public signs of anti-Semitism. With much of American Jewish life centered on the State of Israel, Kaplan's theory of the Jews as a people received fresh substantiation. Surprisingly, reconstructionism now had less intellectual appeal than in its early, radical days. Kaplan's message about the significance of ethnicity had been absorbed by the major religious movements while its sociological reinterpretation of Judaism was discounted by a generation largely critical of science.

Despite his own goals, future Jewish generations may well consider Kaplan more important as a theologian than as a social philosopher. His effort to rethink the ideas of the Jewish religion in naturalistic terms remains one of the distinctive, creative theological options available to inquiring Jews.

Fashioning a Naturalistic Jewish Theology

Naturalism begins with an act of humility. The human mind cannot provide answers to ultimate questions like, What is the essence of being human? What is death? Why is there evil? What are the limits of our freedom? Most important of all, reason cannot tell us what God *is*. We cannot understand ourselves, much less comprehend God as God truly is. Agnosticism is the only honest posture on the metaphysical issues concerning God—existence, nature, will. Working from our own experience in this world, we simply cannot know anything substantive about God.

Kaplan is not stymied by his intellectual realism. Rather, it prompts him to distinguish between a belief in, and a conception of, God. The belief precedes the conception. Faith is an intuitive human response to the universe. Ideas of God result from people's seeking to understand the world in a way that will allow them to live the fullest possible life. They are the outward cultural expression of inner experience; hence, ideas of God need to be socially understood. Knowing how God functions in our lives is, in essence, all we need to know about God. Belief in the Divine confirms and motivates our drive to self-fulfillment. A naturalistic faith will begin with our highest human hopes and identify God with them.

Belief in God is a corollary of our search for self. The self can fulfill itself only by dependence on the external world, by trusting that nature supports its inner upward strivings. To affirm that creation is hospitable to human growth is not an assertion about ultimate reality. Kaplan is not offering a proof of the existence of God, though he says we all need religion. He is only positing that our nature drives us to live abundantly and we therefore naturally trust that reality enables us to do so.

Kaplan's View of God

In what sense, then, does Kaplan use the word "God"? He rejects any description of God as personal, for to him a personal Divinity is an anthropomorphic one. No naturalistic thinkers could accept such a God. Some philosophers have therefore identified God with strictly impersonal scientific concepts such as force or energy. Kaplan rejects this view on two grounds: first, as an unwarranted metaphysical assertion, albeit a naturalistic one; and second, because it renders God morally neutral. Kaplan's God must be related to human self-realization and that, Kaplan believes, inevitably has an ethical component. For him, God is everything in nature we rely on to fulfill ourselves. Kaplan condenses that into, "God is the Power that makes for salvation." The assertion is remarkable. No other Jewish thinker has ever given a definition of God. Kaplan has done so not because he believes that these eight words are adequate to describe God, but so that he can rationally communicate his basic religious insight to others.

God is not a mere wish or an illusion. The term refers to those real processes in nature that support our efforts to live abundantly. Our faith is subjective in being based on our hope that we might fulfill ourselves. It is objective because by God we mean those forces in nature that make it possible for us to achieve our ideals.

Kaplan cannot be criticized for speaking of his God as real. What should not be assumed as a consequence is that God is *a unity that is real*. Kaplan abets this possible misinterpretation by referring to God in terms that seem to describe an entity. He calls God variously the Power, the Process, the Force, with both article and capitalization indicating he is referring to a special "thing." Unity in Kaplan's conception of God cannot be a description of God's being but only of our way of looking at Divinity. Kaplan makes no statements about God's nature for that would be metaphysics. Asserting the unity of God reflects the consistency of our inner, subjective response to the universe. In its objective, "real" sense, the term "God" refers not to an entity, but to many different forces in nature—hence, to disparate objective realities. We may summarize, then: insofar as Kaplan's God is real, God is not one, and insofar as God is one, God is not real. Many Jews have found this idea an insuperable difficulty in Kaplan's conception of God.

A second problem arises from his view of the function of the God-idea. If one can accept the reality of Kaplan's God, one has faith in a God who is fully impersonal. Anthropomorphism and naive religiosity are immediately ruled out. But can an impersonal God involve people personally? Or, conversely, can people take personally an impersonal God? Indeed, what happens to our standards of human development when God is declared to be impersonal? Kaplan's response is in terms of his definition: God is those natural realities that promote the highest human values. Hence the impersonality of God does not vitiate the importance of full human personhood. Kaplan's critics then charge that this God cannot serve as a model for people to emulate for it is only a means we have created for our self-fulfillment. Can one worship such a Divinity?

Humanly, a religion centered on an impersonal God seems a contradiction in terms. Religion either touches all one's heart, one's soul, and one's might, or it is nothing. Why should one be utterly involved with a God who is utterly unresponsive in return? Kaplan does not see why the impersonality of God should create such a problem. God is no more impersonal than any other lofty idea. People take their country very seriously. They address it personally and speak of it with deep affection. They will even give their lives for it. God, being far more involved in human existence, should be even easier to relate to personally.

Kaplan's Theory of Evil

Kaplan reinterprets all the major themes of Jewish belief. Of particular interest is his treatment of the problems of evil, prayer, the chosenness of Israel, and Jewish law.

Kaplan's theodicy is kept thoroughly rational by his again substituting function for metaphysics. Had he approached the question metaphysically, we might expect him to say that God cannot be held responsible for the evil in the universe because God is not omnipotent. Kaplan's God is finite, limited to those powers in nature that make for human fulfillment. If God is restricted to what makes for good, how then can we blame God for the evil that befalls us? Kaplan does not take this approach, apparently because it would imply that he has a metaphysical knowledge of precisely what God is and is not. Instead, he prefers to deal with the functional question of how we should meet evil. He worries lest evil deprive people of the will to better themselves or their world. Regardless of our suffering, we need to find sufficient faith in the positive aspects of the self and nature to continue to fulfill ourselves. We transcend evil by not letting it deter us from further self-realization. Here Kaplan yokes his theory of human nature to the liberal's moral argument that evil is primarily a challenge to our ethical courage and creativity.

Kaplan saw no need to modify his views about God and evil as a result of the Holocaust. The history-ruling God that some people now said was dead, Kaplan had given up years before as unbelievable for any person of sophistication. The suggestion that the world was empty of God, specifically that it was morally and humanly neutral, contradicted everything Kaplan understood science to teach about human nature. A negative "faith" would function counter-productively. It would confirm people's fears that the universe was bound to frustrate their efforts at self-actualization. Their consequent passivity and resignation would be utterly unworthy of human beings as conscious moral agents. The Nazis had used their freedom of will to become murderers, and the leaders of the democracies, by doing nothing, had acquiesced in their evil-doing. No iniquity, regardless of its horror, proves that our ideals are false or cannot succeed. To the contrary, we indignantly protest the Nazi savagery and recognize the paramount importance of fighting evil everywhere precisely because we know the evil that people can do. Moral activism, not metaphysical speculation, is the fitting human response to the problem of evil.

Kaplan's View of Prayer and Chosenness

Kaplan's treatment of prayer is a logical outcome of his view of God. Prayer must be understood in terms of the worshiper. Kaplan states boldly:

> All thinking—and prayer is a form of thought—is essentially a dialogue between our purely individual egocentric self and our self as representing a process that goes on beyond us . . . when we wish to establish contact with the Process that makes for human salvation, we can do so only by an appeal to the higher self that represents the working of that Process in us. From that . . . we seek the answer to prayer.

One prays to oneself, so to speak, but to oneself as a locus of the consciousness of the realities that cooperate with us, those natural processes we call God. Why will we pray if we are only communing with ourselves? Because our nature as self-transcending creatures will always lead us to intense inner reflection about the goals and direction of our drive to improve.

Even so, prayer is not primarily a personal matter. Kaplan stresses its social context. Communal worship not only aids the individual but relieves the single self of the special pressures of private prayer. The group supplies one with perspective, channel, and incentive. No wonder the great religions have always advocated both solitary meditation and institutional services. Jews will naturally wish to express this universal human social need as part of their people. In the Diaspora, synagogue services provide one of the most important regular occasions for Jews to gain a feeling of ethnic solidarity. To give effect to his philosophy, Kaplan and his disciples have composed new prayer books. They are largely traditional *siddurim* with a number of alterations and omissions, as well as some creative additions, all based on Kaplan's teaching.

Neither Kaplan's view of evil nor his view of prayer has called forth such controversy as his vigorous opposition to the concept of the chosen people. He rejects it as an immoral, divisive, arrogant notion. Jews ought to renounce it as generating hatred, or at least suspicion, between Jews and non-Jews. At its best, chosenness may once have meant special moral responsibility and thus presented a spiritual challenge to the Jew. With time, it has become an assertion, even if unconscious, of Jewish superiority. It functioned to give the Jews a defense against their enemies and a rationale for their continued existence. Neither use is desirable or necessary in the modern world. Minorities should be safeguarded by securely establishing democracy. They need no justification for their will to survive. They have a right to do so that derives directly from the natural order of things.

Moreover, the idea that God chooses a people is today as meaningless as the notion that God has some sort of conscious, personal will. The study of comparative religion, Kaplan believes, has demonstrated the falsity of claims to exclusive revelation by the inconsistency of the many doctrines asserted to be "the only truth." The higher ethics of the contemporary world, with their universal horizon, makes such tribalistic notions unthinkable.

Any religion genuinely interested in the unity of humanity should renounce particularistic doctrines of salvation. The Jewish people, which has suffered so grievously from those who held exclusivist ideas, and whose civilization has been permeated by ethics, ought to take the lead in this direction. Kaplan concedes that a sense of unique communal purpose does offer added inducement for Jewish living. Let the Jews choose a vocation for their people but not disguise it as a supernatural act of God. By an open, communal decision, let them dedicate themselves to serve humankind. Since nationhood has often meant chauvinism, exemplifying the moral potentialities of collective existence could be a worthy goal for Jewish life.

Law in Kaplan's Reconstruction

A similar liberalism pervades Kaplan's conception of Jewish law. He demands that the law serve the needs of the people, not that the people serve the institution of the law. He would modernize it by making it entirely voluntaristic and eliminating any sense of compulsion behind it, either heavenly or human. An active community can be built in stages. In the beginning we must try to help Jews regain a strong loyalty to their people. Then they will naturally want to express their human concerns in Jewish fashion. As participants in Jewish civilization they will also want to share in Jewish religion. If its practices are made as meaningful as possible and if pluralism in ritual is accepted, many could be won to faithful observance. A democratic assembly of the organic Jewish communities should lead this process. Their legislation would determine what constitutes "law" for Jews today. Because these would now be living folk decisions, they would carry special weight with all loyal Jews.

Kaplan maintained this liberal position consistently though it brought him into tension with the Conservative movement, with which he was long associated. Its position on Jewish law was more traditional, holding that contemporary decisions be fixed by a body of rabbinic experts and interpreted by local rabbis. The theological issue of the source of the law's authority was bypassed in the hope that enough Jews remained loyal to the classic Jewish legal process to accept as binding modern decisions made in its spirit. Kaplan was scornful of this theory. Limiting change only to what the traditional processes of the law might allow is often retrograde (as shown by the problem of granting women full-scale rights in Jewish religious life). Kaplan's protests against the Conservative movement's failure to develop new patterns of practice were ineffectual. He and his followers finally decided to develop their own institutions to further Reconstructionism. Their pattern of observance is considerably more liberal than that sanctioned by the Conservative movement. For the time being, that is as much of the Jewish community as has been brought into Kaplan's democratic process of setting contemporary Jewish law.

In sum then, Kaplan utilizes a comprehensive humanistic framework for his interpretation of Judaism. All our knowledge of history, of society, of the self and its development is relevant to his modernized Judaism. Every aspect of Jewish communal, cultural, and spiritual life is touched and affected by his reinterpretation of the Jewish heritage. He has not hesitated to adopt positions previously unknown to Jewish thought, many of them quite unpopular. His philosophy is irradiated by his integrity and commitment. Yet it is Mordecai Kaplan, the person, who has been his most extraordinary creation. The seriousness and formality of his writings generally mask his warm and lovable nature. In the various decades of his long life, the man himself was always present, giving, open. He was that rarity, a genuine person—and rarer still, an authentic modern Jew. His words were the words of naturalism but their overtones echoed Sinai in a harmony many American Jews appreciated.

Questions Jews Ask About Kaplan

Having demonstrated in great detail what naturalism might make of Judaism, Kaplan has convinced his critics that it cannot adequately explain the nature of Jewish life.

Kaplan begins his thought with a general understanding of humankind and moves on to justify the continuation of Jewish life. In typical rationalistic fashion, he has greater confidence in the superior truth of a universal theory—sociology—than he has in a particular tradition— Judaism. The abstract, broad-scale approach commends itself not only as modern and scientific but because of its greater comprehensiveness.

His critics charge that in beginning with the abstract Kaplan has ignored another strand in modern thought. Other thinkers have argued that truth never is available in a general form. In reality, truth is inevitably particular. Thus, religion in general is something only academics talk about. The rest of us know "religion" through particular religions. If truth is to be found in specific instances and not just in abstract theories, then Judaism has as much right to determine what is valuable in modern thought as modernity has to instruct Judaism on its proper form. Why should Judaism be so obsequious to modern social science when it is ethically agnostic and denies the realm of the spirit? If anything, science's moral neutrality has become one of the great human dangers of our age. Humankind, teetering on the brink of nihilism, needs its religions, including Judaism, to give it an independent source of value. Science might then not abuse its awesome new power over nature and human life so badly in the future as it has done in the recent past.

Critics also deny Kaplan's view that people by their very nature are oriented to self-fulfillment. The American dream of happiness through self-improvement has proved deeply disappointing. Most lives necessarily remain unfulfilled since worthy human goals are infinite. Kaplan's optimism seems naive. Traditional religion balanced a ceaseless, unsatisfying servitude to self-fulfillment with a serene joy in the fact of being. Over the ages, religion has proved most valuable to people by helping them deal with an existence that was not ultimately self-validating. A mature view of life and religion needs both dark and bright tones.

Kaplan rejects the new realism as unnatural. He insists science has discovered certain lasting truths about basic human nature. Leaving aside the issue of whether psychology has demonstrated that there is an essential human "nature," Kaplan's use of science itself has been challenged. He treats it as if it were prescriptive, assuming that the patterns it shows people have followed are the ones we must or ought to utilize in the future. But what of human freedom? Once we know the way social forces have operated, do we not have the possibility of choosing to act against them? For example, in a world desperately in need of internationalism, perhaps separate peoples are an anachronism we should now speedily transcend. Kaplan appears to have turned description into command, deriving a moral "ought" from what merely happened to be the case.

Besides, Kaplan's social science derives from its earliest modern discoveries—those of Durkheim and Sumner. Decades later, many truths that he accepted as permanent are rejected altogether or subsist in one theory among many. His very claims for the reliability and consistency of the social sciences are rarely heard among the practitioners themselves.

Finally, the entire Kaplanian discussion of human nature is dominated by the term "self-fulfillment" or its equivalent. He apparently thinks its meaning is self-evident. In a simpler day, it may have been. In a time beset with identity crises, little is more problematic. Surely the self is not an entity in us. If it is a potential, how shall we know which of our drives and powers properly fulfill it? Nature only gives us conflict. Unless we have a standard external to our troubled selves and on a superior level, how can we ever know what fulfillment might be? Since Kaplan's God is interpreted in terms of human self-realization, God cannot set a goal for us. Kaplan's God disappears, the critics allege, just when our society needs God the most, when we no longer are certain what we ought to be.

Criticisms of Kaplan's Judaism

Kaplan's proposals for the reconstruction of Jewish life have also drawn rejoinders. One arises from his strict identification of peoples and religions. Kaplan maintains that if America is to become a proper civilization it needs to develop its own faith—what recent followers of Durkheim have termed its "civil religion." Until that has been fully accomplished, Kaplan contends, American Jews have good reason— and democratic warrant—to live in their two civilizations. Kaplan's antagonists have not been persuaded by his plea for dual cultural life. If Americans as a people ought to develop their own religion, should not American Jews give their major energies to that goal? They have a special inducement for such concern. By finally being part of a mature American folk they could end the perils of minority status. To respond that every people ought naturally seek to survive disregards the utterly unnatural, incomparable persecution of the Jews. Without a compen- sating reason for remaining Jewish, morality dictates that this dan- gerous social status, being a Jew, ought to be brought to an end.

Furthermore, if the Jews are primarily a folk, then their secular activities are as valuable as their religion. Is folk dancing the Jewish equivalent of study of the Bible or Talmud? The great American Jewish folk act is gossiping over coffee after synagogue services. By contrast, the worship rarely gives most Jews a strong community feeling. Should prayer, then, give way to more socializing? Kaplan properly feared that considering Judaism a "religion" might lead to a loss of ethnicity. To make religion only the first of many folk activities seems to delimit it unduly.

Two theological criticisms must also be noted. God once functioned in people's lives because they believed, consciously or unconsciously, that God was real. Can Kaplan's God have the same effect on people's lives when they know God's unity is only a mental construct and God's reality is a disparate series of natural processes? To argue from our alleged need for a God is already to lose the case. Of course, we moderns would like to believe in God and know that our efforts to live abundantly are supported by that God. Having been trained by Feuerbach and Freud that all our talk about God is only a projection of ourselves into a cosmic realm, we are skeptical about God. The more we hear about human needs the more we wonder whether God is real. Only when we are convinced that God is not just a mental prop we have created will God be significant enough to us to affect our lives. Functionalism does not allow us to avoid the metaphysical issue.

The concept of the chosen people also seems poorly handled by Kaplan, certainly in its historical development. Rarely has religious particularity been as hedged by moral considerations. The prophets categorically denied that Israel's chosenness supervened God's justice. The Rabbis repeatedly defined chosenness as receiving Torah and hence being obligated to do commandments. Jewish "superiority" to others was occasionally asserted as a response to the persecutor, not as a product of Jewish theology. In any case, giving up one's doctrine is no way to change general social realities. A doctrine ought to be evaluated in terms of its intrinsic merit, not in terms of what one hopes other religions will do about their similar beliefs. At this point the dangers of dealing with religious truth essentially in terms of its social context become vividly clear.

The very intensity of the criticism testifies that Mordecai Kaplan has made a lasting contribution to modern Jewish thought. His legitimization of a secularized Jewishness enabled many post-immigrant Jews to integrate into American culture while retaining Jewish self-respect. When religion was on the defensive from a metaphysically imperialistic science, he created a theology in which a de-anthropomorphized God could be understood in terms of human needs. In a day when liberal Judaism and Zionism seemed intellectually incompatible, he found a way to combine a strong Jewish ethnicity with a fully universal faith. In a troubled and confused time, Mordecai Kaplan had the daring and capacity to confront his people's problems realistically and to propose solutions. For decades he challenged the will and the intelligence of all who cared about Jewish life. His unique combination of Jewish heart and mind remains a spur and a challenge to all succeeding Jewish thinkers.

PART III
The Six Systematized Positions: Nonrationalistic Models

6

The Pioneer
Existentialist:
Franz Rosenzweig

SOME Christian theologians—Sören Kierkegaard or, centuries before, Augustine, or, more recently, Karl Barth, for example—have been connected with existentialism because of its characteristic criticism of the human situation. The existentialist analysis exposes our bent for self-deception and self-exaltation, giving the doctrine of original sin fresh meaning. Suddenly, liberalism's doctrine of humankind's perfectibility seems a rationalization of our aggressive self-esteem. Classic Christian terms such as "sin," "justification," and "redemption," seen in an existential light, take on a contemporary, personal tone. More, they explain much of recent history. Social analysts, political scientists, and other intellectuals who normally eschew theology have turned to Christian existentialism to comprehend a humankind that could produce the horrors we have seen. By contrast, religious liberalism's essentially optimistic view of people has failed to account for the depth of malevolence in educated, cultured people.

The general Jewish view of humankind differs radically from that of Christianity and many scholars consider this difference the root disagreement between them. For Judaism, sin is heinous but not the central reality of humanity's relation to God. The classic Jewish sources reveal no more than an intellectual flirtation with the doctrine of original sin. They depict human beings as pure-born and fully capable of responding to God's demands. Even should one sin, one

125

retains the capacity to reconcile oneself with God through the practice of *teshuvah*, repentance (better, "turning"). Judaism rejects the concept that people are sinners, either in essence or by the necessities of existence. In Jewish usage the word "salvation" does not, therefore, customarily denote helping sinful individuals justify themselves before God, their judge. With its more positive attitude to the human situation, how can Judaism appropriately utilize existentialism to explicate Jewish faith?

Many thinkers also insist that Jewish modernity and rationalism are inseparable, that reason has played an indispensable role in the development of modern Judaism. Historical analysis demonstrated that Jewish practice and belief had changed over the centuries, suggesting the validity of contemporary adjustments. Philosophy argued that an unchanging ethical devotion was central to the Jewish tradition whereas the ritual forms in which it was expressed were secondary and ought to be adapted to a new social ethos. Reason also motivated the Jew's continued rejection of Christianity. Miracles—the virgin birth, the incarnation of God in human form, the resurrection, the ascension—are central to Christian teaching, as is dogma (e.g., that God is a trinity that is yet a unity). Any rational mind, operating without prejudice, should deny them. Ethical monotheism, particularly in its rationalistic reinterpretations, posed no such difficulty. If anything, reason spurred the Jews to adhere to their minority faith.

The Place of Rationalism in Jewish History

Even a cursory view of its history refutes the notion that Judaism has historically been as rationalistic a religion as has been suggested. If reason is identified as the kind of systematic, abstract thinking associated with Greece, then its use in Judaism is late, not early; sporadic, not continuous; syncretistic, not indigenous. The Bible is not a philosophic document but a collection of histories, stories, law, poems, and wise sayings.

Philo aside—he remained unknown to Jewish tradition until modern times—rationalist expositions of Judaism arose only in the ninth century C.E., a thousand years after the last biblical book was written and centuries after the editing of the Talmud. Moreover, this rationalist awakening took place not in response to a Jewish need, but at the polemical prompting of, and as a response to, the Moslem culture in which Jews then found themselves.

Similarly, today, the Emancipation brought Jews into a society that alleges a high regard for rationality. Jews again had recourse to philosophical patterns of self-description. From roughly the fifteenth to the eighteenth century, there was little or no Jewish philosophy, though much speculative Jewish mysticism. Thus, Jewish history offers ample evidence to refute the contention that Judaism cannot be divorced from rationalism.

The gains rationalism brings to Judaism—a changeable tradition and a rejection of Christianity—might equally well be accomplished by a nonrational existentialist theory of Judaism. Franz Rosenzweig was the first Jew to explore this intellectual possibility.

Beginnings of Jewish Existentialism

Rosenzweig was born in 1886 and died at forty-three in 1929. His Jewish background was inauspicious. He was the only child of a reasonably well-to-do German family, with typically little interest in Judaism but great devotion to German culture. After a shift from medicine to philosophy, he wrote a doctoral dissertation published under the title *Hegel and the State*. The work evoked considerable acclaim and influential professors were ready to sponsor his teaching at a university, though Jews were still unwelcome there, particularly in that native discipline, idealistic philosophy.

Rosenzweig rejected a career as a professional philosopher because of his turn to religion. He gained his intellectual maturity by giving up the rationalistic gods of his early philosophical faith. His major contribution to religious thought, *The Star of Redemption*, was written during World War I. Many thinkers then were seeking a substitute for idealistic rationalism as a result of its failure to prepare them for the human realities they had experienced. Rosenzweig's book must be read less as an existentialist statement than as a German idealistic philosophy seeking to overcome itself.

The young thinker opens his argument with an uncommon philosophic topic, death. Why, he ruminates, should it trouble the individual? If Hegel is correct that all people are included in the Universal Spirit that is working its way through history to ever greater self-realization, why should they be disturbed at dying? Their cosmic significance will not perish, for their individuality is carried along by Absolute Spirit on its purposeful way. Death cannot rob individuals of their part in its magnificent, all-encompassing, forward flow.

What poor consolation is such philosophy, as we contemplate the frightening reality of our inevitable, ever-nearing death!

Surely an individual's disappearance has no real significance for idealist philosophers, for they dissolve its reality into an idea and turn our concrete existence into an abstraction. In an instant the hidden function of Hegelian philosophy is revealed. It exists to help people convince themselves that death is meaningless and may conveniently be ignored. Such philosophy is generated by our fear of dying and our unwillingness to face it. We are terrified lest we be forced to acknowledge the startling paradox of our individuality. Nothing in the world is as real to us as our own being—and we are steadily losing it. No abstract concept, no matter how universal or all-embracing, can ever be as significant as that. No idea can ever match the reality of "me" here and now. Proper philosophy—"existentialism"—begins with the reality of this incomparable but perishing self, with the recognition that true existence is concrete, individual, and particular, not abstract, general, and universal. Rationalism can no longer be a useful way of contemplating existence. A new sort of thinking must now begin.

The Three Givens of Existence

Death makes us aware of the first given reality of being, the self. Similarly it discloses that the world, too, has existence in its own right.

Some idealist philosophers were so taken with the creative power of reason that they had reduced "the world" to the intellectual construction of reality created by a human mind. Rosenzweig argues that "the world" is real even as the self is real. Individuals can have a separate existence because they are independent of the world about them. Thus, our death fills us with anxiety but the death of "the world," were we able to survive it, has another effect upon us. The self and the world are different and distinct. Neither is a creation of our reason or will. Both are simply there, realities given with our very existence. They precede our reason. Hence the hardheaded thinker must cope with them.

How can this be explained? How can one make sense of the existence of two such irreducible realities? German idealistic philosophy tried to do so with its concept of the Absolute whose universality embraced them both. The concept of the Absolute did give a comprehensive meaning to existence. In the process it robbed persons and the world of the individual reality that it reserved for itself alone. The significance it had claimed to confer, it thus subtly took back. Rosenzweig concludes that we must renounce traditional philosophy's goal and hope: a single concept universal enough to embrace persons and the world in their distinct realities. Instead, we shall understand them only when we acknowledge a reality beyond them and independent of them. Religion calls it God. As suddenly as that, without proof or definition or even pointing to any special realm of religious experience, but simply by contrasting the work of modern philosophy with the reality of human existence, Rosenzweig posits a real, existing, independent God.

Rosenzweig's does not begin with Decartes' notion of an empty, doubting mind. He posits three given, distinct realities: first, "me," the individual (which he calls "man"); second, the world (in which one lives out one's existence); and third, God (the ground and guide of all existence). Rosenzweig once termed his method of reaching these three entities "absolute empiricism." That is, they were the unavoidable realities yielded by a direct confrontation of the conditions of personal existence. We, the world, and God are simply there. Our reason cannot hope to explain them in terms of some master abstract principle. Ideas are always less than life. Responsible thought must build upon that recognition. The task of philosophy is humbly to follow after what exists and utilize reason to explicate its structure insofar as that is possible. This approach is proto-existentialist, the sort of thinking that a few years later Martin Heidegger and others would systematize into what we call existentialism. Commenting on his own thought, Rosenzweig also described his intellectual approach as a "new thinking," a methodology that made the situation of one's actual life the basis for all one's ideas.

Some Characteristics of the New Thinking

We cannot use European philosophy to capitalize on Rosenzweig's insight into what is given with existence itself. If the individual self is its very core, the new thinking must be personal, not impersonal, as philosophy customarily is. It must proceed in terms of particulars, not in terms of the universal categories rationalistic thinkers utilized. It must be open and dynamic, thus able to cope with living, shifting relationships among individuals, the world, and God.

Rosenzweig found human speech a close analogy to the kind of thinking he was advocating, going so far as to characterize it as "speech thinking." In true interchange the individual is personally involved, not passively present. In the course of speaking, people say things they did not previously know they believed or affirmed. Speaking from one's depth is therefore a variety of revelation. Taking place between partners, speech unites human beings into a momentary society. Dialogue is the living sinew of relationship, binding one partner to the other in genuine togetherness.

Rosenzweig wants to think about human existence in this participating, revelatory, relational way. Note that Rosenzweig proposes not to abandon all rational guidance at the point of human commitment but, beginning there, to construct an intellectual understanding of existence. After World War I other thinkers similarly explored the possibilities of speech as a guide to existential thinking. Martin

Buber's somewhat different exposition of thinking in terms of dialogue has become the most widely known and accepted of these philosophies.

Rosenzweig carried his exposition a bold step further. In effect he tried to create an appropriate logic for existential thinking. He argued that three primary words were necessarily involved in every statement. The first is "yes," the affirmation that something is real, that it has significance. The second is "no," which applies even in affirmation, for it indicates that the object is not something else but just what it is. The final word is "and" since, after all, the thing is both its "yes" *and* its "no."

Rosenzweig's structure for the new thinking is suspiciously close to the rationalistic logic of Hegel. Here as elsewhere, Rosenzweig is not as free of German idealism as he desired to be. Rosenzweig might have responded that Hegel's logic applied so well to reality because it stemmed from the structure of speech, not from purely mental considerations.

One significant example indicates how Rosenzweig's "logic" shapes his religious thought. To say a "yes" about God is to say that God is "there" and real, that God is what God is, thus making God "God." The affirmation also implies a certain "no"—that God is not any one thing, not merely this or limited to that. Transcending thingness, God is free to be and do whatever God wills to be and do. To this must be added an "and." God "is" *and* God is "free." God is the free being, the one whose being is freedom, who, through freedom, expresses God's particular being.

For Rosenzweig, God cannot be mere abstraction, a concept that summarizes or grounds all other ideas. God wills; God acts. In the language of Jewish tradition, God is a living God.

Time and history are critical to this sort of religious thought, for the relations among people, the world, and God are not lived out in static, unchanging being. Existence takes place as dynamic duration and, as the confrontation with death revealed, it finds its meaning only as one event succeeds another. Truth cannot then be merely the logical coherence of ideas or a static correspondence of thought to what-really-is. Truth now must be understood as a true relationship. Truth exists when a self is willing to live it and ascertain its existential reality. The important truths are those on which one stakes one's life. More important truths are those for which one is willing to die. And the greatest truths are those to which generation after generation will pledge its life and for which it will risk its death.

By virtue of God's relation to people and the universe, God is involved in time and works in history. Thus, despite the modernity with which the new thinking operates, Rosenzweig's existentialistic God is a personal God, one very much like the God described in the Bible.

The Three Relationships of Existence

What exactly is the relationship between God and the world? The ancients called it creation and thereby stated a continuing truth. Nature is not independent of God but receives its existence from God. God "calls" it into being and is its source and origin. Creation may largely be spoken of as referring to the past, though it cannot take that meaning exclusively. God sustains creation and keeps bringing new things into being, though largely in a derivative way. As the Jewish morning prayer puts it, properly utilizing the present tense, God "renews each day the work of creation." Nonetheless the creation-relation is fundamentally an event of the past.

The relationship between God and people is revelation. God makes us aware of God's presence and, out of that knowledge, of what is demanded of us. Unlike traditional Judaism, Rosenzweig does not believe God communicates verbal statements. All God gives in revelation is Self, God's being-there-with-us. As we all know from being in love, the presence of our beloved awakens in us a sense of aspiration and unworthiness, of dedication and resolve. Revelation as being-there-together means command, judgment, and acceptance as one. Jewish tradition depicted it in objective, factual terms—"And God spoke, saying . . ." In Rosenzweig's existentialist interpretation, revelation has been given new meaning in terms of personal relationship.

Even as one lives in the present, not in the past, revelation is a very present exchange. It cannot have happened only once or occur sporadically. It must be a contemporary reality—if people will open themselves to it as presence and not as idea. Of course, revelation has occurred in the past and history has been changed when groups have been decisively influenced by it. Such special moments have the quality of a continuing present, for revelation is most appropriately spoken of in the present tense. For Rosenzweig, God tells the Jews today, as at Sinai, what they must do. The contemporary experience of God, not that of the past, is ultimately critical to him, producing a dynamic and evolving Judaism. Rosenzweig's thought indicates that an existentialist theology can generate criteria enabling Jews to deal with the question of meaningful change.

The remaining tense, the future, applies primarily to the relationship between people and the world. Standing before God, we know we must transcend our present level of existence. Our work in the world ought to reflect better our knowledge of God. Each person needs to reach out and find others. Ultimately a community will appear whose members, through knowing one another in full individuality, will live with one another in peace and harmony. In turn such communities will overflow to reach all humankind and then out to nature until a final concord of people, the world, and God is achieved. The relations among the three existential realities are consummated in this messianic fulfillment. The Jewish sages termed this "redemption" and often pictured it as the work of humanity as God's partner in history.

Some people consider messianism impossibly remote and utterly unrelated to our present existence. They underestimate the power of life. It struggles to maintain itself despite all change, to attain permanence amid the flux of existence. A living thing is that unique natural locus where individuality asserts itself, even if only briefly, against unremitting change and decay. Our daily, lifelong experience testifies to our continuous triumph over non-being. We remain; the self continues; life is transcendent. The redemption of the entire world is the ultimate victory of the life principle. Effective only in a partial and incomplete manner now, it will one day be perfected in a harmony of people, the world, and God. Not without deliberate intent does Rosenzweig begin his philosophy with an evocation of death and end it with a call to life, a life dedicated to the work of redemption.

The Star That Illuminates Existence

Rosenzweig's "metaphysics" may be depicted by a diagram. The three realities are set at some distance from one another to indicate their genuine independence of one another. Their active interrelationship must also be indicated. Balancing the static realities and the active relationships, our view of reality looks like this:

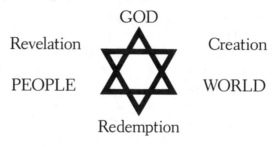

GOD

Revelation   Creation

PEOPLE   WORLD

Redemption

This is the star of redemption!

Rosenzweig's abstract conception of reality must now be applied to history. How did it receive concrete application in time? What do human records disclose of God's acts and people's response?

In pagan cults as in great religions, people everywhere have truly known the living God but only dimly. Rarely have they fully grasped the three realities and their interrelations. A true religion must build its way of life on creation, revelation, and redemption. Many religions have some truth, but thoughtful people will adhere only to those religions that know and live by the star of redemption.

Rosenzweig cannot accept the Asian religions, for they do not know and reflect the dynamic of creation, revelation, and redemption. Rosenzweig also denies the ultimate merit of Islam. Though heir to the Jewish understanding of history, it no longer demonstrates that active, creative relationship with God set forth in the star. He considers Islam's formalized and culture-bound condition a parody of a true religious relationship. Obviously, though Rosenzweig had firsthand experience and academic expertise in Judaism and Christianity, his knowledge of Islam was slight and his contact with it nearly nonexistent.

Two True Religions of History

Though a loyal Jew, Rosenzweig comes to an assertion probably without parallel in modern religious thought to this day. He declared that there are *two* true religions, Judaism and Christianity. Each emphasizes one aspect of truth. Judaism remains aloof from other religions to protect its integrity, to retain its vision against the distortion that would result from adopting perspectives from the outside world. Christianity is expansive, seeking at all costs to win the world for God, even to the extent of compromise or adulteration. Judaism is the fire of the star, Christianity its rays. Neither has the whole truth, for they stand in history, not at its integrated conclusion. Now human beings can achieve only part of the final perfection. To realize the harmony of knowledge and action, of self and community, that is redemption, we must utilize our present religion, awaiting its culmination in messianic days. Only then will we know and live God's truth in all its fullness. Until then we must live in such partial truth as we can find in our finite state.

Many people are shocked to hear that two religions, highly divergent in teaching and practice, are true. That claim defies logic and outrages consistent thought. But not by Rosenzweig's definition: that we find truth not in ideas but only in the concrete living out of history. Which of these religions is finally true can be known only when the many generations over the millennia of history have lived by them and given their lives for their truths. Then either or both, transformed perhaps, will participate in that fulfillment called the Kingdom of God.

Does Rosenzweig's existentialism deprive its adherents of a justification for maintaining Judaism rather than accepting Christianity?

Rosenzweig does acknowledge the legitimacy of Christianity. Considering its history and the lives it has molded, he feels he cannot honestly do otherwise. Must not every believing Jew face up to the significance of Christianity's (and Islam's) place in God's purposes? So, too, the devout Christian must puzzle over Israel's continued existence in faith and service despite its rejection of the Christ. Rosenzweig has given a candid response to a perplexing reality. He would want to know how other modern Jews could give any less positive a judgment.

Rosenzweig simultaneously affirms Judaism's special truth. He would emphatically deny that Christianity is truer than Judaism. It can offer Jews nothing they do not already possess. All they need spiritually is already in Judaism. Indeed, what every Jew has at birth, the Christian must yet acquire, for a Jew is born into a living relation with God, the Covenant. No one is born a Christian, for without baptism one dies a heathen. To become a Christian, one must come to the Father through the Christ. For heathens Christianity is an effective means to God. But what can baptism bestow on a Jew who already shares an authentic relationship with God?

Rosenzweig claimed further that the Jews are already at the goal for which Christians are still striving. Christianity is only on the way to the Kingdom. The church must be reconstituted with each new birth, each generation. It justifies its present unfulfillment by the future return of the Christ. Then Christians will finally be fully united with God. The Jews are in a quite different situation. They are already with God. Having God's revelation, Torah, enables them now to live, so to speak, in the Kingdom of God. This constitutes Israel an eternal people. Time and place, the political and social events that make up ordinary history are of relative indifference to the Jews. Living in eternity, why should they seek temporality? For a Jew, to desert Judaism is not only unnecessary but a retrogression.

The Uniqueness of Rosenzweig's Theory of Judaism

Rosenzweig's existentialism contradicted the theories of Judaism dominant in his day. The liberals insisted that Judaism was a pattern of belief centered about the concept of ethical monotheism. The traditionalists countered that a Jew was identified by observance or neglect of Jewish law. The Zionists rejected both religious positions, affirming rather that Jews were a secular, national group. Loyalty to the folk, its land, and its language was the primary sign of Jewish authenticity. Rosenzweig consciously dissented from all three views while incorporating some of their major concerns. For him, the Jew's religious existence was not simply personal. Each Jew shares the Jewish people's Covenant with God, made at Sinai and renewed through centuries of loyalty and practice. The idea of the Jewish people without God is utterly unknown to the Jewish past and unthinkable in any genuine Judaism. A living relationship with God must be its center and no idea, not even one as noble or exalted as "ethical monotheism," can substitute for it. The Covenant relationship is naturally expressed in deeds and thus Jewish law is its necessary expression. One cannot, however, compromise people's human dignity by requiring them to do an act that, despite knowledge and general commitment, they find themselves unable to do. For Rosenzweig, relationship, not performance, is the test of Jewish legitimacy. He therefore was more concerned with piety and observance than the liberals, with autonomy more than the Orthodox, and with religion more than the Zionists.

Rosenzweig's philosophy grew out of his experience. Immediately before World War I, the young university student had been directly challenged by the religious affirmations of some friends and relatives. Their thoughtful probing destroyed his middle-class, self-righteous secularism and made him see the need of religious commitment. Though born Jewish, they felt one could find living religiosity only in Christianity. Rosenzweig agreed to join them, yet somehow felt it more authentic to do so as the early Christians had done, to come to the Christ as a believing Jew. He spent one last Yom Kippur day in an ordinary, traditional synagogue in Berlin. When the full day of services was over and that day of Jewishness had been lived, the resolve to convert made no sense. He no longer felt that he needed Christianity or that he could ever become a Christian. Rosenzweig never discussed that day's events or described what transpired. His many other writings make plain that religion ought not be based on special experiences, whether the genteel ones of Baeck and Otto, or the extravagant ones of the mystics. He rejects such grounds for a proper faith. For him, being, not feeling, should be our guide. I suggest that, having once opened himself to the reality of living as a Jew under the Covenant, he realized that he had always possessed that which he though he must convert to find. Existence, not experience was critical.

The present task of Jewish leadership, as he saw it, was to lead Jews back to the Jewish roots of their existence. In culture-oriented German Jewry he felt this could be accomplished best through adult education, by exposing people to the ancient sources, wherever possible in the original Hebrew. After his war service he desisted from theologizing and devoted his life to Jewish education, most of it as head of the adult Jewish academy in Frankfurt, which he founded. His philosophy demonstrated that deeds, not ideas, are the primary way a Jew responds to God and he was determined to exemplify it.

Rosenzweig's Debate with Buber

In the early 1920's Rosenzweig had an extraordinary debate with Martin Buber, in which they exchanged a series of letters on the issue of Jewish law. (Rosenzweig frequently used letters to express his ideas, since they allowed him to practice speech-thinking with his correspondent.)

In a long open letter, Rosenzweig challenged Buber to adopt the same standard for Jewish law that Buber had urged Jews to apply to Jewish study. With telling effect Buber had argued against the liberal notion that only the ethical teaching of Judaism was worthy of serious lay study. Jewish history dictated otherwise. The Jews were a people, as the Zionists said, not a philosophic school as the liberals implied. A people records in its literature what it has learned and valued in life. To grasp its folk wisdom, one must study its texts in all their variety, openly and without preconception. To set limits by genre or theme as to what will or will not be of value produces more of an encounter with oneself than with the spirit of the Jewish people. A serious inquirer will first study the material and accept whatever lessons may emerge from the encounter.

Rosenzweig urged that modern Jews come to Jewish law in the same way. They should observe it not according to any prejudgment of what remains valid in it, but insofar as they are "able" to do so. A living, personal relationship with God as part of the Jewish people mandates a life of Jewish duty, of the discipline delineated by the sages. Life under the Covenant is existence under "the yoke of the commandments." The liberals had required only the practice of ethics, judging all other acts by their usefulness in sensitizing one to morality. Rosenzweig now advocated a full-scale commitment to carrying out the traditional law, allowing the doing to produce its own validation.

Buber firmly rejected this line of argument. He wanted no precondition, not even the content of the law, to stand between him and what God might or might not command. In a living relationship one responds to the other in terms of what is demanded of one now, not what once seemed appropriate. A given precept of the law is probably what God once asked Jews to do and may be asking them to do now. It may also not be what God wants now. Buber made a distinction between study and action. Facing a text, one may reasonably suspend judgment about its worth and accept the discipline of giving oneself to the study. Action is different. It involves the commitment of the whole self. Often our deed reveals who we truly are—even to ourselves. When acts are at stake, Buber insists, people can be required to do only what, in their encounter with the Eternal Thou, they find themselves called to do.

In this correspondence Rosenzweig did not develop further his thesis that traditional Jewish law is binding, at least in principle, on non-Orthodox Jews. He could not easily do so because he and Buber shared a common theoretical understanding of revelation and law. Both thinkers affirmed autonomy, that only the immediate moment of relationship with God was authoritative. Only the encounter with God, with its address to the individual self, could command. Once the living moment was reduced to a rule, what had been an authentic behest became an impersonal and hence dead regulation. Or, to put it another way, a law addressed to everyone and thereby to no person in particular had no religious validity. Rosenzweig conceded that command must be existential. (We shall take up this matter again in Chapter 7.)

Resolving the Issue of Autonomy and Law

In other writings, Rosenzweig suggested a way around this dilemma. He did not abandon either his identification of authentic Jewish existence with accepting the authority of the law or his existentialist notion of the personal, present quality of revelation. Instead he argued that in the doing, what previously might have seemed only a lifeless statute became God's personal command to the doer. Against Buber's insistence that the imperative must precede a genuinely required religious act, Rosenzweig asserted that stated Jewish observance, carried out in Jewish being, created its own sense of commandment.

Had he said no more, Rosenzweig would have been an apologist for traditional Judaism. But his position is particularly intriguing since he remained a liberal by dialectically enunciating the notion that Jews need not undertake any duties they found themselves "unable" to do. His comment on the topic was brief and cryptic. He surely did not mean Jews should desist from observances that did not appeal to them. No trivial considerations could carry weight in his serious approach to authentic existence. His personalistic philosophy would normally make the criterion for a proper act the ability to devote one's whole self to it. Against Orthodoxy, Rosenzweig could not demand that Jewish law had sway over a Jew who, at the very deepest level, was "unable" to perform a given practice. In Rosenzweig's understanding, the law momentarily exempted this Jew—and that as a matter of authentic modern Jewish duty. For such a Jew, the unobserved law was in a special category: a commandment, but one "not yet" fulfilled.

Rosenzweig is the only major modern Jewish thinker to have created an unqualifiedly non-Orthodox interpretation of Judaism that takes traditional Jewish law so seriously. He has therefore been highly esteemed by those Jews who see law as the central feature of Jewish history but who no longer can accept the doctrine of its divine origin and continuity. Rosenzweig's intuition in this regard seems in conflict with the rest of his thought and with much Jewish experience. Even as his theory of revelation does not validate Jewish law, neither does observance usually do so. Many well-intentioned Jews testify that doing rarely produces the sense of personal command that Rosenzweig told them would occur. Rosenzweig raised, but could not answer, a question that continues to perplex liberal Jewish thinkers: How can one grant the individual self the dignity of making independent decisions yet require law for the Jewish people?

Rosenzweig's doctrine of the Jewish people has also drawn much criticism. By making the Jews essentially a people of revelation, he withdrew them from normal history. Living in eternity, they had no need for a land of their own or the protection that acquiring their own sovereign state might grant them. Rosenzweig was a confirmed non-Zionist. He saw no significant virtue in ethnicity and he worried lest the revival of the Hebrew language secularize Judaism and thereby empty it of its unique spiritual content. If anything, Rosenzweig seems here to be less true to Jewish tradition than to have made an ideal of Diaspora existence, if not of a Christian theological view of the Jews. Half a century later—in a time that has seen the establishment of the State of Israel—Rosenzweig's attitude toward peoplehood seems particularly naive.

Rosenzweig has had few intellectual disciples. For one thing, his thought, reference, and argumentation are thoroughly Germanic. He has not transplanted well. Many of his key assumptions appear more as proclamation than as the result of reasoning or experience—for example, his treatment of God's reality. His later, Jewish, thought also suffers from being developed only in fragments. We often cannot tell what he meant and do not know how we can apply his works to our quite different situations.

Rosenzweig's own life was powerful argument for the value of an existentialistic commitment to living as a Jew. In 1921 the first signs of a progressive paralysis were detected, and as the years wore on he became completely incapacitated, barely able to move a finger, finally able to signal with only his eyes. Despite this disability, he lived until

1929, and did so as an incredibly active, concerned, creative human being. With his wife's aid, he wrote innumerable, discursive letters, reviewed records and books, and worked with Martin Buber on a new German translation of the Bible. A circle of friends, admirers, and disciples gathered around him, offering him the Jewish community that was basic to his being. The various accounts of the group who regularly came to Rosenzweig's home and enabled him to carry on his Jewish practice are among the most moving documents of modern Jewish life.

Rosenzweig's thought stands on its own as a special example of Jewish existentialism. That his life bears its own special testimony to the validity of his ideas is an existential consistency one hopes to find in thinkers but dares not expect. For Rosenzweig, death ended existence only as people know it. It could not overcome life itself.

7

Religious Existentialism: Martin Buber

EXISTENTIALISM proceeds from the premise that the whole person, not merely one's mind or conscience or emotions, must be the standard of our thought and action. By analyzing the structures of human existence and describing our existential needs, it provides a new justification and elaboration of religious faith. Though this emphasis on the self gives existentialism great power, it also produces its great weakness. Turning to the person may teach the necessity of belief; it tells us nothing about the proper substance of our affirmation.

With attention concentrated on the virtue of faith, every religion seems acceptable, even the most bizarre. If existentialism only produces faith in faith, it can support great evil. Nazism had a powerful effect on many Germans. Its ideology seemed a saving truth to vast numbers, even though it produced a corrupt society and a ravaged continent. Is there no guidance to what is worthy of our existential commitment or why our personal stand in faith should be here rather than there?

If human existence were rationally comprehensible, our concerns about the content of faith could receive sure and explicit answers. Classic philosophy utilized the mind to supply us with judgments about life that were as dependable and certain as the logic upon which they were based. If existentialism is correct, the human condition cannot ultimately be explained in purely cognitive constructs, no matter how grand. Despite the pain, we must surrender the hope that reason might yet give us the safety and assurance of having an intellectual understanding of existence. If we are honest with ourselves, we will acknowledge that our lives always retain a substantial element of risk and venture.

Recognizing the difficulty inherent in their position, various existentialists have sought to explain what constitutes a worthy faith. Negatively, they have proceeded by offering an intensive analysis of the depersonalization of the individual in contemporary society. By exposing the ways we have been robbed of our sense of personal dignity and unique identity, they have pointed to needed social change. Positively, working from their new insight into the self, they have suggested what it means to be a genuine person, to have true relationships and to create a social order that fosters authentic individuality and community. No one has contributed more to this project than Martin Buber.

He was born in Vienna in 1878, and until his death in Jerusalem in 1965, his life was marked by his steadily increasing influence. Before World War I, he was already a significant figure in European and Jewish intellectual affairs. His writings on religion and culture, religious socialism, and particularly mysticism, appealed to the broad public engaged in spiritual search. In the Jewish community, he was an early adherent of Zionism and a leader of its cultural activities. His emergence as an existentialist came with the appearance of his brief classic *I and Thou* in 1923. In the following decades, he applied his new theory to every aspect of human and Jewish existence. No Jewish religious thinker since biblical times more substantially influenced his culture than did Buber, though it must be noted that his influence outside the Jewish community was much greater than that within it.

Origins of Buber's Thought

Buber's thought shows no symptoms of the personal or social trauma often called a "failure of nerve." He came to existentialism in the decade following the appearance of his mystical work *Daniel* in 1913.

Buber once related an incident that was symptomatic of his development from one concerned with immersion in the All to facing real people in their immediate situation. In late autumn 1914, a young man came to see him. Buber had just spent a morning basking in mystical exaltation. Still warmed by his intimate communion with God, Buber received the youth cordially and answered his questions in friendliness. Afterward Buber was troubled. He realized that he had not truly heard or genuinely responded to his caller. The young man obviously had questions he burned to ask but could not articulate. The older man, more concerned with the afterglow of his morning rapture than with the person in front of him, had inhibited rather than promoted their exchange. Sometime later, Buber heard from his friends that his caller had died in the war. Experiences such as this forced Buber to the admission that mysticism, far from disclosing reality to us, obscures it. The people who confront us moment by moment and make their demands on us are far more significant than any subjective occurrence might be. Authentic human existence, Buber realized, is found in "meeting," in the reality that arises between people, not in a reality suggested by theories or sensations.

Some scholars have maintained that Buber's ideas developed from his early and lasting affection for the Hasidic movement. None has shown how Hasidism might engender Buber's philosophy rather than offer convenient illustrations for it. The possible Jewish roots of Buber's unique insight into the human condition remain unclear. Yet his affirmation of the interpersonal as more significant than purely individual being repeats the priorities of traditional Judaism. A religiosity that can obscure one's responsibility to one's neighbors is uncongenial to the Jewish spirit. In stressing engagement, rather than solitariness, Buber affirmed the Jewish heritage in a new, existential way.

Buber directs our attention to the inner life of personal relationships. This idea has led many critics, particularly rationalists, to call his teaching mystical. This term can easily lead to profound misunderstanding. If a mystic is one who wishes to transcend individuality by union with Deity, Buber is no mystic. He envisages meaning as arising from what transpires *between* two persons. One must take this statement literally. If either person does not steadfastly maintain individuality, there is no meeting, only merging, probably the submerging of one in the other. Rather than surrender oneself in dialogue, Buber believes that only maintaining one's particularity while sharing it with another truly calls relationship into being.

Persons, Not Ideas, Are Critical

With intellectual communication no substitute for person-to-person encounter, Buber sometimes writes in an odd style. Seeking to direct people to I-Thou meeting, he cannot convey his meaning in impersonal, objective, philosophic prose. He presents his comments on the human situation in short, poetic observations, more musing than arguing with his reader. He had no desire to be considered a theologian or philosopher as he did not want academic convention to keep him from engaging reality or his readers. Again, a personal experience is illuminating.

Buber once gave some lectures attended by working men. Recognizing they were uncomfortable in the milieu of the university students, he later met them at a separate place. In response to his presentation, one man commented that he did not require a hypothesis such as God because he felt at home in the universe. Buber responded with a withering refutation of all the man's preconceptions, particularly his naive insistence that sense perception exposes reality. After Buber's philosophically devastating speech, the man said, "You are right." And then Buber knew he had been wrong. He had merely convinced the man that he needed a new set of ideas, perhaps even that he required a concept of God. But Buber's goal had not been conceptual; rather, it was to bring the man to a personal relationship with God.

In moments such as these Buber came to know the vast difference between knowing an idea and knowing a person. Buber's fame derives from his unique twofold understanding of relationship, which may with some liberty be called his theory of knowledge.

Our Dualistic Approach to the World

Buber suggests that there are two ways of knowing or relating to the world. The more obvious one, on which we base our everyday lives, Buber terms the "I-It" relation. People usually relate to things by observing them, examining them, testing them. They are measured, taken apart, put back together again and thus comprehended. Doing this can involve ingenious manipulation of the object or the use of sensitive instruments to yield a precise understanding. During this process we make a conscious effort to put a distance between ourselves and the object we seek to understand in order not to disrupt our perception by emotional or personal involvement. As a sophisticated technique, this becomes modern science. On an ordinary level, it is our common modern manner of relating to our surroundings.

Buber does not belittle the value of this kind of knowing. Without objective understanding, people become the victims of superstition and magic, never attaining the freedom that a scientific understanding of the natural order makes possible. Technology may have caused many problems but those who daily benefit from its wonders—enough food to eat, pure water to drink, medicines to cure disease—should not condemn it as worthless.

Buber can pinpoint our difficulty with objectivity. It arises when advocates of the I-It relation imperialistically claim it is the only legitimate form of knowing. The dogma is highly tempting. Dispassionate observation offers to give us control over the world. Place the tremendous social and economic power of a technologically oriented age behind this proposal and the drive toward the dominance of the I-It becomes almost irresistible.

Buber adamantly refuses to accept the sovereignty of the I-It relationship. Consider again the two incidents previously described. Are detachment, analysis, manipulation capable of opening us up to the human being who stands before us who might, if we are accessible, speak to us from the very depths? In special circumstances we may agree to be treated as objects, for the I-It relation may disclose which chemicals or operations are indicated to remedy certain of our disabilities. Normally, we are offended when someone who should treat us as a person will only relate to us as if we were a thing. Then we know that the I-It relation cannot enable us to know a person as a person.

Think of a common personal experience. Something troubles you deeply and you want to discuss it with someone. You hesitate talking to anyone about it but finally know you must and you go to visit a certain trusted person. After the ritual preliminaries and the pause in which you summon up your courage, you begin to speak. What you wanted to say comes slowly at first, but then more easily, perhaps in a rush. You begin to say things that, to your surprise, you did not know you wanted to say. Now that they have come out, you realize that they are even more important than what you had consciously intended to say. You are speaking from someplace very deep within you when you suddenly notice that your friend is staring at the run in your hose or the pimple on your chin. You break off speaking; you probably cannot continue. If he asks why you stopped and you respond that he was not listening, he may be shocked. He may even be able to repeat your last words. It makes no difference. You came to have him listen not merely to your words, but to *you*. That is why no long letter, no telephone conversation, no casual meeting could substitute for a face-to-face meeting. You wanted him to pay full attention to you—and he didn't. How frustrating such an encounter can be!

Genuine Meeting, the Less Common Experience

You know what did not happen because you have occasionally had the opposite experience. You try to talk to someone but you simply cannot express what you want to say. The words will not come. You say many things, even wrong things, but never what you really had hoped to say. In the midst of your frustration you may stop and have the joy of realizing that your inarticulateness makes no difference. Your friend understands what you want to say, even though you never put it into words. You know that. You know that your friend understands you. More, your friend knows that you know that he or she knows. And *you* know *that*. The two of you have truly come to know each other. In authentic encounter—meeting, dialogue, relationship—two individuals come to understand and appreciate one another, not just the words or signs they exchange. Buber called this the I-Thou relationship.

Encounter arises in a far different way than does I-It knowing. It demands participation, not distance; giving oneself, not objectivity. If the other person is to know you, and not merely part of you, you cannot hold back part of yourself from the communication. You can be truly known as a person only when someone knows you as a whole and that can happen only when one is addressed by another person and responds on that level.

Buber cannot, therefore, accurately describe the I-Thou relationship to us. If all of you is in it, there is nothing kept back to observe and record what is going on. Many people say they cannot even dimly recall an I-Thou encounter. From earliest childhood, we have been trained to remain on guard with other people. In everything we do, we keep part of us on sentry duty, hoping we are being properly noticed, fearful lest we blunder, wary of the great judges within and without us. This inner-outer, schizoid existence may have its virtue as making possible the objectivity that can bring stability and structure to our existence in the I-It realm. (Thus, I must watch as I write these words to make certain that they are set down in correct grammar and syntax, that they are logically ordered and properly convey my understanding of Buber's teaching.) In personal relationship such detachment is fatal. Operating behind our facade we wonder who is really behind the limited self the other has disclosed to us. Mask encounters mask, not I-Thou ("you" singular), you in all your individuality.

Some Signs of Genuine Dialogue

Much of what people value most in I-It knowing disappears in the I-Thou realm. Precision is impossible and public communication is difficult. Language cannot easily convey so uniquely personal an experience. Perhaps that is why all cultures have honored good poets and considered music indispensable. Ultimately, the I-Thou relationship is ineffable. My description here and Buber's own writing cannot substitute for your personally experiencing it or recalling having done so. They are meant as helpful gestures, offered in the hope of pointing you toward similar events in your own life.

Buber himself would object to characterizing his basic insight as a distinction between knowing objects and knowing persons. He maintains that the form of our relationship is not determined by the apparent nature of the partner. Just as one may have an I-It relation to a person, so one may have an I-Thou relation with an object. Many people occasionally respond to nature with I-Thou sensitivity and others have a similar openness to ideas, to art, or to other cultural activities.

I-Thou relationships yield far more significant meaning than do those that remain I-It. Becoming a person fully and seeing reality in responsiveness impress one with a richness of quality in oneself and thus potentially in all things. To take the climactic case, love brings us incomparable affirmation. We know ourselves and another to be of inestimable worth. Our world is full of such value, given or achievable.

Love also commands. We must live up to the self we have come to know ourselves to be, through our relationship. Our beloved may legitimately make demands on us and we quickly come to know what is expected of us. For fear of shattering our relationship, we will feel obligated to do certain acts and refrain from others. No verbal exchange may occur to define our duties. Sometimes articulation blemishes rather than enhances our communication. In any case, the dearer the person, the more responsible we will feel. Now we know when we revert again to the usual I-It situation that it is not ultimate. Rather, what we discover on the uninvolved, analytic level receives its proper human context from what is revealed to us in true dialogue.

As desirable as it may be, the I-Thou encounter cannot be forced. A person is essentially free or effectively an object. To demand other people to be fully present or to manipulate them to do so denies their freedom and destroys the possibility of an authentic encounter. All we can do is try to remain open to dialogue. Knowing that it occurs and remembering our previous experiences can help us stay available for a fresh meeting. Fortunately, the I-Thou moment often comes on its own to grace our lives with its gift of meaning.

Buber envisions life as highly dynamic. We cannot persist in the I-Thou experience but continually revert to the I-It. For all the loss entailed in that movement, it blends continuity and structure with glimpses of value and direction. At any moment we may again be relating to the world in I-Thou fashion. Encounter comes and goes in quite prosaic fashion. It involves no mystic state, no emotional peak. It is an ordinary ingredient of our lives when, say, we spend a few moments with someone we truly care about.

We Come to Know God As We Come to Know People

Buber declares that we need to relate to God in an I-Thou way if we wish to know God at all. Most philosophers have sought God in I-It terms, as if God were an object. Turning God into a thing is idolatry — the most fundamental denial of God's reality, according to the Bible, though the modern images are mental, not stone or wood. If God is not known as objects are known, our customary intellectual questions about God sound misplaced. We would not ask them about any given individual. Does one prove the existence of a person? Can one give the concept of one's sweetheart or the definition of one's friend? Persons can never adequately be conceptualized. They are found, addressed, lived with, and only then truly known.

Far more important, intellectual understanding is not a prerequisite of relationship. People cannot know everything about their prospective friends before they put their trust in them. Despite our necessary ignorance, we rightly reach out to one another and accept the risk of life's most significant commitments. Our minds may help us live responsibly but if we limit living to what is rationally conclusive, we shall not be fully human.

Buber's argument is simple: apply the wrong way of knowing to people or to God and they remain hidden. Reach out to God as one does to another person, and a surprising yet obvious fact emerges: God may be found everywhere. We discover God in the same place we might make a friend, wherever we are, as ordinary as that might be. We do this in the same way we reach out to another person, not by forcing the encounter but by being there and letting whatever happens happen. Religion ought to be a commonplace, the basic stuff of everyday existence. The point could not be more important.

Buber Is Against Special or Religious Experiences

Buber rejects the term "experience" for the I-Thou relationship. He is wary of its romantic, sensual connotations. He wants to make certain that we do not identify encounter with God as an exceptional event— one characterized, perhaps, by tingles or tongues, overwhelming bliss or overcoming power. Perhaps dialogue with God will leave a residue of serenity; it will certainly command one involved in it. If we measure significance by sensation, we shall utterly misunderstand the I-Thou relationship with God. The analogy with love or friendship is exact. Coming from a chat with a person we hold dear, we are certain our companion is, as we often now say, "a real person." Not because gongs chimed, or a ray of sun broke through the clouds, or because of any other romantic sign or event. Persons met—that is all, and everything. So it is with God. Most religious traditions teach that if we would but turn to God, in whatever ordinary place we find ourselves, God would be there with us.

People often prefer to have a special realm for God—most likely in the secret hope of confining God to it. To recognize God's presence in our ordinary lives would mean exposing ourselves to the responsibility and spontaneity of genuine relationship. Religion, our institutional way of relating to God, easily becomes an elaborate scheme to limit God to given times, acts, and places, excluding God from interfering in the rest of our lives. Religion, like theology, may easily become the foe of the religious. On the whole, Buber advocates abandoning religion in the hope that we will once again be open to personal involvement with God.

What should one expect from an encounter with God if not rapture and ecstasy? Many people wait for words. Taking the Bible literally, they assume they will hear a voice. To them dialogue must mean a verbal exchange. The remembrance of human relationship should disabuse us of such mythic expectations. Encounter may begin with words, but if it is limited to language, it may never proceed very far. In our moments of greatest intimacy, what is most binding and mutual is expressed silently. Thus, when we undergo great sorrow or suffering, words tend only to belittle reality. Good friends know when not to talk—yet, they also intuit how important it is for them to be there. Were they not present, there would be a painful emptiness that even mute presence fills with comfort and consolation. Presence, not verbiage, is given when I and Thou commune. "I" know that "Thou" art with me—and I with Thee. From being there with one another—and that alone—all else derives. Seeking God, we should not await a voice but only God's presence, God's being there with us—no more but also no less.

For some few people, finding God ends all doubt and answers all questions. Most of us are not so blessed. Our faith remains mixed with questioning, our moments of certainty alternate with new skepticism. Buber's own understanding of faith as relationship makes understandable this strange dialectic.

Love always provides the best analogy. Many a marriage survives the shocking discovery that one's spouse is capable of hateful and abusive acts. How can people face that and still say they are in love? Their confidence in one another is not ended by such a trauma because they set love into the totality of their relationship. Their love grew on those many repeated moving occasions when they found themselves truly I-to-Thou. Now, momentarily standing in I-to-It negation, they trust that it will pass and the confirming I-Thou will return as it has before. When faith in the dialectic departs, love is gone.

Encounter with God follows the rule that we cannot abide in the realm of the I-Thou. God's presence gives way to God's absence, a loss made all the more severe since, unlike the beloved, God is never present as a body. In Buber's pregnant phrase, God is the Eternal Thou, the only Thou we know that never becomes an It. God being absent, we have no immediate warrant for faith. When our doubt arises in the context of trust that we will yet find God again, disbelief is painful but acceptable. Every serious personal relationship knows such oscillation between its highs and lows. Faith, Buber opines, is not a permanent state, something gained once and forever like a college degree. It is like a great love, found and lived in a continual alternation of knowing and wondering, losing and regaining, and believing and doubting and believing once again.

Buber's Understanding of Evil

Before the Holocaust, Buber explained evil as the result of our refusal to relate to one another personally. When we can treat people as abstractions and thus deal with them impersonally, exploitation and manipulation cease being sins. As soon as we face outsiders and enemies as individuals and open ourselves to them as persons, we cannot easily continue treating them with indifference or hostility. Human interaction can counter hatred since relationship is the foundation of morality. Conversely, willfully withholding oneself from others is the first step on the road of evil.

Buber suggested that immorality arises in people in two stages. In the first, we are merely aimless. We cannot make up our minds what to do. We are victims of the infinite possibilities that human freedom opens up to us, and we can do nothing. Our evil consists of our passivity. In the second stage, we do casual, occasional evil acts, eventually even being untroubled by willful and habitual wrongdoing. At that point, we have allied ourselves with the demonic in us and have dehumanized ourselves—at least for the present.

Persons being ultimately free, we can always stop and change our ways. We "turn" back to other people—and to God. The Rabbis termed this act *teshuvah*, repentance, or in Buber's existentialist reinterpretation, the "turning." If we will make the effort, relationship can be restored. God, Buber taught, fulfilled the Divine responsibilities in the relationship with people by always remaining available for its restoration ("atonement"). The difficulties in finding, maintaining, and reconstituting the Covenant were always on the human side. Instead of turning to God, the everlasting open One, we resolutely turned away.

After the Holocaust, Buber could not remain so optimistic. He no longer was able to declare that it was people's fault if they lost faith or did not find God present in their lives. The unbearable evil of the Holocaust forced Buber to the tragic recognition that God sometimes, somehow withdraws from humankind. What could be more evil? Buber used two images to describe this. The blacker one was biblical: God sometimes hides God's "face" (presence) from people. The other was a bit more positive. To use an analogy from nature, in radically evil times, God is eclipsed. God is not dead, then, for though we stand in darkness, we await God's return. Buber did not seek to explain this. Instead, like a faithful, wounded lover, he neither lied about his pain nor abandoned a relationship that was real though incomprehensible.

Buber does not propose to explain why in normal times, God is so readily available. He does not argue that God, in some metaphysical sense, *is* a person. All objective assertion about God deviously turns God into an "it." As an existentialist, Buber can only speak of the reality we know as part of our living experience. Thus, what he can profess is that we know God the way we know persons. He further maintains that when persons encounter one another truly, God is also present.

Describing so subtle a presence is even more problematic than trying to find words for a direct I-Thou encounter. Buber says that in true meeting we may sense an other, who stands behind the dialogue partners and makes it possible for them to meet one another. People who are blocked from approaching God directly should try the path of love and service to their fellows. Often the best way to bring people to God is not by describing the I-Thou relationship but by making oneself personally available. Should the encounter occur, not only will the basic paradigm of meeting be experienced but an intimation of God's presence will be gained.

The New Spirit of Liberal Piety

Existentialism's personalization of religion gives it a tone that, though modern, has many traditional echoes. For example, it mandates personal piety without the encumberment of an anthropomorphic God. To avoid describing God as a person, some theologians have insisted on an impersonal understanding of God. The intellectual gain was generally exceeded by the human loss, most people finding it difficult to relate personally to a God who is neutral to them. Buber predicates a God but does not mean that literally. All literal statements are I-It—hence, in Buber's philosophy, they are necessarily false, including all anthropomorphisms. When understood as I-Thou poetics, anthropomorphic statements may direct us with great power to the God who is known as persons are known.

Another example of the personalist reinvigoration of tradition is found in its attitude to the Bible. Liberalism was based on the Bible's being a human work. It was the greatest book humankind had created in the course of its spiritual development. Why that was so, why the modern classics—Darwin, Freud, Dostoevsky, Ibsen—were not really more relevant to the religious quest of people today than Holy Scripture never could be explained. Buber's view of revelation enables the religious person to take the Bible seriously, though not literally. The words are human, but they result from authentic encounters with God. They are unique in human literature in their transparency to what transpired between the prophets and God. Reading them today in I-Thou openness, we can often recapitulate the experience that engendered them. Over the centuries, the Bible has brought people into relationship with God in a way that no other literature has ever done or is ever again likely to do.

Something similar happens to the practice of prayer in Buber's reworking of it. People have often turned prayer into a means of appeasing God or flattering God in the hope of gaining favor. In reaction, modern philosophers have limited it to an exercise in mental hygiene or the integration of one's inner resources. Buber's Eternal Thou can as little be manipulated as can anyone with whom we wish to have a genuine relationship. More, God cannot now be denied independence, the critical characteristic of one who participates in dialogue. Answering our prayers cannot now mean that God does what we ask. When one always must do what another requires, it is slavery, not covenant. God, too, must be granted the freedom to answer our petitions, even to give a negative answer by saying "No." We pray not for results but to renew the most important relationship of our lives. In prayer we seek to open ourselves up to God's presence. Learning again that God is with us in what we are going through provides all the answer a mature person can ask for.

Having the classic religious terms and practices revitalized creates a contemporary religious practice that is more pious than the older liberalism and more believable to moderns than unrefurbished traditionalism.

Relating Religiosity to Reality

Too many people never go beyond this point in Buber's thought. They are fixated on what may be called Buber's theory of religion-in-general. Since it can produce a warm involvement with God and people, since it knows no limitations of circumstance or situation, it possesses broad appeal. Many Americans particularly esteem Buber because he seems to justify religiosity rather than religion, the private practice of the I-Thou rather than institutional pieties. Buber is not that unhistorical. Because he is an existentialist, Buber concerns himself with religion in the concrete, lived human situation. He probes humankind's actual experience with God in time, climaxing in the record given in the Bible. By I-Thou standards, it is the Bible that best tells how God was first fully known. Reading its pages with I-It eyes, as is done in so-called scientific biblical study, yields data only of some antiquarian interest. It necessarily caricatures the Bible's own concern, the continued involvement of the living God with individuals and a people. Read with I-Thou openness, the historic reality and contemporary truth of the Hebrews' experience with God are revealed.

The Covenant of Sinai, the climax of the exodus narrative, was a unique event in human history. At the mountain, the raggle-taggle band of erstwhile Hebrew slaves, moved by the incredible experience of exodus and the leadership of a man of extraordinary vision, entered a Covenant with the one God of creation. This was no mere ritual of offering sacrifice and accepting legislation so as to give structure to the mob. True, through rites and laws a new nation emerged to seek its destiny. It did so out of the unique consciousness that this people, Israel, had faced and known God. In the strange and overpowering events they had experienced, the Hebrews had become open to the presence of the Eternal Thou operating in their history. At Sinai, corporately, in one great moment of recognition and acknowledgment, they, individually and collectively, bound themselves to God. They pledged themselves, as a nation, to be God's own people, to serve God in human history, to carry the knowledge of God in their midst and exemplify it before humankind. They dedicated themselves to this service until all people would similarly recognize God and live in that knowledge.

What was not specified at Sinai became clear to the people of Israel through its history in the wilderness and on the Land. Much of its education in the meaning of the Covenant came from suffering and chastisement. The Sinai–golden calf–punishment–return cycle runs through the Bible. The genius of the Jewish people was not that it was inhumanly saintly but that it never fully broke its relationship with God. It acknowledged God's truth even when that truth was used to condemn it. Its glory arises in turning its chastisers into its heroes. Other historic religious movements have kept their inspiration alive for two, perhaps three generations after their founder. Israel's span of fresh revelation runs through at least eight centuries after Moses. Despite backsliding and stubbornness, even Exile, the people, as a people, managed to return to God and renew the Covenant. In those historic trials the people of Israel mastered the art of maintaining loyalty to God and their destiny despite the tribulations history might bring. Succeeding generations built their lives as a folk on the Sinai experience and through their reliving of it knew that it was true.

The Covenant Remains the Basis of Jewish Existence

The Covenant relationship is the foundation of Jewish existence. It has taken different form as Jews have moved from one society and culture to another. Sometimes it has not been expressed in its full power, only again to burst forth with renewed vigor, most recently, according to Buber, in the Hasidic movement.

Buber declares that Israel's Covenant with God is as alive and needed today as it has always been. Humankind remains radically unredeemed. People do not know the Eternal Thou. They do not seek to treat all others as "Thou's" and bring community, the Messianic Age, into being. With the major forces of society moving in totalitarian and technopolitical directions, Israel's stubborn loyalty to humanity through God is desperately important. Christianity may be a true faith, but it is mediated and indirect, essentially individual and not strongly social. Israel's faith is direct and communal; it has not been superseded or rendered obsolete.

Today, the Jewish people faces a major spiritual danger. In the secular Western world one's nation and one's religion are kept in separate spheres of existence. Buber derides this as blasphemy. Exiling God from social existence to the halls of institutions set aside for that purpose desecrates human life. Everyone suffers when such radical secularization occurs, as is obvious from the continuing efforts to remove human considerations from the realm of politics and think essentially of what is most efficient or technically desirable. The Jews should be particularly disturbed by this trend, for their unique character and historic destiny derive from the biblical fusion of religion and nationality so as to set an example for humankind.

In medieval times, the Jewish community was able to integrate folk life with religious understanding. In the emancipated modern world, that unity is no longer visible. In the State of Israel many insist that Jewishness is adequately expressed as civic loyalty, God being a private if not irrelevant matter. Elsewhere in the democracies, Jewish identity is defined largely in terms of an institutional religion, one that often lacks an inner sense of God's presence and an outer commitment to social responsibility. Buber, the Zionist and believer, demands that the two realms interpenetrate. When he immigrated to the Land of Israel, he aroused considerable hostility by insisting that Israeli politics be humanistic. He advocated a binational, that is, joint Arab–Jewish, state, as the only legitimate way of dealing with the just claims of both peoples to the land. Buber was also critical of contemporary Jewish religious life. He saw its primary stress on the observance of Jewish law as divorcing religiosity from the broader realms of modern existence. Worse, the practices had as good as become ends in themselves and thus an impediment rather than a help to gaining the presence of God. In this situation, Buber refused to accept any objective, external set of standards to structure his service of God, and he did not follow Jewish law.

Problems with Buber's Philosophy

The major critics of Buber's existentialism see its personalistic gains more than offset by its intellectual and Jewish failings. The central issue is structure. His opponents judge Buber's ideas too insubstantial to be considered a serious system of thought and are disturbed that his theology is individualistic to the point of anarchy, thus Jewishly inauthentic.

Intellectually, the clash is the familiar one between the schools of rationalism and existentialism. Personalistic, its reasoning is so subjective, its logic so individual, its categories so fluid, how can one know what the thinker truly has in mind or be able to debate it? If the I-Thou relationship is ineffable, how can Buber or anyone else talk sensibly about it? No one denies an individual's right to create an evocative, private pattern of speaking about life and its meaning. Buber wants his thought to be taken more seriously than that yet refuses to accept the usual standards of evidence and clarity employed in intellectual intercourse. This line of attack may be pressed home on two specific fronts, ethics and coherence.

Making the I-Thou relationship the basis of ethics conveys no useful content to anyone seeking moral guidance. Its subjectivity does nothing to prevent possible horrible abuses. The fanatic and the inquisitor regularly claim a private sense of God's authorization. Reason alone provides an objective defense against the fiendishness propagated by self-delusion. Rejecting rational ethical rules for commands, which arise only in a given situation, removes our best check on the demonic potential in all of us.

Buber could not deny that his antagonists understood him correctly, and this admission is particularly troublesome since the problem of evil is not academic in our generation. Buber's own efforts to rule out intolerance under his system are impressive yet inconclusive. His most telling response might be that the greatest evils of our day have come from *applying* reason, not giving in to subjectivity. Auschwitz and Hiroshima are equally results of deliberation and calculation. Many of our current social problems arise from our zeal at rationalizing human affairs. Human reason and its rules are not immune to our talent for perversion.

On the other hand, following the dictates of the I-Thou involves an element of freedom and, hence, risk. The risk of evil may be mitigated by Buber's principle of applying to the I-It world the values learned in one's I-Thou moments. We should always strive to accept others as fully human and treat them with mutuality and responsibility. This behavior would surely create a greater moral climate. Of course, such a procedure converts the I-Thou encounter into an I-It law, a move inconsistent with the fundamental premises of Buber's theory. Consequently insofar as Buber can respond to the critics of his ethics, his system loses coherence. But Buber claims to be not a system builder—which he considers an I-It intellectual goal—but one who lets thought follow the realities of human existence.

Do We Live in One World or Two?

Buber's dualism has also troubled many thinkers. Our world, as he describes it, seems to be two discrete entities, differently encountered and differently structured. One is in either the I-It or the I-Thou realm. They never intersect or merge. How can one gain a comprehensive understanding of so contradictory a universe? If the "logic" of the two is radically dissimilar, what becomes of the fundamental unity of existence that most people desire and philosophy has always prized?

As applied to God, the puzzle deepens. In the realm of the I-Thou, we may know God as the ground of all that is, the source and foundation of all existence. But we cannot know God that way in the world of I-It. God does not enter the world of the I-It, for, by definition, the Eternal Thou is that which can never become It. As long as we look with I-It eyes, we never see God at all. Then how does God relate to the world of I-It? What is God's place in that dimension of being in which we must spend most of our lives?

Buber might respond that he is not a metaphysician and has not alleged that the I-It world is real. He is only describing one of our "attitudes" toward the world, a sort of Kantian analysis of how we think, not of reality itself. This turns Buber into an idealist philosopher, a stance that contradicts his insistence on turning to our concrete existence to search for truth.

He might also argue that while the I-It world is real, so to speak, the I-Thou world is "more" real; that is, it provides the greater context within which the I-It world must be comprehended. But that is just what we do not understand. How can the Eternal Thou be related to a world in which God has no place and in which God cannot be seen? As science increasingly supplies mechanical or electrochemical explanations of phenomena, the world of I-It seems ever more fully closed to God's entry. If that world has reality, how does the Eternal God rule it, guide it, provide for it, or simply enter it to make the I-Thou possible? The least charge one can make against Buber is that he does not take the scientific view of reality very seriously and disposes of the issue by assigning it to a second level of significance.

Buber could give no further rebuttal. This anxiety about dualism had little meaning for him. He was satisfied to take our strange dualistic situation simply as he found it. He cared more about living in sanctity than about attaining a unified intellectual world view. His critics doubt that such a divided understanding of reality, for all its high humanity, will satisfy the modern mind.

Can There Be a Serious Judaism Without Law?

The major Jewish criticism of Buber is directed at his rejection of the validity of Jewish law.

His controversial stand emerged most clearly in his famous correspondence with Franz Rosenzweig on this issue. Their debate hinged on the place of corporate experience in personal responsibility. Both men agreed that their relationship to God was part of the Jewish people's Covenant. They had no difficulty with the individual Jew's need to study and personally appropriate Jewish literature without preconception as to what might "speak" to one. In that realm, discipline legitimately preceded meaning.

Rosenzweig then analogously urged such a standard with regard to Jewish law. He admitted that revelation was only personal, that we are required to do only what we know God wants of us. He further acknowledged that law was the aftereffect of encounter, not its content. God did not reveal the rules themselves. People created them, having been involved with God. With all that, he argued that a Jew was bound in principle to live under the law, that the classic codes had authority over the individual even though some of their regulations did not "speak" to one's personal sense of duty. Rosenzweig called for doing the law first and awaiting its personal validation in the process of its performance.

At this point, Buber demurred. He insisted that action involved the fullest commitment of the whole self. No external criterion should therefore be permitted to interpose itself between the I and what the Eternal Thou might now be understood to command. Perhaps a given law might serve to open the individual Jew to the presence of God. Once, such an encounter gave rise to the practice and gave it legitimacy. Where one still retained that connection, the law was valid. Otherwise—the usual case—it was impersonal and hence invalid. All such structures place barriers between the individual and the Eternal Thou. Buber thus denied that, in principle, Jews were obligated to perform the stipulations of the Jewish law. Indeed, considering its present proponents behavioristically rather than spiritually directed, he was an opponent of observance as a means of revitalizing Judaism.

A *Personal Response to the Problem of Law*

I have argued that Buber is inconsistent in this area. He predicates Israel's Covenant as corporate reality that continues from generation to generation. In some sense, the people of Israel's religious destiny is distinct from the decisions of individual Jews. There must be, then, a level where the individual as such is not the final arbiter of appropriate behavior under the Covenant. If not, Jewishness should be subject to judgment just as every other social accident is and therefore could be discarded, to the point of ending the Covenant. Yet Buber often indicts modern Jewry for its refusal to identify individual Jewish being with personal acceptance of Israel's Covenant. He implies that one's individual being has a corporate dimension. One is true to oneself as a Jew, therefore, only as one is true to one's folk. There cannot be any ultimate distinction between the two aspects of Jewish existence.

Much of the ambiguity and tension of modern Jewish life arises from struggle to pacify the warring parts of the Jewish soul. If so, Buber is overly strict in limiting legitimate Jewish responsibility to what the socially isolated I "hears" as it stands over against the Eternal Thou. Existential Jewish duty results rather from what the I-Jew is called upon by God to do in the I-Eternal Thou relationship. That may not generate external law but it authorizes common patterns of practice, for the Jewish "I" does not function in utter isolation, but as part of the Covenant community.

I am suggesting that the Jewish I in an I-Thou relationship is substantially determined by being situated in the people of Israel's historic-messianic relationship with God. Support for this inference exists in the unexpected, variant description Buber gives of the personal exchange between good teachers and their students. Buber denies that effective education can be confined to I-It competencies. It must help students become persons. Teachers need to find ways to engage their students as "Thou's." Buber surprisingly maintains that teachers should not make themselves fully present to the pupils. Rather than become friend or companion, a "Thou," teachers must always maintain a certain distance from their students or they will be unable to function. In the classroom the I-Thou relation is real but one-sided.

This account violates Buber's regular dictum that only with both persons fully present can "I" meet "Thou." How then can teachers evoke the students as Thou's while denying full mutuality? I believe the answer is to be found in the concept of role. Teachers enter the classroom precisely in order to teach, pupils in order to learn. Teachers can be true selves in teaching only as they follow their vocation, not as they abandon it to be persons-in-general. To borrow a kabbalistic conception, teachers constrict their full personality for the sake of accomplishing this important task, teaching. In the task, good teachers can find themselves as selves and not as "it's." As teacher-selves they offer but do not complete the mutuality that makes a genuine I-Thou relationship possible. Perhaps this concept violates Buber's canon that only the presence of the whole self can make the I-Thou relationship possible. If so, then I have only reduced but not eliminated the inconsistency he introduced into his thought when he sensitively described the reality of the fulfilled student-teacher relationship.

As I see it, then, a Jew is one who stands athwart the Eternal Thou, not as universal self, but as Jew-self, individual and member of a people simultaneously. The Jew's duty will always be as much a matter of folk as of self, as much a matter of what the Covenant of Sinai requires of me at this particular moment as of what I personally feel as commanded. Such covenantal existentiality does not restore the complete validity of traditional Jewish law or reestablish a basis for objective, impersonal standards of Jewish conduct. It does channel personal autonomy in terms of God's demands as the Covenant people ought to respond to them. Buber did not go this far, but those whom Buber has made self-consciously believing Jews may now well learn it from him.

8

Neo-Traditionalism: Abraham Heschel

IF THE BIBLE is our standard, Martin Buber has the most classic theological stance of any of the liberal Jewish thinkers. His God is real and personal, far more like the living God of traditional Judaism than any idea, mystery, or process could be. His concept of the people of Israel encompasses its multifaceted nationality without belittling its relationship to God. In revitalizing the ancient sense of Covenant through his understanding of personal relationships, he showed a way beyond universalistic religiosity, or secularizing particularity.

What Buber did not do was far from insignificant. His philosophy has the least power of any liberal doctrine to validate Jewish law or communal standards. Cohen knows social ethics to be required; Baeck adds the obligations imposed by mystery and shared with a unique people; Kaplan makes the folk authoritative for all who are its healthy members. Buber, in his strict immediate individualism before God, is the most antinomian of them all. He acquires a rich Jewish faith at the price of any rule or norm of Jewish obligation.

Traditional Judaism gave precedence to action over belief when a conflict between them was unavoidable. Here again the flaw of the classic liberal theological strategy reasserts itself. Jewish reality is unilaterally subordinated to modern truth, in this case Buber's understanding of the I-Thou relationship. Inevitably, one or another fundamental aspect of classic Jewish faith has been slighted, thus prompting efforts to create a more adequate contemporary Jewish theology. Baeck went beyond Cohen to restore a felt relationship with God. Kaplan

167

added ethnicity, and Buber reaffirmed the Covenant as a relationship between two real and independent entities. Yet in taking modern Jews that far in belief, Buber makes the issue of Jewish practice so central that his version of Jewish duty—for all its inner possibilities of development—must now be surpassed.

The realities of Diaspora Jewish existence lend special urgency to the creation of a ground for community norms of practice. If Jewishness is merely a personal, existential stance, though related to the Jewish people, what will give structure to Jewish life in the Diaspora? In what sense do these Jewish individuals function as the people of the Covenant? Buber, though recognizing this problem, wrote very little about the possibility or method of creating a vital Diaspora Jewish life. His Zionism called for living among other Jews, on the land of Israel, a situation that he hoped would keep radical individualism from destroying the people he cherished. Diaspora Jews, facing the fragility of their communal life, know that the corporate Jewish act establishes and signals their continuing peoplehood and relationship with God. Without a repertoire of communal practice, Jewish existence off the land ceases to have meaning. Those American Jews who seek to reclaim Jewish identity in depth find no theological issue more pressing than that of the proper form of Jewish observance and the authority behind its delineation. As long as liberal Jewish thought redefines Judaism by an externally determined, perhaps secular criterion, how can their concern ever receive a significant response, much less an answer? They require a post-liberal approach to Jewish theology, thus setting its central problem in the last decades of the twentieth century.

Heschel's Unique Stance and Style

Abraham Joshua Heschel consciously devoted himself to creating a philosophy that learned from the liberals but reversed many of their basic premises. He used the intellectual tools of modernity to move beyond his predecessors' procedures to a contemporary justification of traditional Jewish faith.

Heschel was a professor of Jewish ethics and mysticism at the (Conservative) Jewish Theological Seminary of America from 1945 until his death in 1972. His apparently odd combination of competencies reflects a biography and career devoted to commonly divergent religious interests. Scion of a distinguished Hasidic dynasty and steeped in Jewish learning of the Eastern European style, Heschel gained a doctorate from the University of Berlin with a phenomenological study of prophecy. His piety unshaken by the move to the West or the university, his earliest publications dealt with technical problems in medieval Jewish philosophy. Another stream of his researches focused on Hasidic leaders and doctrine. While his thinking reflected Hasidism's emphasis on subjective piety, his major books sought to provide an intellectual structure for Jewish faith. In person, he powerfully communicated the possibility of mystical awareness, yet he was also the Jewish thinker most actively involved in such public issues as civil rights, the Vietnam War, and the oppression of the Soviet Jews.

He was a superb stylist in Yiddish, Hebrew, German, English, and, it is said, Polish as well. He published in all those languages and his linguistic brilliance was an integral component of his method of communicating the proper depth of modern Jewish faith.

Readers can so easily be overcome by the unique quality of Heschel's word play that they miss the cognitive development going on behind it. To complicate matters further, Heschel develops his ideas in an uncommon manner. Modern arguments normally proceed in linear fashion. One sentence follows another cumulatively, each thought building on the previous one until the conclusion is reached and, by this process, considered well established. Heschel rejects this procedure as inconsistent with his understanding of religious insight. His paragraphs may deal with one theme, but their sentences are radial, not additive. They center on a given motif, pointing to it or away from it so as to disclose various of its facets. By a sort of sculptor's shaping, the notion itself appears. In the same way, the paragraphs that combine to form a section—and the sections that constitute a chapter—are not joined in ladderlike progression to reach a new level of thought. They multiply the insights and expand the vision, evoking rather than demonstrating, disclosing but not delineating. Yet, unlike Buber in *I and Thou*, Heschel carefully builds a logically ordered intellectual system in his major books. His work *Man Is Not Alone* bears the subtitle, *A Philosophy of Religion*; and its more substantial companion volume, *God in Search of Man*, is subtitled *A Philosophy of Judaism*. The books are philosophy in a very special sense, for Heschel repudiates the self-sufficient rationalism with which that term is usually associated. More helpfully, he used the term "depth theology" to describe his intellectual method. In common with the religious existentialists, he believed thinking ought to proceed from one's given human situation, analyzed to its deepest roots, which were, for him, religious.

Though Heschel utilizes the customary existentialist attacks on scientism and rationalism to clear the way for his teaching, he refuses to accept the human self as an independent given and to think in terms of it as Buber and Rosenzweig do. Instead, selfhood prompts Heschel to wonder and gratitude, and hence to God, who becomes the fundamental axiom of this thinking. Heschel's unique sense of the radical "depth" of the self transforms person-centered existentialism into "theology." He reverses the standard liberal argument and denies the legitimacy of arguing from human experience to the reality of God. This inversion of an accepted point of view is common in Heschel's writing. He wants us to change our perspective totally in order to comprehend Judaism. Heschel's unique style seeks fundamental change, not a mere alteration of substance. Once he has established his religious premises, Heschel explicates them as rationally as he can. His philosophy consists of thinking about their content and consequences in a way that is coherent with them and acceptable to any open mind.

Heschel's Three Paths to God

Heschel predicates three ways to religious truth: through nature, revelation, and the holy deed. In the pious life they operate as one. Due to our modern spiritual disabilities, we find it desirable to analyze them separately, identifying what each lends to and borrows from the other two.

Were mysticism not so easily misunderstood, Heschel's first, most generally available path might be termed "mystical." He exhibits an extraordinary sensitivity to the hidden reality inherent in the seemingly ordinary. He denies that one must attain a special level of experience to know this. The religious perspective is quite normal. If anything, such a response to the universe is the natural one, as children and primitives show us. Modernity has trained us to repress our instinctive awe at the world and our part in it. Our most important spiritual task today is to liberate ourselves from the scientism that has taught us an unnatural skepticism. Then we will once again ask with a higher incredulity: Why is there anything at all? Why is it so wondrous, so unexpected? Why do we human beings have this astonishing power to ask and marvel? Regaining "radical amazement" will enable us to be true to ourselves and open to the reality of God.

Heschel's felicity for images is most impressive as he seeks to arouse a reader dulled by the secular demythologization of nature. Argument will not work. It does not evoke awe, only another level of technical understanding. Heschel writes to illuminate, and like the great painters and photographers, he makes us see anew what we have blindly glanced at a thousand times before. In an age so jaded it has forgotten that nothing should be taken for granted, Heschel's approach to reality must be called therapeutic.

Regaining the Wonder That Anything Is

Heschel directs our attention not only beyond rationalism to experience, as Baeck did, or onward to encounter, as Buber did, but away from ourselves altogether. Personhood is too wondrous to be accepted as self-evident. Our reasoning, our sensitivity, our ability to engage in dialogue are not self-evident principles from which we can confidently search for meaning. They themselves refute all liberalistic complacency. Whatever we might choose to start us on our religious quest itself is given to us and directs us to its source. Nothing is self-explanatory; everything points beyond itself to a Giver. God necessarily precedes every effort we might make to search out Divinity. God must, in a post-liberal way, be understood as an "ontological presupposition." That is, God is the basis of any being, the utterly basic premise for anything that is. Only when we affirm God's greatness and reality do we ourselves, and our minds, our sensations, even our doubts and our skepticism, become worthy of serious self-investment. God is the premise of our existence, not the possible outcome of our inquiry.

A God so fundamental to our lives is far beyond human powers of description or definition. God overwhelms every effort to explain God, for the very act of explanation itself drives us to its Divine ground. Heschel denies that we are capable of useful judgments as to what God is like. The God who gives us our capacity to judge ought rather to fill us with a sense of the Divine greatness and glory. Our most exalted praise is necessarily an understatement. On this first level, Heschel brings us to God's sublimity. With this preparation, he can move forward in a way the liberals could not, to proclaim the reality of a contentful revelation.

The Move from the Universal to the Particular

Modern theologians who must come to terms with the universal phenomenon of true religion must then validate their specific religious tradition. For Cohen, particularity was as good as a historic accident. For Baeck, spirit enters history through groups. For Buber, the people of Israel had a unique ethnic response to God's presence. For Kaplan, Jewishness is a matter of social form, which in itself is a necessity of nature. Heschel explains the ubiquity of faith on the level of radical surprise. It provides him with a broad base from which to appreciate the variety of human religiosity. How then does he validate his particular Jewish faith? He is too traditional to accept a liberalistic explanation of Jewish identity. While existence reveals God universally, "there is no speech, there are no words," but these are granted with revelation. The greatest miracle in the Bible is the Bible itself! In it, what was perceived mutely in creation rises to the level of direct communication. Through its pages a new type of religious understanding is born, one that can recognize the truth of radical amazement but also knows the direction of its fulfillment. Moderns can hardly be expected to recognize God's revelation if they have not been awakened to its possibility through knowing God's nearness. Until then they consider the Bible another technical problem, a set of conundrums about literary sources, the dates of their editing or the social setting that produced them.

When one's understanding begins with the God who grounds all being, an encounter with the Bible is itself a revelation. Reading its words, one quickly recognizes that our private intuition has here been given its fullest exposition. Now we are prepared for its central, astounding claim: instead of a human quest for religion, the Bible declares that God has been in "search of man." People in the Bible are as we know them. They seek to avoid God and, failing that, rebel against God's rule. God will not be put off. The God we know from our openness to self and creation comes to people to command and console, to judge and forgive, to direct and give hope.

So traditional an affirmation of biblical revelation instantly raises the old liberal questions concerning the humanity of the biblical text. Heschel will not deny the human element in Holy Scripture but this should not obscure its Divine origin or accuracy. When we read its books in openness to the One who speaks through the text, we will realize how much more it knows than we do. If radical amazement replaced scientific dogmatism about what could have happened in ancient days, many of our modern questions would vanish.

Prophecy, the Ultimate Act of Sympathy

Heschel's unique conception of prophecy ingeniously resolves the problem of an accurate Divine revelation cast in human form. Heschel deems the prophet to have attained a special height of religious sensitivity which he calls "sympathy." The subjective overtones of that term properly indicate that prophecy transcends all cognitive enterprises and lies beyond technical analysis or explanation. The prophet is turned toward God in utter existential depth and is responsive to what is happening in the Divine. Prophetic sympathy has nothing to do with human emotionalism, self-abandon, or ecstacy. The prophet remains sufficiently self-possessed to respond to God as an individual, sometimes to the point of resisting or arguing with God. A contrast with Buber's theory of I-Thou encounters will clarify the distinctive intellectual contours of Heschel's formulation.

Three major differences must be noted. Heschel claims a certain reflective or cognitive aspect to the prophet's experience. Taken within the context of sympathy, we may say the prophet gains understanding. The prophet does not merely encounter God person-to-person but gains knowledge about God. Second, Heschel assigns God a far greater role in the moment of prophetic sympathy than Buber finds in the I-Thou relationship. God's reality dominates the prophet, though not to the point of the prophet's loss of self. How can God, the one real Master of the Universe, the presupposition of every aspect of human existence, not be the overpowering, overwhelming reality of such a situation? Third, Buber claims, the prophet experiences God's presence only during the encounter and later provides a personal, verbal expression of what transpires. Heschel disagrees. The prophet accurately records what God is going through or demands at a given moment. Though expressed in a personal style and in the symbols of the culture, God's reality, not the prophet's person, determines the message. The prophet reliably recounts what God wants of us. Sympathy is receptivity to God, not projection of self.

Heschel's position has, therefore, fairly been described as a sophisticated fundamentalism. The biblical text is taken as true to God's own reality without requiring a defense of every aspect of our Hebrew text as the equivalent of a photocopy of God's dictation. Heschel's differences with the religious liberals are clear-cut. More certain of human reason or experience than they are of God, liberals mandate substantial human initiative in determining what religion ought to be. Heschel knows that God has disclosed to us what believers ought to know and do. God's revelation, not human creativity or conscience, ought to determine the content of religion.

God Has Feelings, Particularly About the Good

Two consequences of Heschel's theory of revelation give his philosophy distinctive shape. First, we may be astonished but we ought not deny the steady prophetic pronouncement: God has feelings. Again and again, the prophets describe God as distraught, unhappy, angry, indignant, and, less frequently, overflowing with tenderness, compassion, mercy, or affection. With some embarrassment, liberals have termed these "anthropopathisms" and considered them, when not mere poetry, a symbolic way of pointing to transcendent reality. Heschel will have none of this. The prophets may speak poetically but their concern is truth, not literature. Indeed, we can now see that to speak of revelation as sympathy meant that the prophets felt what God felt; they had *syn-pathos* ("together-feeling"). God is a God of pathos, of emotions, for that is the God the prophets described.

Heschel sees no need to apologize for what seems to nonbelievers and liberals a mythological notion. To the contrary, he vigorously rebuts the idea that God would be superior for not having feelings. Such a stand has no Jewish foundation. Greek philosophy derogated emotion as a source of wisdom, and the Stoics, in particular, spread the idea that a calm detachment from one's feelings is the best way to face life. As philosophers became more rigorously intellectual, they created the idea of God being impassable, insensitive, and emotionally unreactive. Jews should not let Hellenic predilections outweigh the clear message of prophetic revelation, especially when they contradict major commitments of the modern mind. Thought without emotion is a caricature of personhood. Worse, the proliferation of people who merely function in roles or efficiently pursue calculated ends is one of the great evils of our era. Our major social task is to restore people to full personhood. Pathos, not distance, needs to play a major role in our lives.

The same is true of our icy God-ideas. We have become as unfeeling as the God in whose rationalistic image we have sought to recreate ourselves. In our urge to become whole as persons again, we are responding to the reality the prophets long ago accurately described. We ought to be feeling beings, for God is a God of pathos.

Heschel's second emphasis is surprisingly liberal. Having established the accuracy of the prophetic message, he might have then devoted himself to discussing the teachings of Moses, "the chief of the prophets." Instead of concentrating on the Torah, Heschel gives most of his attention to the later prophets. He reiterates all the familiar themes of "prophetic Judaism" so powerfully enunciated by Hermann Cohen. God's feelings are aroused by human action, in most cases by their ethical or unethical conduct. We can judge the heinousness of our sins by the intensity of God's reaction. Unethical acts are not a petty annoyance to God and righteousness does not evoke casual Divine satisfaction. When we judge the prophetic accounts of God's reactions to our behavior as extreme, we only testify to our loss of a proper measure of their cosmic importance. Nothing is more important to God than ethical conduct between human beings on a social and personal level. To be sure, Heschel rejects the liberal thesis that ethics alone is revelation. God's self-disclosure produces one body of truth in which law is the central substance and ethics the most significant concern. Heschel is unique among those who have upheld the accuracy of the biblical message, in giving ethics this predominant place. And his teaching was made all the more impressive by his record of political activism.

Responding to the Holocaust He Escaped

The Holocaust death-of-God discussion of the late 1960's did not cause Heschel to revise his philosophy. In one respect, his attitude toward evil was essentially that of the liberals: evil results from the human abuse of the freedom God gave us. For God to take away that freedom because we have badly abused it would itself be evil of God. The world's indifference made the Nazi bestiality possible and Heschel made that destructive moral sloth the model for his calls to humanity and Jewry to take action against the evils around them.

In another critical respect, Heschel struck out on his own. The liberals, judging people to be basically good, assumed that education and culture would bring humankind to behave ethically. Heschel, here reflecting his Hasidic background perhaps more strongly than anywhere else, was no optimist with regard to human nature. He considered the evil urge in people to be far more sinister and effective than the liberals had ever imagined. He believed it affects everything we do, even our righteousness. He acknowledged a close affinity with Reinhold Niebuhr's Christian theory of human nature as existentially though not biologically fallen. But for all his realism about the human will to do evil, he never claimed people were sinful in essence. They always remained free to return to God and, with prayerful effort, to do the good. The Nazis could not blame their perverse human nature for what they did. They were fully responsible for it. They chose to perpetrate the Holocaust and "rationally" determined to keep it going at all costs. Their awesome guilt is a direct consequence of their moral freedom.

Heschel denied that people had a right to question God about our suffering. Apparently he did not think us righteous enough to offer such challenges. He certainly believed that God was so much greater than we are that we should maintain a respectful, appreciative silence in God's presence. Interestingly, too, he did not apply his theory of God's pathos to the problem of evil. In talmudic times some Rabbis assuaged the agony of the Exile by saying that God accompanied Israel in *galut* and shared its sufferings. Heschel could not bring himself to explicitly revive that idea. Perhaps he felt our pain was too great for such consolation. Or his general reticence about speaking about what God does may have kept him back from such a theodicy. Or, he did not essay the stance of a modern Job or Levi Yitzchak because he knew too well that God was the very premise of our doubt and indignation. Having lost much of his family in the Holocaust, he suffered greatly over it. His sense of our proper humility before God kept him from writing very much about it.

We Meet God in Doing the Commandments

Revelation is only the second of the three paths Heschel sees leading to God. Heschel could not stop the development of this thought at this point, for Judaism is not the only religion of biblical revelation. Christianity, perhaps even Islam, could join Judaism as a religion seeking to be faithful to the prophets. Heschel was open to the truth in these traditions and frequently participated in interreligious activities. Yet he also affirms the distinctiveness of the people of Israel's relation to God. The move from revelation to holy deeds, the third level of religiosity, finally exposes Heschel's doctrine of particularity.

Traditional Judaism is grounded on the revelation not only of the written Torah, but of the oral Torah as well. The writings of the Rabbis and the rabbinic traditions down to this day have God's authority behind them. If the recognized rabbinic authorities today speak in God's name, then only such changes as they allow are authentic Judaism. If, as the liberals argue, all the Rabbis operate with is essentially human power, then past decisions may be altered and contemporary ones disputed if there is good reason. Heschel maintains the inseparability of the written and the oral Torah but does not explicate his meaning. He merely notes, "The prophets' inspirations and the sages' interpretations are equally important"—an Orthodox stance. At the least, his theory of revelation would substantiate right-wing Conservative Judaism. In any case, he teaches that for Jews, the fulfillment of the Bible is the Rabbis, not the Gospels or the Koran.

He mitigates this doctrine in two ways. First, he insists on a careful distinction between revelation and interpretation. The former is quite limited in extent when compared with amplification by the Rabbis. Perhaps Heschel implies that the process of interpretation might permit us to move on to practices somewhat different from those previously sanctioned. He further argues—with considerable vigor and passion—that ethics should receive priority in the life of Torah. He claims this has traditional warrant and illustrates the inner tension in the Bible and Rabbinic literature that led many great teachers to assert the preeminence of the ethical. Despite these liberalistic concerns,

Heschel never specifically indicated when and under what conditions he would countenance a break with rabbinic law.

Fulfilling the commandments brings one to God. Neither experience nor existence nor encounter but devoted doing is the central concern of Judaism. Heschel produces a phenomenology of observance that opens up the inner life of the pious and moves beyond the liberals' concern with the doer to what transpires between the believer and God during the holy deed. Modern students of religion usually concentrate on religious feeling or faith. Heschel examines the sacred act as the meeting place between God and humankind. Heschel, fully self-conscious of this uncommon approach, summons Jews not to the risk of faith but to a "leap of action."

In a pious deed, we confirm and fulfill the fickle subjectivity of faith. We transcend our limited selves by responding not to our desires but to God's. The climax of human religiosity is learning to make God's needs our own, to want so much to do what God wants that we are continually doing it. In such responsive living our private relationship with God is renewed for Jews as individuals and a community. Observance is the ongoing renewal of Israel's ancient Covenant with God.

Heschel does not insist that emphasis on works is distinctively or exclusively Jewish. Though he speaks of *mitzvot*, divine commandments, and cites rabbinic sources liberally, he refers continually to "man," not to the Jew in this analysis. Perhaps he is making room for that understanding of Christianity that sees gospel as including, if transcending, law. Perhaps he only wishes to show the universal human effect of Jewish living. Whatever the reason, Heschel's third way of coming to God is most fully expressed in the traditional Jewish observance of law and commandment. Heschel's system reaches its goal in identifying the particular Jewish way of life as an incomparable response to the revealing God, a position anyone with general faith now ought to be able to see.

Where Is the Jewish People in This System?

The revelation to Israel dominates Heschel's understanding of Judaism. The Jewish people, as such, hardly has an independent role in his thought. It remains utterly subordinated to the will of God as revealed to the prophets. Heschel devotes less than a dozen pages to people-hood in his major books. He almost certainly adopted this stance to counteract the stress on Jewish ethnicity of his faculty colleague, Mordecai Kaplan, which appealed to many American Jews. For Kaplan, Judaism is the folk culture of the Jews of which religion is but one part, if the most significant. Heschel quietly polemicized against ethnic humanism by reducing to a minimum the Jewish people's role in creating Judaism. God's will, not folk creativity, determines what the Jewish people ought to be and do. His early books say little about the ethnic themes so critical to Kaplan—land, language, the arts, and community organization.

Heschel's unconcern with ethnicity was more likely a factor of his desire to be faithful to Jewish tradition. A comparison with Rosenz-weig is instructive. Both men believed, unlike the rationalists, that revelation was the necessary foundation for an authentic Judaism. Heschel's conception of prophecy is more traditional than Rosenz-weig's because Heschel defended the content of the prophetic mes-sage. As in Rosenzweig's case, the focus on revelation produced an unusual attitude to time and history. Rosenzweig had argued that the Jews transcended these normal attributes of existence. By virtue of following God's commands, the people of Israel was, so to speak, already living in God's Kingdom and thus on the plane of eternity. Heschel analogously argued that Judaism is primarily a religion of sacred time—as per the commandments—but not concerned with space. The Jewish tradition did not disparage spatiality, for it was an attribute of the creation God had called "good." Contemporary civilization, however, has invested itself most heavily in the spa-tial aspects of existence, thereby robbing humankind of its special quality, the immediacy and will connected with time. The command-ments do the opposite. By making the Sabbath a pivot of daily life, Judaism placed a premium on time, specifically by asking people to sanctify it by holy deeds. The secular existentialist lament, that mortal existence is given only for our destruction, is transformed from a source of despair to a motive for acting as God's partner in complet-ing creation.

Rosenzweig did not hesitate to accept the non-Zionist consequences of centering Judaism on revelation. When the core of Jewishness is sanctifying time through commandments, space becomes almost irrelevant. One can be observant anywhere. In that respect, Heschel's philosophy, like that of Rosenzweig, provides a firm foundation to Jewish life in the Diaspora. It also produced an intellectual challenge for him when Jerusalem came into Jewish hands in 1967 and subsequent interreligious discussions raised the issue of its return or internationalization.

The difficulty is elegantly simple. Jerusalem is fixed in space. The New City, which had always been under Israeli control, though only some yards from the Old City, is simply not to be equated with it. If Judaism is essentially a religion of the sanctification of time, why should world Jewry insist on continued control over an undivided Jerusalem, particularly when it remains so contested a bit of space? Heschel might have answered that, for all its emphasis on time, God's revelation also deals with space, focusing specifically on the city of Jerusalem. To such a Jewish dogmatic claim others would respond with their own religious counterclaims, thus negating the effect of the argument. Heschel proceeded phenomenologically, explicating what Jerusalem had meant to the Jews throughout their history and the spiritual effect it has on Jews today. No other religion has anything like this unique attachment to the city, a fact implying that Jews have a special right to sovereignty over it. His images are moving and his language, as always, evocative, but no case emerges from them. Phenomenology may disclose one's inner reality but that may not persuade the reader. Heschel has no universal basis for special claims of space. Lacking an effective theory of Jewish ethnicity, he cannot insist upon the central role of the land of Israel or the city of Jerusalem in Jewish duty.

Speaking from Faith to Those with Many Doubts

The mutually reinforcing movements from nature to revelation to deed give Heschel so great a sense of certainty that he regularly speaks with an assurance that can easily disturb inquiring readers. Worse, he often insists that the only choice open to us is one between his view and an absurdity (e.g., either the prophets are accurate or they are mad). He continually dismisses the validity of questions posed from a liberal perspective. Again and again he begins an insightful discussion of a modern problem, shows its implications, and, just as one expects that he will respond to them, he says instead that from the standpoint of faith that is not the real question at all.

When one is fresh to this technique or when the insight is quite striking—religion is not man seeking God but God in search of man; the Bible is not human theology but God's anthropology—the effect can be quite telling. As with a Zen koan or a Hasidic master's epigram, enlightenment may strike through the dramatic reversal of perspective. Repeated use of this device, particularly in works that call themselves "philosophy," makes many readers uncomfortable. Thoughtful people tire of having their questions dismissed as meaningless if not foolish, especially when they do not arise from individual whim but from the major intellects of our era. Unease speedily rises to irritation when positions other than the author's are dismissed as "arrogant," "absurd," "insane," "incredible." Heschel is so certain of his faith that alternatives are simply untenable. Yet not infrequently in the modern world, the product of thoughtful skepticism (e.g., the universality of genuine ethics) has turned out to have more religious significance than the inherited pieties of a given tradition (e.g., the autocracy of religious leadership). Heschel often makes no contact with people who do not have as firm a belief in God's revelation as he has. Accepting religious experience only as fulfilled in biblical revelation takes away much common ground he might have had with the serious modern inquirer. His faith may demand it, but it sets a major obstacle in the way of his addressing people raised in a secular ethos.

Problems with the Reliability of the Bible

When Jews raise objections to Heschel's manner of argument, their negativity might be dismissed as the result of self-hate or some other

form of venality. The critics press on to reject the Heschelian interpretation of revelation on the substance of the case. Rationalistic
antagonists will marshall the data of biblical literary criticism to argue
for the human origins of the prophetic texts. A more telling case can
be made from inside Heschel's system. By Heschel's own standards
some of the most compelling prophetic passages challenge the Godly
authenticity of others. Granting that God has pathos, what shall we
say about the accuracy of the prophetic descriptions of God's hot
anger? Heschel answers that God's wrath, unlike ours, is never out of
moral control. God keeps it under ethical constraint. The Divine
indignation is only another form of God's justice, now passionately
applied because people have done awful deeds.

Most readers, even traditional ones, have read the texts differently.
The prophets seem rather plainly to say that God, having rightfully
made demands and quietly waited for people to fulfill them, has finally
lost patience with us. God therefore proposes to visit the people of
Israel with an awesome destructiveness that far exceeds compensatory
punishment. Indeed, the prophet may hope that the threat of God's
overwhelming displeasure will cause Israel to repent. Read this way,
the prophetic pronouncements about God's wrath are a moral embarrassment. An angry judge is a contradiction in terms because genuine
anger always results in injustice. It contaminates the deserved with the
undeserved, adulterating this moment's deserts with recompense for
past events, confusing this person's guilt with the evils inflicted by
others, real or imagined. If one did not need to defend the accuracy of
the prophets, one could see the morality behind the prophet's dismay
at the people's continued obstinacy. Heschel must defend God's anger
to preserve the reliability of prophetic sympathy and thus the doctrine
of revelation on which his system rests. If his explanation of God's
anger is unconvincing, his entire intellectual structure falls.

The liberals may have made too little of God and too much of
humankind. In all integrity, they could not accept biblical text and the
rabbinic tradition as God-given or God-empowered. Slavery might be
condoned by people in a given historical situation; it was not God's word.
Women might be treated as legally separate and hence unequal until
recent times; any suggestion that this is God's permanent command

must be repudiated. When such troublesome laws are integrated into what we have learned about the growth of all human practices, they become more understandable if less authoritative than of old. Now radical amazement strikes us because the Hebrews, though so much a part of Near Eastern civilization, managed to be so incredibly different spiritually. Again, though the Jews have been intimately affected by every society they were dispersed to, they remained true to their Covenant with God. The humaneness of the religion itself becomes an invitation to awe.

Heschel's moving validation of a neo-traditional Judaism is unparalleled in twentieth-century Jewish thought. No other thinker has yet presented a systematic defense of Judaism based on God's revelation of the written and oral Torah. Against those who have felt that modernity necessarily implied some version of liberal belief, Heschel carried through the central project of modern Jewish thought by providing a theology of classic Judaism. Even those who cannot accept his system have learned much from him about the spirit that should inform contemporary piety and observance.

Heschel challenges Jews moving from liberalism to greater traditionalism to decide whether personal autonomy should usurp the place of God's revelation. Does an authentic Judaism require the acceptance of God's law as revealed to the prophets and interpreted by the Rabbis, or may it derive from our present-day human understanding of what God demands of us as members of the Covenant people? Heschel grandly made the case for traditional Jewish faith. No one who seeks to reestablish liberalism or to validate classic Judaism in another way can ignore his passionate case for seeking God's perspective. And everyone can benefit from the example he set of the pious Jew as an involved human being. No Jewish community figure of recent years better demonstrated how a believing Jew ought to respond to the crises of our time. His integration of Judaism and modernity in his life was itself a monumental accomplishment.

PART IV
The
Contemporary
Agenda

9

Confronting
the
Holocaust

SINCE Abraham Heschel, no Jewish theologian has presented a full-scale, distinctive exposition of Judaism that has occupied the center of Jewish intellectual attention. The work of Jewish thought has continued, if anything, in a more varied, vigorous, and sophisticated form than previously, but it has been scattered and thematic rather than concentrated and systematic. No topic has drawn more attention and been discussed in greater depth than the theological implications of the Holocaust. Tracking this debate is more than technically difficult; it is humanly daunting. Most of the thinkers involved admit that the Holocaust overwhelms them. They also consider it their Jewish duty to try to come to terms with it, even tentatively. These factors make summarizing this discussion particularly difficult. Nevertheless, a number of basic intellectual positions, often identified with certain protagonists, have emerged over the years. During the 1980's, however, a certain repetitiousness came into the theological writing about the Holocaust despite efforts to find a less inadequate language for the old overwhelming trauma. Perhaps this may be understood not only as testimony to the awesomeness of what happened but as a sign of a certain religious transition. That is, the Holocaust, like other elemental communal religious experiences, had begun evolving from a living question to an accepted ritual. This perspective does make it somewhat easier to track the central theses of the discussion.

187

1945–1965: *The Two-Decade Silence*

We begin with a historical puzzle. What caused the hiatus in time between the end of the Holocaust and the beginning of the discussion? Not until the mid-1960's, twenty years after World War II, did the Holocaust become a central topic in Jewish religious thought. Elie Wiesel's *Night* appeared in 1960 to little notice and the articles that Richard Rubenstein wrote then (later gathered with others into *After Auschwitz*) awakened little debate. Why?

Most observers have given a psychological answer, one not without moral overtones. The Holocaust had so traumatized us that we repressed it as too painful to bear. As it receded in time and our anguish lessened, we could open up to the terrible hurt and let it into our consciousness. Surely this is true of the survivors. Only in recent years have they found the inner strength to speak out. With the exception of Elie Wiesel, none of the thinkers presented in this chapter was in the death camps, though several fled Europe before the mass murder began.

For most American Jews, the silence resulted as much from guilt at their inaction as from their identification with those who suffered and died. American Jewry had all too readily followed the advice of their leaders who, despite evidence of unprecedented mass extermination, acquiesced to the government's demands for silence and concentration on the war effort. For two decades guilt grew as they realized how great an evil they had abetted. The therapy for that festering wound was exposure—and the new Jewish devotion manifest throughout the Jewish community.

The Cultural Context of the Change

The psychological analysis is persuasive but I believe it improperly isolates Jewish experience from its American context. Though I agree with Irving Greenberg's plea that the Holocaust should lead Jews to break their fawning dependence on modernity, I do not see our change, as he apparently does, as an internal Jewish community affair.

I believe our Jewish turn inward arose substantially as part of a shift in the American ethos that made it socially acceptable for Jews to face up to the Holocaust and its implications. Against Greenberg, I view our very discussion of the Holocaust not as a withdrawal from modernity but as another sign of our continuing involvement in it.

As a result of the civil rights movement, the United States entered a period of ethnic reassertion in the early 1960's. Black civil disobedience shattered the notion that minorities had to be well behaved. Etiquette was revealed to be a means of keeping the underprivileged powerless. Polite silence at one's continuing disabilities was no longer considered a reasonable price to pay for having been granted some rights. Blacks, Indians, Poles, and other groups became conscious of their guilt and anger at the servility they had gratefully undertaken. Public complaint and hostility to leaders became common; attacks on supposed friends who deserted others in a time of need were heard; and comparisons with Nazis and the Holocaust were a steady theme of minority invective.

American Jews had arrived at the mid-1960's with a new self-confidence. They were unexpectedly influential in the society and probably its single most affluent religio-ethnic community. Once that status would have enjoined a more neurotic conformity. Now it meant being secure enough to speak out.

In my opinion, the old Jewish inhibitions were finally dissolved by the popular acceptance of the Protestant death-of-God movement. Most Americans—and Jews—considered the American Jewish community a religious group. With Judaism one of the country's three great religions, the Jews, despite small numbers and endemic unbelief, had extraordinary social position. Consciously and unconsciously, they tended to emulate the dominant, Protestant mood. In the leading liberal churches this now shifted from a pronounced theocentrism to a death-of-God theology that was quite different from the atheism of another time. Its adherents proposed to stay in the church and rebuild it, in Dietrich Bonhoeffer's words, "as if there were no God." Once religion without God became acceptable in the paradigmatic group, the Jewish release was complete. Jews were bold enough ethnically to attack all anti-Semitism and religiously free to do so in terms of giving up belief in God. Richard Rubenstein writes that he was surprised when William Hamilton, the organizer of the death-of-God movement, identified him as the Jewish counterpart to the Protestant thinkers, but he soon recognized, within limits, what he shared with them. Once again, particular Jewish experience participated in, yet extended, what was happening in the civilization generally.

The Influence of Elie Wiesel

The pivotal figure in the resulting intellectual work is Elie Wiesel, though his works on the Holocaust are mainly fiction. They are not entertainments but learned and reflective narrative explorations of the range of responses one might make to the Holocaust. Wiesel has often characterized his role as that of a witness. His effort to give truthful testimony has been agonizing. How can an author avoid reducing the terror in order to have its horrifying message widely heard? Wiesel's painful effort not to bear false witness is the standard by which the integrity of all who discuss this topic is measured.

In only one of his books has Wiesel permitted himself to describe the suffering during the Holocaust. *Night* is autobiographical and depicts the reactions of a pious teen-ager as he goes from his sheltered village existence to Auschwitz and thence, astonishingly, to liberation. I will not say more for I do not want to give anyone an excuse for not reading the book or contribute to lessening its impact. A number of its passages have already been cited so frequently they have become our Holocaust clichés, thus being emptied of meaning—exactly the problem of authenticity that so agitates Wiesel.

In *Night* Wiesel enunciated many of the themes around which his writing centers. The death camp experience was unutterably evil. No previous human experience or imagination of suffering explains such horror. Auschwitz, the symbolic name for all the ghettos and camps, was a unique event in history. More, it was revelatory. Now everything in human life must be seen through its lens. That is not meant as hyperbole but as fact. Auschwitz is the new Jewish Sinai; it must set the context and content of contemporary Jewish views of God, humankind, religion, and Judaism. By that standard we can no longer be satisfied with the old Jewish apologies for God's bungling of reward and punishment: life after death, suffering out of love or for the sake of others, redemption by the Messiah, and the like. They are not utterly false, yet after the Holocaust they are empty. Nothing makes sense any more—even the very act of trying to make sense of things. In the face of such evil, one may well wonder why one should bother with the world of history. But despair too is wrong. It makes the Holocaust more reasonable than existence. We must live—but what can it mean not to despair after the Holocaust? The question haunts Wiesel's work and life.

Wiesel believes there are no "answers" to the Holocaust. He is not even certain we have the right questions. He restlessly moves from one aspect of it to another, afraid to come to rest at any intellectual point and by such relaxation betray the fathomless terror Jews knew. Again and again he suggests that a species of intelligent madness is the most appropriate response to the Holocaust. Were we capable of becoming appropriately deranged, we might see in what now appears to us as blackest night. Philosophers who seek to "explain" the Holocaust are engaged in a self-contradictory project. Madmen are more truthful witnesses to the insanity we lived through.

The final word cannot be insanity, else how would we write fiction or try to face life? A cruel duty is laid upon the survivor, not to forget, and not to let the world forget, as it would dearly like to do.

Continuing Work of the Survivor-Witness

Night is the first book of a trilogy whose second volume is *Dawn* and whose final part, *Day* in French, is entitled *The Accident* in English. The increasing light is intentional. *Dawn* treats the partial answer to suffering of a people's national revival in its own homeland—an "explanation" made almost as irrational as the Holocaust by the violence it precipitates. In *Day*, the protagonist confronts the redemptive kindness of a doctor who fights death with all his might and thereby shows the goodness yet to be found in life. *The Town Beyond the Wall* contrasts helping a human being with the iniquity of spectatorship. In acknowledging the power of personal responsibility, Wiesel finds himself open to a positive relation with the God with whom he remains in conflict. By the end of *The Gates in the Forest*, the survivor, racked by the ambiguities of life and the guilt he bears, becomes sufficiently positive in his ambivalent relationship to God to recite the *kaddish*, that extravagant praise of God Jewish mourners offer. And having faced the dead and the God who brings death, he is able to take up marriage and procreation, the primal burdens of life.

Each novel discloses a partial truth and leaves one recognizing how fragmentary our understanding must remain. The ultimate irrationality of existence was given unusual expression in *A Beggar in Jerusalem*. This novel interprets one of the most joyous events in Jewish history, the return of the Old City of Jerusalem to Jewish sovereignty in 1967. It is the only one of Wiesel's novels not written in a realistic style. The swirling, uncertain, dreamlike narration communicates the madness that alone can cope with the paradox: the generation of ultimate suffering has been granted unexpected happiness.

In the late 1960's Wiesel began publishing in other forms. His addresses and articles on the Holocaust, his response to contemporary Jewish issues, most notably a powerful book on the resurgence of Jewish life in the Soviet Union, and his retelling of biblical, talmudic, and Hasidic tales now were increasingly brought to the public. This continuing Jewish devotion puts into relief the one question that never occurs in his work: Should the Jewish people and tradition continue? Wiesel's categorically positive stance toward Jews and Judaism is no narrow self-assertion of ethnicity. His quest is thoroughly universal. He wonders how anyone can affirm life after the Holocaust. He takes it for granted that if there is any proper human response to Auschwitz, it will also be true for Jews. At the same time, since no one knows human suffering better than the Jews, their wisdom is humankind's best source of insight into the mystery called existence. To Wiesel, every Jew and the Jewish people itself are holy. Promoting Jewish survival is an unshakable dogma after the Holocaust.

Issues Posed by Richard Rubenstein

For all the influence of Wiesel's work, the theological discussion of the Holocaust has not centered about it because its format is intentionally ambiguous. Instead, Richard Rubenstein's book *After Auschwitz* focused the significant controversies of the late 1960's and shaped the form in which they developed. That volume collects articles written over the six years when Rubenstein was evolving his radical Jewish theology. Readers today sometimes find it difficult to determine the position at which he ultimately arrived, though his later writings partially clarify this. Rubenstein agrees with Wiesel that Auschwitz is our Sinai. The refusal of contemporary Jewish theologians to listen to its voice is a damning indictment of anything they might now be shocked into saying about it. Rubenstein proposes instead to make its revelation about the human situation the basis of his illusionless Judaism.

The evil the Nazis perpetrated upon the Jews requires, at the very least, that Jews give up any claim to be chosen. In the Western mind, as in much Jewish teaching, chosenness means suffering for God's sake. Persecutors may then have an easy conscience because suffering is the divinely appointed Jewish role. After Auschwitz such attitudes are intolerably offensive. Rather than give any comfort to the oppressor and validate indifference to the victims, Jews should renounce the notion of their appointment as God's suffering servant.

Rubenstein's opposition to chosenness did not arouse much conflict. It had long been reinterpreted, as in Mordecai Kaplan's case, to the point of repudiation. Such connection as it had retained with suffering had largely been severed by the events of the Holocaust. Some traditionalists, such as Harold Fisch, Eliezer Berkovits, and Irving Greenberg, have tried to recast the doctrine of necessary Jewish suffering without legitimizing persecution, but none of these views has been widely discussed or accepted.

A major controversy broke out over Rubenstein's rethinking of belief in God. He argued that the Holocaust invalidated all the classic Jewish positions regarding God and evil and requires us to reject classic Jewish faith in God. Rubenstein remained a religious thinker, albeit one whose idea of the Holy Nothing was disturbing to the average Jew, though his reworked understanding of the Jewish people and of Jewish practice was far more recognizable.

The First, Negative Assertions

Rubenstein denies that any of the old Jewish theodicies, the defenses of God despite evil, are tenable after Auschwitz. On occasion he remarks that the death of one innocent child should have been enough to refute them. (Such comments imply, against his normal stand, that *all* evil refutes theism; the Holocaust is not unique but merely gross.) That the Nazis' bestiality was just compensation for Jewish sins; that God must allow such evils so as to preserve human freedom; that it taught a valuable lesson to the world; that God tests our faith; that God has compensated the Jews for their suffering by giving them the State of Israel; or that the Holocaust brutality can be expunged by the bliss of the world-to-come—all are morally unbearable notions. No God who did such things would be worth worshiping. Further, to take refuge in traditional humility and say that God's ways are infinitely beyond us is an utter abdication of our human judgment and of the victims' human dignity.

Rubenstein calls on us to reject the God of traditional Jewish theology. He makes two quite different statements of his position, one doctrinal, the other a social observation. The former was most concisely put this way:

> Traditional Jewish theology maintains that God is the ultimate, omnipotent actor in the historical drama. It has interpreted every major catastrophe in Jewish history as God's punishment of a sinful Israel. I fail to see how this position can be maintained without regarding Hitler and the SS as instruments of God's will. The agony of European Jewry cannot be likened to the testing of Job. . . . The idea is simply too obscene for me to accept.

In a number of other places Rubenstein similarly objects to what he understands to be the normative Jewish teaching about God's control of history.

Rubenstein does not equate giving up an old doctrine of God with denying God's reality. Atheism involves a metaphysical certainty, a negative one, which is incompatible with Rubenstein's existentialist, person-based thought. Instead, he makes a temporal, immediate judgment concerning our post-Holocaust period. He continues,

> No man can really say that God is dead. How can we know that? Nevertheless, I am compelled to say that we live in the time of the "death of God." This is more a statement about man and his culture than about God. The death of God is a cultural fact.

This too became a steady theme in his thought. Most Jewish thinkers considered these two assertions faulty but I think it will clarify Rubenstein's total position better if we immediately consider his positive teachings.

Recreating Judaism Around the Holy Nothingness

Auschwitz should lead us to agree with the French existentialists Sartre and Camus that "we stand in a cold, silent, unfeeling cosmos, unaided by any purposeful power beyond our own resources." But Rubenstein is not an atheist. There is, after all, not nothing but something. The source of that being is the focus of Rubenstein's religiosity. He is wary of applying positive terminology to it lest he mask the negativity revealed by Auschwitz and the death that awaits all created things. Borrowing a theme from Jewish and general mysticism, he terms the object of his reverence "the Holy Nothingness." "In the final analysis, omnipotent Nothingness is Lord of all creation."

An inverted messianism results from this. In discussing Christian death-of-God theories, he wrote, "There is only one Messiah who redeems us from the irony, the travail, and the limitations of human existence . . . the Angel of Death. Death is the true Messiah and the land of the dead the place of God's true Kingdom. . . . We enter God's Kingdom only when we enter His Holy Nothingness." Rubenstein does not seek that Kingdom "because I prefer the problematics of finitude to their dissolution in the nothingness of eternity."

Though no supernatural basis for Jewish continuity exists, the Jews, compelled by history to be Jews, should now affirm their Jewishness to attain self-protection and mutual caring. The State of Israel models a transformed Jewish identity because it reasserts the naturalness of being a Jew and gives proper attention to one's body and a connection to the soil. With chosenness abandoned, the State need reflect no special standard of quality. It rightly does whatever it must to ensure its survival in an amoral universe.

The Jewish religion should continue as a means of helping individual Jews meet life's inevitable traumas. In so unfeeling a cosmos, people need to share with one another to gain the human strength required to face the existential challenges of life. Human beings, having great emotional depths, will benefit from a religious life rich in ritual and myth, particularly those that do not neglect their primitive impulses. If Jewish theology and practice can be transformed, Judaism has much to offer Jews.

Why These Were Not the Relevant Issues

Rubenstein has often expressed surprise that, as the Jewish death-of-God discussion developed, he became increasingly marginal to it. At first, many Jews responded positively to the morality of his attack on the silence of other thinkers and the inadequacies of the traditional theodicies. Ever since modernization had taken hold, Jews had cared far more about ethics than about God. But the death-of-God discussion soon moved off in other directions.

Rubenstein's first argument, the rejection of a rigidly controlling God, was never disputed because modern Jews had not espoused it. Some sages of the "*yeshivah* world" and some Hasidic leaders, such as the Lubavitcher Rebbe and the Satmarer Rebbe, have declared that the Holocaust was God's punishment of the Jews for their nonobservance. Almost all modern Jews agree with Rubenstein that such a view of God and the Holocaust is utterly unacceptable.

This judgment is not a new one. Modern Jewish thinkers had been revising their concepts of God through much of the twentieth century to avoid any mechanical connection between God and human suffering. The God of Cohen, Baeck, Kaplan, Rosenzweig, Buber, and other such thinkers was not the "ultimate, omnipotent actor of history." No one who accepted their ideas had a God-concept that required Rubinstein's radical revision after the Holocaust. Except at some atavistic level, even the masses of modernized Jews no longer had believed in a God who operated every historical occurrence. The major response of modernized Jews to the Kishinev pogrom of 1903 — the "holocaust" of its day—was a call for Jewish action, not cries of self-incrimination or arguments justifying God.

By 1966, when Rubenstein's book appeared, most American Jews were so thoroughly secularized that, in my opinion, their "faith" was usually some variety of agnosticism. The announcement of God's death only added a historical-moral proof to those other arguments that modernization had long since convinced them were cogent. To that extent, Rubenstein's second statement of his case, that we live in a time of the death-of-God, confirmed their experience. Since then, another cultural change has taken place. In recent years, not the bleak absence of God but God's immediate, felt presence in charismatic movements, cults, and mysticism has characterized American religious life. "The time of the death-of-God" passed rather quickly. Most Jews consider the lessons to be derived from Auschwitz less ephemeral than that and so their search moved elsewhere.

The Failure to Provide an Adequate Ground of Value

I have argued that the most significant Jewish religious phenomenon of our time was the erosion of Jewish agnosticism. Intellectually, I ascribe it to the confrontation with nihilism that Rubenstein's thought generated. In the heady days of confidence in human rationality, we were comfortable being unbelievers for we could count on the eternal validity of ethics. But Rubenstein's cosmos was utterly devoid of moral standards or values. In that respect he accurately reflected post–World War II secularity. Unlike in Hermann Cohen's era, human rationality no longer implied ethical commitment. Reason meant logic and tight thinking, not moral law. As Sartre taught, values were now only what a person chose wholeheartedly to do. By that standard, one had every right to be a Nazi, an outcome utterly unacceptable to those morally outraged at Auschwitz. Any theory of ethics that reduces the distinction between the murdered and the murderers to a social or historical accident is contemptible. The difference between a Nazi and a Jew testifies not merely to our upbringing but to something in the ultimate nature of reality itself. Against the drift of much of modern life and thought, many Jews found themselves believing in the claims of a realm of human value that no longer had a rational foundation. Confronted with Rubenstein's claim that the Holy Nothingness is indifferent to good and evil, a good portion of our community had to acknowledge it believed in a trans-rational, commanding absolute good. For us, that meant a belief in something very much like what previous Jewish generations called God. Astonishingly, the very discussion that sought to lead Jews away from God led them, like many others in this period, back to God.

Rubenstein sought to meet this problem of the loss of moral standards by arguing that a commanding ethics may be derived from the human body and the self. Had that project succeeded, he would have solved one of the most pressing intellectual problems of Western civilization, namely, providing a secular justification for stringent obedience to moral imperatives. Rubenstein's book on this topic, *Morality and Eros*, convinced few thinkers. With the ethical consequences of his thought nullifying the very moral outrage it had raised against Auschwitz, Rubenstein's ideas increasingly lost their appeal in the Jewish community.

The social factor in this change of perspective must not be overlooked. Gross immorality invaded much of American life in this period, manifesting itself most dramatically in sexual license, drug abuse, and wanton violence. Few people could avoid the problem of a compelling ground of moral values. An amoral universe validates doing anything one can get away with, even holocausts. Many Americans knew they must reject any view of reality that taught no serious set of limits and had few standards of quality. With rationalism and other forms of secularism unable to deal persuasively with this intuition, a turn to religion began and grew during this period. We shall return to this topic at the end of this chapter and in Chapter 10.

Fackenheim and the Modern Loss of Revelation

Emil Fackenheim's essays soon became a source of the most significant themes of the continuing Jewish discussion of the Holocaust. Ever since the late 1940's, he had been a leader of the existentialist revolt against the rationalist establishment of liberal Jewish theology. Fackenheim, who taught modern philosophy at the University of Toronto, utilized his considerable technical expertise to criticize the generally accepted axiom that a modern Judaism had to be a religion of reason. He argued that all authentic religion, certainly Judaism, is based on revelation. Religious rationalism, by basing itself on human reason, had grossly overestimated our human powers and paid too little attention to God's reality. Until the mid-1960's Fackenheim's most influential work focused on restoring God to an appropriately prominent place in the liberal Jewish religious consciousness.

Fackenheim largely accepted Martin Buber's theory of revelation for he particularly admired the way the I-Eternal Thou encounter preserved individual autonomy while yet making God an active, independent partner in the process. Buber had suggested that God gave presence, not words; people provided the language and content. Because God was available, the Divine-human relationship could arise and engender a compelling but non-Orthodox variety of revelation. The reality and immediate presence of God was therefore a critical element of Fackenheim's two-decade battle with the theological rationalists.

Confronted by the issues raised by Wiesel and Rubenstein, Fackenheim felt he must substantially rethink his position. The biographical background is pertinent: a German, one of the last men ordained a liberal rabbi in Berlin and briefly confined in Sachsenhausen after the November 1938 Nazi outbreak, the Kristallnacht, he barely escaped to Canada before the war broke out. Opening himself up now to the

Holocaust, Fackenheim conceded that Wiesel and Rubenstein were right: God was not present in the Holocaust. What, then, was one to make of this event or of the understanding of Judaism?

In our bewilderment, tradition offers little help. After previous catastrophes, great Jewish spirits have written of God's presence in judgment or in consolation. We cannot do that, not because of some lack of spiritual capacity on our part, but because the Holocaust was a unique act of evil. Here too Wiesel and Rubenstein were right; Auschwitz exposes us to a qualitatively new and unprecedented dimension of suffering. Fackenheim is therefore intellectually outraged by the liberal sentimentality that brackets the Holocaust with any human disaster we seek to condemn. For all their moral odiousness, calling either Hiroshima or *apartheid* another Holocaust betrays an effort to avoid the uniqueness of the Nazi barbarity.

Arguments for a New Level of Evil

No other Jewish thinker has explored as has Fackenheim what we might mean by saying the Holocaust is without parallel and what follows from that assertion. Obviously, we are not referring merely to numbers or its unexpectedness or its methodical execution. All such matters amplify common cruelty; they do not specify what constitutes the Holocaust as a unique evil. Fackenheim identifies two factors in the Holocaust that newly transform the old problem of suffering. The one stems from the charge leveled against the Jews. Their alleged guilt was independent of their conduct or beliefs. In previous persecutions—say, in the Middle Ages—Jews could often save their lives by conversion. The Nazis condemned the Jews because of their biology. Having one Jewish grandparent became a sentence of death. Being itself was made a capital crime and there was nothing one could do about it. That, Fackenheim argues, was a uniquely evil act.

His other line of argument points to the will of the persecutors. The Nazis knew the evil they were doing. They were educated people whose moral consciousness was shaped by a Christian culture, yet they calmly, routinely proceeded to process the mass murder of Jews. They even did so after continuing the extermination made no sense. During the last stages of the war, when trains were desperately needed for immediate military purposes, the Nazis refused to divert them from transporting Jews to the death camps. The hatred of Jews transcended the drive to self-preservation. They must have kept killing from a demonic desire to do evil for evil's sake, to commit the ultimate sin, a thoroughly evil act done for a thoroughly evil purpose. Nothing like that had ever happened in human history.

With God withdrawn and inaccessible—no small part of the agony—and in the face of this incomparable evil, one might have expected the Jews to despair. But the events of Jewish history, as theologians read them, are often more numinous than Jewish thoughts. Though the Holocaust itself discloses no transcendent meaning, Fackenheim detects a new "revelation" at the base of the Jewish people's response to it. By what logic can one explain why the Jews did not turn their backs on life after the Holocaust? Why, despite all that they had seen and suffered, did the survivors insist on resuming Jewish existence? And, most surprisingly, why did they choose to be Jews in a more self-conscious, manifest way than they had before? On some unconscious, spiritual level, they *had to do* what they did. For them to allow the Jewish people to die would have been to complete the Holocaust. That was inconceivable. Individual Jews might be so traumatized they could not care any more about being Jewish. The people itself somehow summoned—or was given—the strength to deny Hitler the ultimate triumph. Absolute evil had aroused absolute commitment.

The Nature of Post-Holocaust Judaism

Fackenheim provides an explanation of this incredible act of self-transcendence. Though God was utterly silent, the Jews heard an absolute command come forth from Auschwitz. To emphasize its Torah-like status, Fackenheim has termed it the 614th commandment (though he seems to consider it the most fundamental of all the commandments today). He hears it as having four components. Jews are forbidden "to hand Hitler posthumous victories." Rather, they must survive as Jews. They must remember the victims. They must not despair of God "lest Judaism perish." In this formulation Fackenheim explained to the Jewish community the impetus that motivated its extraordinary postwar return to Jewishness and continues to energize the best of Jewish life today.

Fackenheim drew three consequences from his reoriented belief and these remain basic to his community leadership and intellectual work. First, he no longer finds it useful to distinguish between religious and secular Jews. Earlier, when arguing for the centrality of revelation in Judaism, he had demeaned Jewish secularism. Seeking to come to terms with the Holocaust, his criterion of Jewish loyalty had changed. Though God is no longer present to reveal, Jews respond to the "commanding voice" of Auschwitz. Any Jew, regardless of label, who helps preserve and maintain or, better, enriches the life of the Jewish people fulfills the supreme Jewish responsibility of our time.

The second consequence he derives from emphasizing peoplehood is a new regard for the State of Israel. It is the ultimate fulfillment of the 614th commandment. Nothing else Jews have done so fully sums up, expresses, and symbolically projects the Jewish people's rejection of death, its return to life, its willingness to face the ambiguities of history, and its insistence on remaining visibly, demonstrably, proudly Jewish. The State of Israel is the incomparable answer Jews have given to the incomparable evil of the Holocaust. Fackenheim therefore considers the State of Israel incomparably sacred and demands that every threat to its existence be fought with the utmost Jewish dedication.

This faith is easily misinterpreted. Fackenheim is *not* suggesting that the founding of the State of Israel was God's way of compensating the Jewish people for its suffering. He spurns any such suggestion as morally repugnant, as does Wiesel. He considers such compensation theodicies another effort to compromise the radically unique evil of the Holocaust. The two events have a bearing on one another but each must be understood in its own distinct terms.

Third, Fackenheim concludes that the test of good faith of Gentiles who enter discussions on Jewish matters is their willingness to face up to the Holocaust. When people admit that they were, or are, prejudiced against Jews, one knows with whom one is dealing. Far more pernicious is the attitude of those who are so proud of their decency and good will that they are blind to their complicity in Jew-hate. We must never forget how the liberal democracies impeded the entry of refugees to their countries and later would not bomb death camps. Non-Jews must make plain their attitudes toward the Holocaust and the State of Israel if they would truly talk to Jews.

Christianity must stand under special scrutiny in this regard. The Nazis were not Christians in any normal sense but had it not been for centuries of Christian anti-Jewish teaching, the Holocaust could not have happened. Worse, the church as an institution did not oppose the Nazi degradation of Jews or later, when it became known, their extermination. Occasionally Christians behaved nobly, sometimes even giving their lives to help Jews or call attention to their plight. Most Christians quietly accepted what happened, thereby condoning and abetting absolute evil. Until Christians are willing to come to terms with the anti-Semitism implicit in much of the church's teaching and confess the guilt the church bears for its sinfulness during the Holocaust, Jews cannot give any spiritual credence to Christianity or its leaders.

The Debate Over Fackenheim's Position

Much of the thinking that arose in response to Fackenheim's point of view has sought a way to restore the dead or absent God to post-Holocaust Judaism. Michael Wyschogrod's trenchant criticism of Fackenheim's arguments is an important case in point. Wyschogrod points out the logical difficulty involved in inferring a positive command from a negative experience. Boldly paraphrasing the Jewish experience, he asks, If stamp collectors were subject to a Holocaust, would the remaining stamp collectors be required not to hand the tyrant posthumous victories? Would they be under a command to carry the special burdens that come from competent stamp-collecting?

Wyschogrod wants to focus our attention on the way a happening might become a commandment of overriding power and authority. In the Jewish case, he does not see why we must say that Jewish secularists heard a "commanding voice" from Auschwitz. Yiddishists, Hebraists, Zionists may now want to go on being Jewish for many of the same reasons as before the Holocaust. Only people who believe in a Transcendent Commander will divine in the decision to-be-a-Jew-despite-everything a response to an absolute, categorical command. The Torah-like imperative is a result of one's prior perspective. It does not stem from the historical experience of Auschwitz or the response to it. In themselves, they remain as ambiguous as all events. The notion that Jews are hearkening to an absolute command makes sense only when one begins with belief in a commanding God. We may not understand God's relation to evil but we nonetheless know what we must do in response to it—a human situation with many precedents in Jewish history.

Wyschogrod also rejects the notion that the Holocaust is a qualitatively unique event of evil. He can understand why Fackenheim is particularly concerned with the Holocaust and why, as against the many monstrous occurrences in recent history, a Jew would want to assert the special quality of Jewish fate. From an ethical point of view, that is, from the standpoint of universal human suffering, Wyschogrod does not see how Fackenheim can substantiate the moral individuality of the Holocaust.

I believe the argument can be carried a step further. Fackenheim's two efforts to validate the singularity of the Holocaust seem faulty to me. That no other people has been singled out for destruction, simply for existing rather than for what they did, seems incorrect. In the history of tribal and national antagonism, one people not infrequently proscribes the members of another people merely for not belonging to its kin.

Less easy to decide is the proper interpretation of the will of the Nazis who carried out the Holocaust. I do not mean to detract from either the perversity of the crime or from its unique significance for the Jewish people when I say that I do not find the charge of an unprecedented Nazi will to do evil convincing. The Germans often made what I consider irrational, because self-damaging, decisions in order to continue the Holocaust. I do not see that they did so to do evil as such. Rather, they obsessively pursued their murderous project because they believed their propaganda that the destruction of the Jews was more important than the possible defeat of the Reich. They persisted in their paranoid devotion to ridding the world of its major enemy. Their words and acts fully accord with this interpretation. Like others who have administered terror, they acted in dedicated pursuit of what they, with demonic misjudgment, saw as the greatest good. I despise what they did but my revulsion is insufficient reason to transform their acts into a uniquely qualitative evil that might in consequence thereby attain uniquely commanding power.

Greenberg's Radically Reinterpreted Orthodoxy

Irving ("Yitz") Greenberg's thought about the Holocaust may perhaps best be understood in terms of an earlier theological emphasis and a later communal one that developed out of it. He was one of the earliest thinkers to say that Auschwitz is the transforming religious experience of our time but he does not give it precedence over Sinai, as do Wiesel, Rubenstein, and, arguably, Fackenheim. Early on he spoke of it rather as having inaugurated a "third cycle" of Jewish history—Sinai and the destruction of the Second Temple having started the other two. Just as they initiated a reshaping of Jewish life, so must this awesome experience. He retains the major categories of classic Jewish faith but subjects them to radical reworking in terms of the Holocaust. His early thinking is therefore dialectical, balancing the claims of his Orthodoxy and Auschwitz one against the other.

Though Rubenstein asserts that traditional Judaism is no longer believable after Auschwitz, Greenberg finds no reason to explain why the Holocaust does not shatter rather than reshape his Orthodoxy. He only suggests that the contemporary traditional Jew believes in a modern fashion, on the basis of "moment faiths." Explicitly crediting Buber, Greenberg says there remain times when God is known and present, though there are others when one finds oneself in the cruel world of the Holocaust. In Greenberg's case, the occasions of validation still supply the context for coming to terms with the times of doubt and disbelief.

Additional ground for the assertion of a dynamic traditional Jewish faith may be found in Greenberg's vigorous, continually reiterated polemic against modernity. The first lesson that he would have Jews—and all others—learn from the Holocaust is that our wholehearted embrace of modernity was a major blunder. Western secular civilization has shown itself to be deeply demonic and capable of the most monstrous inhumanity. The form and operation of the Holocaust are the conhsummation of centuries of Western religion, intellectuality, science, and technology (a theme also dear to Rubenstein). For Jews to have given up their tradition for such spiritual trash seemed to Greenberg at this stage unutterably tragic and in need of thoroughgoing reversal. Somewhat like Fackenheim's argument that utter tragedy can be converted into energetic devotion, Greenberg hoped that convincing Jews to give up their dependency on Western culture would lead them back to traditional observance.

He largely abandoned this polemic strategy in his later thought, most likely as a response to the emergence of an activist right-wing Orthodoxy that rejected pluralism and democracy. The most dramatic manifestations of this phenomenon were seen in extremist acts in the State of Israel. Some believers now insisted that tradition rejected Western political openness as an appropriate basis for a truly Jewish society. At the same time, more subtle pressures were being exerted against Orthodox modernizers and the non-Orthodox everywhere else in the Jewish world. It became clear to Greenberg that he was, for good Jewish reasons, far more committed to modernity than some of his early polemics indicated. This realization had a significant effect on his later thought and was one reason that his major strategy for winning Jews to Jewishness now became enticement, showing how good it can be to be an observant, learned Jew.

The Early Theological Emphases

Greenberg agrees that we are in a post-secular time and that compelling moral affirmation can be based only on a relationship to God. He goes further, arguing that the establishment of the State of Israel validates continued faith in God. As Jewish tradition should have led us to expect, a redeeming act has "matched" the catastrophe. Almost all Jews consider the State of Israel central to their Jewishness and most believe it to be a balance for the horror of the Holocaust. These sentiments do not lead to belief in God by any large number of Jews, particularly the Israelis who remain resolutely secular. Perhaps Greenberg still maintains this faith, for his religious appreciation of the State of Israel has not faltered but it is an argument not often heard in his later thought.

To revise his traditional faith in God, Greenberg utilizes models derived from Job and Lamentations. These justify, in ways quite familiar from liberal theologies, the *search* for faith against confidence in established doctrine and find argument with God a legitimate Jewish way of maintaining a relationship. Despite Rubenstein's strictures, Greenberg offers a defense of the Jewish people as God's suffering servant. Anti-Semitism's eerie quality derives from its satanic theological basis. Because the Jews are a witness to God and testify that the world remains unredeemed, the nations hate them. On a practical level as well, the Jews are a likely target for whatever demonic impulses inhere in a culture. Jewish suffering is not therefore senseless but an active part of the Jewish people's service of God. A limit to such suffering must be invoked, for, as the Holocaust showed, "when the suffering is overwhelming, then the servant must be driven to yield to evil. . . . The redemptive nature of suffering must be in absolute tension with the dialectical reality that it must be fought, cut down, eliminated."

Positively, Greenberg maintains that after Auschwitz our central religious affirmation is the creation of life. By having and properly rearing a child, one shows a primal hopefulness and decisively rejects all that the death camps stood for. For Jews, whose numbers have been radically depleted, propagation is a primary obligation. Simultaneously, any cultural or religious activity that devalues the worth of human beings or any group among them must be adjudged anathema. From there it is a simple step to the elimination of the secular-religious dichotomy. Anyone who desists from murder or exploitation or, better, who is dedicated to the care of people, must now be regarded as a God-fearer. With humanism now an acceptable piety, Greenberg can identify the State of Israel, despite its committed secularity, as a religious institution. Like Fackenheim, he sees it as the Jewish people's supreme, life-generating response to the Holocaust. He goes beyond Fackenheim by suggesting that in itself—the Holocaust aside—the founding and continuation of a Jewish state on the sacred land is numinous. It must become a generative premise for the construction of an adequate modern Jewish theology.

Berkovits' Argument for a Holocaust Theology of Faith

Eliezer Berkovits, also an Orthodox rabbi, sought to revise Holocaust theology more than traditional Jewish faith. Born in Hungary in 1900, he died in Jerusalem in 1992. Having himself escaped from Europe only in 1939, he felt the agony of the Holocaust in a most personal way.

Berkovits could not understand why many thinkers insisted that God was not to be found in the death camps. Many people who were there had the opposite experience. To be sure, a good number did lose their old beliefs and values but numerous others did not; some few even found faith there or later. For them, God was available and this knowledge enabled them to bear their suffering, often with nobility. If anything, the records indicate that in these dire circumstances traditional belief stood up better than modernist and liberal world views, which rather easily collapsed. The Jewish death-of-God theologians have simply ignored this data. Berkovits laid down the principle that those who were not there, but passed the murder era miles away in safety, should be most restrained in making dramatic, negative claims about its lessons.

Berkovits contended that our Holocaust theology began with the wrong premise. It extrapolated from the experience of the disillusioned to create a vision of the cosmos that necessarily then had no God. Surely there is nothing new and certainly not revelatory in evil's producing a loss of faith. Disbelief is the common situation of secular humankind; under the blows of the Holocaust, modernized unbelievers would naturally lose whatever faith lurked in their psyches. What naivete about the human condition has led our thinkers to suggest that negation ought to awaken our awe?

Should we not, however, be astonished by the many people who maintained their faith despite everything the Nazis did to them? Their spiritual accomplishment in our time, in their situation, is breathtaking. In this argument Berkovits did not indulge in pathos. He did not try to wring from sentimentality what intelligence and conscience deny. Rather, he reverently called our attention to the common saints and everyday heroes of the ghettos and death camps. Their unwavering devotion is awesome by any standards. And Berkovits demanded to know why they should not be the foundation of our religious reconstruction after Auschwitz. If the commanding voice of Auschwitz calls us to maintain faith with the victims, they above all should be our models. We should remember them in the most significant possible way, by trying to emulate their faith. Should we find belief difficult—Berkovits admitted understanding is utterly beyond us—we ought to give their affirmations more credence than our doubts and honor their memories by patiently awaiting the return of faith.

The full force of Berkovits' negative feelings as a result of the Holocaust was directed against Christianity. Fackenheim and Greenberg have felt a positive obligation to challenge Christians (who would speak to Jews) to acknowledge the depth of Christian religious anti Semitism and its role in making the Holocaust possible. They have made the repudiation of any vestige of Christian anti-Jewishness, the acknowledgment of Christian guilt for the Holocaust, and an appreciation of the State of Israel to post-Auschwitz Jews the conditions of contemporary Christian–Jewish dialogue. Berkovits denied that Jews and Christians can have any significant interchange whatsoever in our generation. The obloquy and persecution of pre-Hitler years should themselves be sufficient to prevent any self-respecting Jew from taking seriously present-day Christian declarations of a change of heart. After Auschwitz and the Christian silence during it and the subsequent threats to the State of Israel, how can any rational person take Christian declarations of good will as anything more than desperate efforts to bolster what is left of their decaying self-image? That some Christians still seek to convert

Jews to their faith rouses him to fury. His cry, "All we want of Christians is that they keep their hands off us and our children!" must rank as one of the strongest rejections of interchange with Christians to appear before the English-reading public.

A Limited God, the One Rational Religious Answer

Rationalistically minded Jews have not been impressed by any of these arguments for continued belief in God today. They do not see how thinking people can be asked to believe what they cannot understand. For them, reestablishing faith depends on finding a new conception of God, one that establishes value while making intelligible the occurrence of evils such as the Holocaust. (Rationalists cannot, in principle, accept the notion of the Holocaust as a radically unique act of evil since terming it unique excludes it from universal categories of explanation.)

The alternatives for a rational theodicy are limited. Thinkers after the Holocaust can hardly say that evil is unreal and claim to be realistic. They might follow Rubenstein and deny that God is good, but saying that destroys the ultimate qualitative distinction between Nazis and Jews—an unacceptable position for those morally indignant at the Holocaust. That leaves only the possibility that God does not have sufficient power to stop all evil. Instead of being thought of as omnipotent, God should be conceived of as finite or limited. God cannot "do all things" as Job thought, and thus great evil sometimes occurs. With God's power limited, human moral action becomes all the more important if the world is to be redeemed.

Belief in a limited God is not without warrant in the Jewish tradition. The Bible unequivocally states that God granted the very first human beings the power to do or not do God's commands to them. The biblical authors thereby implied that they believed there were limits as to what God could, perhaps would, do. Various rabbinic statements and some of the ideas of Jewish philosophers and mystics similarly restrict the Divine power. None of the modern thinkers we have previously discussed, except Heschel, makes an unequivocal claim for God's omnipotence.

Mordecai Kaplan, at the other extreme specifically, identifies God as referring only to the helping powers in nature, thus resolving by definition the classic problem of evil. A number of other pre-Holocaust thinkers taught that God was finite. Henry Slonimsky had elegantly described God as growing in history through human moral acts.

Hans Jonas' Construction of a Limited God

One intriguing outline of a finite God is that of Hans Jonas, who taught philosophy at the New School for Social Research with a particular concern for the philosophy of science. In his Ingersoll Lecture, "Immortality and the Modern Temper," Jonas described a God in keeping with the naturalistic view that all causes must be internal to the world. Unlike Kaplan's God, who is entirely immanent in natural processes, Jonas suggested that God created the world but, once having ordered it and its values, God allowed it full independence. After creation, God is never a natural cause. But unlike the Deists' God, who no longer is involved with the creation, this God, because of values, remains "concerned" with what happens. God's own future, so to speak, has become conditional upon what transpires in creation, particularly once human beings evolve who are free to determine its outcome by their action. Jonas' God may be said to be dependent on creation, as against biblical faith, in which all created things depend on God. Jonas could also say that God "cares" what takes place in history, for the future of values depends on it. In this context, metaphorical by contrast to Heschel's literalism, God suffers with every ethical defeat in human history.

When, then, the Nazis abused the freedom natural evolution gave them, we cannot hold God responsible. The fact that God did not act to stop the Holocaust, or did not take away the Nazi's freedom to do evil, or did not miraculously save the Jews, or did not manifest the Divine presence in some spectacular way in the death camps, is not irrational. A God who violates or vitiates human freedom is not the sort of God morally dedicated people would want the world to have.

We are overwhelmed by what our people suffered but can take some consolation from knowing that God's own future was damaged by the Nazi bestiality. We can also understand why Jews and others ought to respond to the Holocaust by fighting every vestige of Nazism or sign of its reappearance. Jonas' lecture does not develop the particular Jewish consequences of his idea of God but it could easily ground a defense of the State of Israel as a major agent of God's work in history.

For all their intellectual appeal, finite doctrines of God have been difficult to accept. In Jonas' case, the rationalistic appeal of limiting God is compromised by the inexplicable reversal of God's energy after creation. By having the creator God suddenly withdraw from nature, Jonas saves God from utter immanence while giving the cosmos independence and people freedom, yet establishing the transcendent authority of immanent values. Jonas himself was forced to admit that the expansion-contraction description of creation involves a mythic, not a rationalistic model of creation, specifically the Jewish notion of *tzimtzum*, God's self-concentration.

Substantively, too, finite theories of God undermine Jewish messianism. Can we still believe that the ideal will one day be made reality if we must depend on humankind to achieve it? After all, the Holocaust has taught us about the limited moral steadfastness of even good people: Should not those whose God has limited power to overcome evil join Rubenstein and despair of human history? Classic Judaism had faith in people because they were in Covenant with God. What their righteousness could not accomplish, God's power would ultimately complete. Can any doctrine of hope today dispense with God's help even though we cannot explain just how God acts or why God's saving influence is seen only sporadically and after long delay?

Diverging Paths in Later Holocaust Theology

These themes have dominated theological writing about the Holocaust. Sometimes new language gives them fresh poignancy or a different midrashic or philosophic elaboration endows them with new power. The underlying ideas, however, have remained pretty much as laid out in the early years of the Holocaust discussion. Indeed, it seems fair to suggest that a certain ritualization has come to dominate abstract statements about the continually fading event. The same range of ideas and images recurs in the continuing effort to cope with the mystery of such extraordinary evil or to find a rational explanation for it. Surely that is the common path religions take, turning into rite what can be communicated and exposed only in this sacred manner. So communal ritual acts like lighting six candles for the six million—typically, a custom of unknown origin—and sounding familiar themes about the horror now commonly supplant theology with act.

Three exceptions to this observation must, however, be noted. One is Irving Greenberg's notion that the Holocaust made the Covenant between God and Israel essentially a matter of Jewish will. Another is my contention that the Holocaust ended our faith, not in God, but in humankind and its messianic capacities, turning us from secularity to spirituality. Quite independently David Blumenthal of Emery University has sought to relate this religious reversal to the issue of interpersonal abuse.

Greenberg's later thought has come to a radically unanticipated conclusion: he has moved beyond a reconsideration of his understanding of the rabbinic doctrine of *mitzvot*—commandment—to a rejection of it. The sages teach that at Sinai, God, the one and only sovereign of the universe, imposed commandments on the people of Israel. To be sure, there was a compensating teaching that the people agreed to the Covenant and its laws. Nonetheless, God's sovereignty dominated biblical and rabbinic images of God and was the basis of God's properly enforcing the commandments by rewarding observance and punishing sin. But, Greenberg inquires, if the Covenant calls upon the Jews to exemplify God's goodness in history how can it include a possibility of the Jews' being destroyed? One might demand sacrifice of those one cares for, but not suicide. So God may no longer require us to be Jews, and we can no longer think of God as one who commands us. As he puts it, "If the Jews keep the covenant after the Holocaust, then it can no longer be for the reason that it is commanded or because it is enforced by reward or punishment."

God does not vanish in this Judaism without *mitzvot* but God is now the lesser and more passive partner in the Covenant. God is, as it were, the Powerless One who cares that the people of Israel succeeds in its covenantal mission but who can do nothing to help, guide, sustain, save or vindicate it. Rather, in an echo of all the thinkers who have suggested that God's death has for the first time fully enfranchised humankind, Greenberg considers this as giving Jews fully mature responsibility for their Jewishness. Like Fackenheim, he glories in the people's self-redeeming response to Hitler but where Fackenheim still could speak of a voice from Auschwitz that commanded this Jewish response, Greenberg considers the Covenant totally voluntary. We carry it out simply because we want to do so, or, as Greenberg says in one of his few explanations of why Jews should continue living the Covenant, "God was no longer in a position to command, but the Jewish people was so in love with the dream of redemption that it volunteered to carry on its mission."

Greenberg sees another great value besides responsibility emerging from this view: it legitimates Jewish pluralism. If the will to continue being a Jew is the one great response to the Holocaust, then any manner of doing so must be considered praiseworthy. Every Jewish act, even a small one, should be greeted with a certain Jewish enthusiasm for it testifies to the Jewish will to continue. This openness to many ways of being Jewish legitimates democracy among us and authenticates a community structure where the will to participate is the effective criterion of one's Jewish acceptability.

It is difficult for the non-Orthodox reader not to see this line of thought as the post-Holocaust response of a sensitive, caring Jew to his Orthodoxy. Greenberg's revolutionary attitude toward commandment is not a response to the kind of modernized God and sense of commandment found in moderns like Cohen, Baeck, Kaplan or Buber. That God only "commands" non-verbally, is largely withdrawn from the operation of history and definitely not an agent of reward and punishment though still the foundation of Jewish obligation. Confronting the Holocaust with an Orthodox faith that expected God to save the Jews from their enemies and reward their observance, Greenberg seeks with dauntless courage to come to terms with the ashes of that old theology. Boldly his revisionism centers not on the insoluble problem of evil but on the more central Jewish issue: What must we do?

His theoretical proposal, that we take Jewish duty entirely upon ourselves, has found few adherents either in Orthodoxy or among the non-Orthodox. Traditionalists see it as eliminating the root of all Jewish teaching: that God gave us the Torah and still commands our obedience to its precepts. Moreover, they, like caring non-Orthodox Jews, have seen the deleterious results of Jews thinking that whatever they want to do as Jews is as good a Judaism as any other. Such humanistic Jewishness may well generate a faithful non-Orthodox remnant that is recognizably Jewish—but for how long and with what spirit? As time lessens historic memories, as sociology devalues ethnic discipline and as democratic acceptance continues opening broad opportunities, the evanescence of a human-centered Judaism seems inevitable.

Was It God We Had Lost Faith In?

My view of the theological effects of the Holocaust is quite different. In order to present it in its proper context I must reserve its exposition for Chapter 12, where I explain my postmodernism, yet since the contrast to Greenberg is so sharp, I want to introduce it here. The discussion of the Holocaust has taught thoughtful moderns little about God that we did not already know. For nearly a century their leading teachers had reinterpreted traditional Jewish belief out of respect for science and in response to Nietzsche's cultural arguments for atheism. Then, as our confidence in human capability became less absolute, our atheism dwindled to the agnosticism that, for some time, was the common attitude of sophisticated Jews to God. Among those who still spoke of God the notion of a finite God was widespread long before mid-century.

Yet why did our theological discussion of the Holocaust so agitate us? I suggest that the Holocaust did undermine our true faith, but the term "God" did not indicate what we believed in, only how important our underlying belief was. The utterly unsettling truth buried under the Holocaust talk about God was that after Auschwitz we could no longer maintain our modernist faith in humankind. For *that* was the operative religion of American Jews. We believed in the goodness of people and trusted that education and culture would guide them properly, while psychotherapy remedied their flaws. We counted on politics to bring the Messiah, with an assist from social science. We followed the commandments of self-realization and looked forward to perfecting humankind. For us, humanity sat on God's old throne. The debate over Auschwitz gradually made us acknowledge our covert religion and confess its untenability. And with that recognition death-of-God theology lost the vitality it had once displayed.

We have not, of course, stopped talking about the religious implications of the Holocaust. Only for some years now the once fashionably radical calls for nonbelief appear irrelevant. It seems a triumph of illusion today to suggest we should still place our ultimate faith in humankind. Rather, it has become disturbingly plain that nothing human beings have long been involved with remains untainted by moral failure. Our government is suspect, our economy exploitative, our ecology destructive, our families troubled and we ourselves conflicted to the point where avoiding depression is a major species of fulfillment. Humanity is no longer the answer but the problem.

Ironically, as we have become strong enough to face the loss of our old covert faith in ourselves, we have discovered that, despite everything, we probably are far less agnostic than we thought we were. When, in moral revulsion against the vulgarity of our society or in rejection of its temptations to paganize, we insist on living on another level of quality; when we insist that our values, for all that they are difficult to define or apply, are fundamental to the universe itself—we base our lives on a transcendent claim of quality laid on human beings, we must respond to it despite the burdens that quest will impose upon us, and we are ready to join those other Jews who now searchingly inquire what being a Jew can mean to them (even as Christians are finding a way back to heartfelt Christian faith). Taking that stance, we are likely at some quiet or critical moment to ask about the root of this crucial belief. What is it, then, that we are trusting in? And more than likely we shall find ourselves realizing that we, in our modern way, are responding to the same commanding presence in the universe to which previous generations of Jews hearkened. In recovering our Jewish identity in depth, we find ourselves on new terms with what our tradition called God.

The almost unbelievable, dialectical outcome of our attention to the Holocaust has been that a sizable minority in the Jewish community is now involved in exploring the dimensions of their personal relationships with God. Through mysticism or the study of texts, in liturgy or Jewish activism, some Jews are seeking to draw closer to what they dimly sense is the still living God of the universe. They do not claim to understand God or to explain God's erratic way in history. The Holocaust remains as disturbing as ever—if anything, more so, for the God on whom they base their lives is also the God of the six million. They only know that God is real and the Covenant continues, and they propose to build their lives on these commitments. Theirs is a fragmentary faith but in this empty era even a partial belief is a lot to have gained.

The critical questions remain as unsettled for us as for prior generations of Jews: Can one believe when one does not understand? How can God now be present, and then, and often, terrifyingly absent? How could God, the God who grounds all values, not have done something, anything to stop the Holocaust, the antithesis of all value? Why do the good suffer?

Is the Good God Also an Abuser?

David Blumenthal has introduced a totally new theme into the discussion of evil and thus into the discussion of the Holocaust: the relation of God to interpersonal abuse. Over against those who have seen the reality of suffering as reason for denying God or radically truncating God's reality, Blumenthal begins with God's existence as a given. His corollary premise is that God is personal. Both propositions are asserted on the ground that they are central to the Jewish religious tradition and reinforced by contemporary religious experience. (This methodology, which he also adduces in discussing the six attributes of God in Judaism, allows me to associate him with what I have termed the "eclectic school" of contemporary Jewish thought. For more on this, see Chapter 14.) He also takes it for granted that God in Judaism is essentially fair, humanly addressable, powerful but not perfect (thus allowing for human free will), loving, occasionally irascible (out of connectedness and love) and a partisan who chooses (e.g., the people and Land of Israel).

These six givens constitute the accepted, essentially unargued context into which Blumenthal introduces what might otherwise be considered a heretical notion, a seventh proposition: that God can sometimes be an abuser. He explicates this shocking notion in his book *Facing the Abusing God: A Theology of Protest*. To understand him one must keep in mind the argument's thoroughly dialectical quality. This theology grows out of intense devotion to God and the Jewish religious tradition. The book opens with a caution to readers that the volume "contains the holy Name of God in Hebrew. Please treat it with respect and dispose of it properly," and it closes with a section of personal prayers to the "Abusing God."

How can a writer so respectful of God then suggest that God is an abuser who needs to be confronted by the abused not only for their therapeutic and spiritual benefit but, as it were, for God's? Two answers convincingly establish his religious right to do so. First, the Bible and Rabbinic literature contain many examples of protest against God for allowing, even bringing such evil. Second, the reality of contemporary experience reveals the extent and varieties of personal abuse.

The protest against God has long been a mainstay of modern Jewish writings about evil and in a quite limited sense this work is an extension of that tradition. However, most of the earlier thought came from rebellious, self-confident secularists still sufficiently attached to Jewish life that they sought authorization from tradition for their heady atheism. In the Holocaust theologies the protest motif sometimes still exuded something of the old heroic romanticism, but as confidence in humankind's judgment waned so did the accusing stance toward God. Blumenthal's religiosity is too firm for humanistic posturing. Rather he writes with a certain pained realism that must be attributed to his great sensitivity to the pain that physical and sexual abuse have caused so many people. God, he knows, must be recognized not only as colluding in this suffering but, in part, as its agent.

His exposition of this theme is particularly effective because he abandons the cognitive exposition of rationalistic theodicies and treats his fathomless topic in a multifaceted way. Thus, in expounding four psalms of protest he presents four types of original commentary. He exchanges correspondence with other thinkers. He provides a dialogue with an adult survivor of child abuse. All this sense of the shatteredness of language and the limits of words is influenced by recent writing about postmodernity, a movement whose European roots have been deeply affected by the Holocaust. (For my interpretation of the postmodern movement, see Chapter 12.) Thus his work is an uncommonly rich and evocative exploration of how a believer can retain piety while remaining fully realistic about people's malevolence to one another and God's own involvement in our human suffering.

No work on this awesome theme can hope to satisfy everyone and ideas with an uncommon shape and content may take a somewhat longer time to find their public. Nonetheless, some issues raised by Blumenthal's work need to be confronted. The basic ones are common to all who start from within a tradition and explain but do not argue for the faith that they take for granted. To some extent this can be justified by rejecting as a vain hope of modernity the possibility that one might begin one's thought with self-evident or necessary premises. To postmoderns some element of will and subjectivity seems necessarily implicated in the most basic level of any serious thinking. The only question that can then legitimately be raised is whether the dialogue partner can accept these premises of the exchange. In this case, Blumenthal invites us, even before discussing the problem of evil, to accept not only God's reality and personalness but six attributes as well. Many people would prefer to bracket any consideration of God's nature or reality until after discussing evil.

The eclectic approach legitimates its theses by culling them from its cultural resource but it does not clarify on what basis it decides on just this text or interpretation rather than its many alternatives. Justifying its foundations would be a lot to ask of a work already so heavy with meaning and interpretation. Yet it is difficult to know how to accept an approach whose fundamental dialectic is clarified only at one and not both of its poles, a problem exacerbated here because the one taken as given sets the context for its radical counterpart.

More specifically it is not clear what this presentation finally has to do with the Holocaust. That theme is introduced early in its pages but largely disappears as the work proceeds. The implication would seem to be that if we understand individual suffering more fully then we will understand social evil as well, an approach that avoids the issue of what the Holocaust uniquely tells us about suffering. Such a move from the individual to the social levels of existence has some merit but many thinkers would deny that the personal can ever fully explain the social realities. It may be that I have raised an inappropriate difficulty and this book is intended as a universalistic discussion of the issue, not a particularistic Jewish one, even as Job is said by a rabbinic source to be a non-Jew. But that seems an unsatisfactory response indeed because one need not be a Jew to consider the Holocaust essential to any Western discussion of the problem of evil. For a Jew not to give it significant direct attention seems, despite the strands of universalism in the Jewish tradition, a strange omission indeed.

This chapter really has no conclusion, for until the Messiah comes evil can only momentarily be kept at bay, leaving humankind perpetually troubled by it. Jewish theology has not considered every question worth answering, nor has it given a definitive answer to all those that are. The problem of evil has had many Jewish responses and much can be learned from them, but a resolution of the issues can come only with the messianic day.

10

A Theology of
Modern Orthodoxy:
Joseph B. Soloveitchik

UNTIL RECENTLY, modernity appeared to mandate the abandonment of traditional Jewish belief and practice. Jewish observance conflicted with the rhythm and style of general society. Remaining distinctive seemed foolish when non-Jews turned out to be humane and Western culture understood the universe far more comprehensively and demonstrably than did Jewish faith. Modern Jewish thought came largely from liberal Jews trying to give intellectual expression to the balance of modernity and Jewishness that most Jews unselfconsciously began to live.

The sociology of adaptation seemed so inexorable that some writers speculated about the length of time it would take for Orthodox Judaism to be reduced to a few European-oriented enclaves. In a stunning reversal of all such predictions, the 1970's began a revival of American Orthodoxy that has made it a vigorous, powerful part of our community life.

One reason for that change, not often remarked upon, was the post–World War II immigration of Holocaust survivors to the United States. Sizable numbers were observant Jews who spurned the notion that they should compromise their Judaism to be more acceptable to a Gentile world. Their presence in the community encouraged those who all along had been fighting the creeping accommodation in American Orthodoxy, whose major symbolic battleground was the mixed seating of men and women at synagogue services.

221

Americanization of the Early Orthodox Immigrants

Sociological observers have repeatedly called attention to the unexpected phenomenon that revitalized Orthodoxy: not immigration but a new mood among native Americans. In their case, a thoroughgoing acculturation has not meant liberalizing belief and practice. Rather, their Orthodoxy stems from deliberate choice, the selection of a life style they believe will be best for them and their children.

One powerful motive for opting for Orthodoxy is the revulsion these American Jews have felt at Western civilization. Where previous generations of modern Jews were eager to be fully accepted, many Jews today are repelled by its general amorality and want to be somewhat withdrawn from it. At its most intense, this feeling leads some to immigrate to the State of Israel; at a somewhat lesser level, some few adopt a Hasidic or other European-oriented life style in the United States.

Being a fully observant Jew commends itself as a good way of participating in general society yet remaining sufficiently different from it so as to maintain one's high sense of human values. At one time Conservative Judaism seemed to have worked out the proper balance between Jewish tradition and American adjustment; for many American Jews it still fulfills that role. But surprisingly, in recent years a good number of Jews have come to feel that it makes insufficient demands for Jewish discipline; that, despite its intentions, it has assimilated too much. Many who now propose to undertake living as Jews wish to do so in as authentic a fashion as they can, which to them means becoming Orthodox.

Authentic Living Seeks an Authentic Theory

Two other factors have influenced this development. One is the growing number of graduates of Jewish all-day schools. They have the learning and skills without which traditional Jewish living might seem burdensome and impractical. Already as children they were often exposed to Jewish role models whose life style they can now adapt to their own temperaments.

The other factor affecting the new traditionalism is the flowering of what has been termed "modern Orthodoxy," the fusion of classic *halachic* Judaism and American culture exemplified best by the graduates and program of Yeshiva University in New York. Its steadfast commitment to Torah does not equate authenticity with a return to the ghetto and a disdain for Western civilization's possible enrichment of Judaism. The modern Orthodoxy that came to maturity in the 1960's established a pattern of American Jewish living that did not compromise with central Jewish disciplines (e.g., *mikveh*, the ritual bath required of women) yet allowed for appropriate modern activities (e.g., *yeshivah* sports activities).

Today Orthodoxy is an appealing option for Jews seeking to base their lives on Judaism. Their search provides the communal base for the search for a theology of Jewish Orthodoxy. The structure of recent Jewish though, mediation between Judaism and modernity, thus remains unaltered in modern Orthodoxy. Its resulting Jewish theology would be of more than sectarian Jewish interest for it speaks to the problem of all inquiring Jews.

An Orthodox Jewish theology would likely have one uncommon characteristic. Most Jewish thinkers have been distinguished by their competence in contemporary philosophy or theology. Their understanding of Judaism has been based largely on *aggadah*, the nonlegal rabbinic material, or on medieval Jewish philosophy. Yet, as Franz Rosenzweig argued in his memorable essay on the proper methodology of Jewish theology, "Apologetic Thinking," all such speculation has little Jewish validity. Insofar as there was authority in the Jewish religion over the centuries, it was provided by the *halachah*, the law that regulated the conduct of the autonomous Jewish community. To come as close as possible to what Jews "had to believe," one ought to explicate the theology implicit in the *halachah*. Rosenzweig and later thinkers left this goal unattained and, thus, seemingly unattainable. Philosophers who could make their way through the swirling currents of the law seemed unable to chart its movements in terms of comprehensive religious concepts, while those who could devise an acceptable structure of modern religious thought generally did not know "the small letters" in which the development of Jewish legal thinking must be traced.

The Rav of the Modern Orthodox Rabbinate

All this made the thought of Rabbi Joseph Baer Soloveitchik of unusual interest. As the leading spirit of the Rabbi Isaac Elchanan Theological Seminary of Yeshiva University and as chairman of the Halachah Commission of the (Orthodox) Rabbinical Council of America, his competence to describe Judaism out of its legal tradition was beyond question. His broad-ranging cultural concerns were amply attested in his lectures over the years, as was his mastery of ancient and modern philosophy. (He won a doctorate in philosophy in 1931 at the University of Berlin with a dissertation on Hermann Cohen's theory of knowledge.) He died in 1993, having attained the age of ninety.

What has thus far appeared of Rabbi Soloveitchik's theology is not easily characterized as a theology of the *halachah*. Some of his writings are directly based on legal materials, notably the accounts of his several annual *shiurim*, his public legal lectures, which focus on specific texts in the Talmud and Maimonides' code, the Mishneh Torah. He gives these an existentialist interpretation. In his general essays, the development of the theme may suddenly include an illustration drawn from the *halachah*. Such mediation of the Western and Jewish traditions is unprecedented. Philosophical readers find concepts illuminated in an unexpected way by examples from a most uncommon source, while the *halachicly* sophisticated reader is exposed to a series of *hidushim*, novel interpretations, based on an existentialistic hermeneutic without parallel in Jewish legal literature.

Despite this interplay of illustration, the relation of the *halachah* to the structure and content of Rabbi Soloveitchik's philosophy is not clear. Occasionally he has used such language as "the Halacha thinks" or "the Halachic idea of." Then the reader, conscious of the author's stature, may perceive a claim that the thought presented is indeed a central element of "the" theology of the *halachah*. The rest of Rabbi Soloveitchik's method throws this supposition in doubt. He never seeks to establish his generalizations by presenting many citations, or by tracing the motif through the ramified Jewish legal literature, or by considering and refuting apparently contrary legal materials. He did not seek to make his case with critical readers but, as one of the master teachers of the generation, he tellingly explicated it. He elaborated a philosophic anthropology (which inevitably involves God) and used the *halachah* to clarify and amplify it—or vice versa—but did not show us how necessary or sufficient is the connection of the one body of thought with the other.

Putting Fragments Into a Whole

This brief introduction has already plunged us into the thicket of problems involved in presenting Rabbi Soloveitchik's thinking. Analyzing these difficulties will itself help us understand his unique position among modern Jewish thinkers.

Only late in his life were a substantial number of his papers published. I have been present when he lectured from a portion of a sizable manuscript, but no book by him has appeared. We must make our judgment of his ideas based on a series of disparate writings whose relationship to one another is not clear. This overview of his thinking is, therefore, necessarily provisional, awaiting the appearance of his posthumous publications.

The problem of the paucity and diversity of sources highlights the dramatic shift in emphasis, if not in thought, from his earliest major publication and the next substantial essays. For nearly twenty-five years those who were not Rabbi Soloveitchik's students knew of his extraordinary intellect through one long paper, "*Ish Hahalachah*" (Halachic Man), published in 1944. In phenomenological fashion, the essay exposed the inner life of the person whose religiosity was channeled and exalted through Jewish law. The author continually contrasted this to the spirituality of those whose lives were centered on religious experience in the subjective, affective sense of the term. The difference between them was far more basic than a simple distinction between intellect and emotion. Thus, he carefully described how the intellectuality of the *halachic* personality has a passional side, enabling it to rise to the level of ecstasy. Both types are, of course, authentically present in Judaism, but Rabbi Soloveitchik extolled the virtues of the *halachic* soul and derogated the spiritual personality.

Most readers thought that Rabbi Soloveitchik had restated the *mitnagdic*, anti-Hasidic, tradition of Eastern Europe and wanted intellect, as utilized in *halachic* reasoning and living, to be the central feature of modern Jewish life. When his later papers appeared, most significantly the lengthy analysis entitled "The Lonely Man of Faith," it became clear that the early impression was wrong. While an overarching intellectuality is manifest in these later publications, they are concerned with facing the conflicted human situation depicted by modern existentialism, not with arguing for a latter-day rationalism. For some years this pattern continued and the most recent essays were the most subjective and personalistic he wrote. We cannot now know if there were major shifts in his thought over these four decades or whether the progress of his thought came about by slow evolution.

Problems of Scope and Style

Even Rabbi Soloveitchik's short papers are not easy to contain in a conceptual scheme. He seems to approach each particular topic from an all-embracing conceptuality but this is only hinted at, not yet publicly elucidated. With its full context unknown, any given paper, for all that it communicates, is not fully understandable. Moreover, a relatively brief paper will have a disconcertingly long reach. Rabbi Soloveitchik would examine various of the conflicts of the soul or of the Jewish people, explicating the dialectic which keeps us in tension and probing how *halachah* helps us live with them. His writing is therefore highly subtle and abstract. An unwary reader may easily lose the path of a careful argument in the course of one of his speculative flights. His breadth of allusion is also extraordinary, including, for example, early Greek philosophers, church fathers, marginal German philosophers, and modern playwrights. (Though his references are apt, he rarely cites or treats these people in any detail.) His utilization of all the genres of Jewish literature is masterful and his sensitivity to biblical texts is utterly uncommon for one whose reputation rests on his interpretations of Jewish law.

These diverse intellectual concerns are expressed in a style that is as distinct as the thought it seeks to convey and enhance. With cognition subordinated to the human being as an emotional, conflicted, aspiring creature, Rabbi Soloveitchik's writing is charged with sensibility, not infrequently becoming passionate. These felling tones are central to the message he wishes to impart. They never lead him to the stylistic extravagances of Abraham Heschel, who made artful word play a major instrument of his effort to bring the reader to an insight that language cannot convey. Soloveitchik agrees that much of our faith and our selfhood is eneffable, but who we are and what we believe can substantially be comprehended by intellect and expressed in words. He does not write in oracular, epigrammatic fashion as did Buber in *I and Thou*. He has greater confidence in human reason than Buber does and the substantial length of some of his papers indicates his hope that additional description or allusion may communicate the elusive personal point he is trying to make.

A Theology of Alienated Jewish Existence

Rabbi Soloveitchik's published papers center on the human condition. They explore what it means to be a person in relation to God (less so to the people of Israel) as Jewish tradition understands it. Their overriding concern is to delineate and accept the contradictions involved in being human and illustrate how the *halachah* understands and responds to our humanity. In specific theme—loneliness, anxiety, conflict—as in general outline, this is philosophic existentialism. With all due regard for the radical religious differences between them, Rabbi Soloveitchik's philosophical content and method are more like Sören Kierkegaard than Hermann Cohen.

One way of comprehending Rabbi Soloveitchik's distance from rationalism is to observe how, consciously or unconsciously, he utilizes and transforms the method of "correlation" that the Marburg Neo-Kantian had developed. Cohen argued that all statements about God should simultaneously be statements about humankind and vice versa, because we know God only through human reason and rational human beings require an idea of God to attain an integrated world view. Paul Tillich, the great modern Protestant theologian, applied Cohen's method but revised it for use in an existentialist framework. Tillich called for rationality, that is, technical existentialist philosophy, to elucidate the important questions raised by human existence. But reason, which has a limited understanding of existence, was incompetent to answer them properly. Instead, the theologian would draw on revelation to respond to them. For Tillich, theology meant correlating Christian revelation answers to the questions intellect asked about existence.

Emil Fackenheim, before his work became Holocaust-oriented, declared that this dialogue between the questions existence raises and revelation answers was the most appropriate framework for creating a modern Jewish theology. He proposed to carry out this program by drawing on the liberal Jewish understanding of revelation. Rabbi Soloveitchik seems quite willing to let modern culture raise issues for the sensitive human being. But he does not allow these to press in on people with covert authority. In his thought, with great consistency, the Torah is recognized as the only legitimate source of answers. Indeed, exposing another "face" of the Torah is traditionally a meritorious achievement. The existentialist questions only provide Rabbi Soloveitchik with a new hermeneutic level on which to demonstrate the Torah's infinite validity.

Major Currents in Soloveitchik's Thinking

Three major intellectual approaches characterize the available papers. The first of these is the acceptance of Kant's dichotomy between the mathematical-scientific world, characterized by causality, and the ethical experience of freedom and self-consciousness. Rabbi Soloveitchik retains more respect for human reason than does the usual philosophic existentialist. He accepts science to the point of labeling as allegory the references in the blessing over the new moon to the ultimate perfection of its "blemish" (the *midrash* says it was originally the same size as the sun). He does not believe that people whose lives are dominated by a rationalistic mentality are thereby unable to find God—another difference with Martin Buber, who felt God could not be met in I-It relations to the world. Rabbi Soloveitchik understands the Jewish teaching that the creation is good to mean that nature as such is not Godless and necessarily profane.

As a consequence of his strong sense of the distinction between the objective-scientific aspect of human existence and its personal-experiential side, much of Rabbi Soloveitchik's writing is dialectical. He sees division and tension in every area of human existence. His thought seems unable to find a resting place. He constantly shuttles from one facet of human experience to another, showing the contrast between them and indicating the severe conflicts we feel as a result.

This sensitivity to our dynamic subjectivity separates him from the Jewish Neo-Kantians. Moreover, while he makes some references to the ethical aspect of being a person, that category is not so central to his discussion of the human condition as it is to the Kantians. From the material available, I cannot tell whether he would argue for the reality of an autonomous moral law for all rational beings (Kant and Cohen) as contrasted to a revealed one (Maimonides, in the name of Jewish tradition). Where Kant and his reviewers considered it axiomatic that the universe was rational, Rabbi Soloveitchik does not see the world and our situation in it as fundamentally comprehensible. Precisely because we are thinking ethical beings, alienation is the essential state of personal self-consciousness.

Rabbi Soloveitchik describes many of the dimensions of this alienation and shows how Judaism responds to it without, in this world, ever overcoming it. Thus, he builds his description of human religiosity on the human experience of loneliness. His mentors in this regard, as he notes already in the 1944 essay, were Kierkegaard and Ibsen, but more especially, Scheler and Heidegger. Since almost no one in the Jewish community then was concerned with such thinkers, his thought was little understood and his philosophic disciples were few indeed. Even today, despite a new openness to theology among Jews, one cannot say that there are many cognitively prepared to follow Rabbi Soloveitchik in his enterprise.

Thinking by Means of Essential Types

These two conceptual motifs—dichotomy and dialectic—are shaped and controlled by the notion of typology. Rabbi Soloveitchik's writing deals only with ideal types. He does not treat things as they are, nor does he abstract certain norms from things. He deals rather with pure forms of existence. These are never found in the world, for all historic phenomena are necessarily imperfect manifestations of the ideal patterns. By elucidating these ideal types we can hope to understand the reality in which we are immersed. Rabbi Soloveitchik's utilization of the typological method is fully self-conscious and he acknowledges being influenced in this regard by Eduard Spranger, whose work *Lifeforms* popularized typology in Germany in the early 1920's.

The typological approach to reality can confuse the unsophisticated reader. Most Jewish thinkers work from historical reality and seek to demonstrate a truth or persuade the reader of an interpretation concerning it. Thus, religious existentialists have argued from the emptiness of the human situation to the necessity of a choice for or against God, insisting that in the ultimate decision we will not opt for meaninglessness. Because Rabbi Soloveitchik often moves quickly from his pure, theoretical types to the real situation of people, he may incorrectly be understood to be engaged in this sort of argument. In fact, he does not seek to move skeptics to faith or to give convincing answers to those troubled by doubt. He only explains; he makes no direct effort to convert. He speaks as a man of faith about his faith, not about the reasons why those who stand at its periphery should accept it. Typology serves him as a means of interpreting the Bible or the *halachah*. Where others see only story, morals, or practice, he detects essential truths about the human condition. He is the great elucidator of traditional Judaism's implicit teaching about ideal human types. For one who believes that God has given Torah and commanded us to search out its meaning, that would seem an appropriate form for Jewish theological activity to take.

His method is often also more strictly phenomenological. He describes, in as rational and communicable a fashion as possible, his experience as a human being and believing Jew. He makes no direct claim that everyone must see what he sees or that his is the only true understanding. He only tells us about the religious life, his life—but surely in the hope that the cogency and insight of the picture he has drawn will move us to recognize it is true of us as well.

The Basic Split in Human Nature

Rabbi Soloveitchik discerns a fundamental dualism in human nature which he explicates in terms of a typology he detects in the creation stories. The Adam of one of these accounts is man the maker, controller, and user. Blessed by God with intelligence, he strives to conquer the earth and use it for his good. In this labor he achieves the dignity that lifts him above the level of the brute and makes him truly human. He is thus a social being, for community is useful in difficult projects and it provides for the exchange by which he can express his accomplishments. Though he can set moral norms for himself and experience aesthetic creativity, these do not bring him ultimate satisfaction. He knows his limits, so that, even in the modern situation, he comes looking for God. The trouble is that he insists on understanding God in his own manipulative terms. That is a contradiction that cannot be overcome and which sets up his conflict with the Adam of the second account of creation.

This pure type is of another orientation. He is submissive, for he knows himself to be the servant of God. He is less concerned with creating his own world than with accepting it as God has made it, for he sees God and hears God's command in every aspect of it. In this intimate relationship with God he comes to know himself as an individual and recognizes his uniqueness. So to speak, this gives him his true being and is therefore the most important reality of his life. Yet it is inexpressible, lying beyond all cognition or verbalization. So too, personal verification is a matter of utter isolation, for he can never fully share his certainty with anyone or communicate it to another. Graciously, God provides a setting, Covenant, in which he can ease loneliness. God, "He," becomes the link through which an "I" and a

"Thou" can confront each other. Every genuine community of faith exhibits this tripartite relationship. Only there does the man of faith find companionship and community, though never the overcoming of his ontic singleness.

A contrast with Martin Buber is instructive. Buber had said that while the partners in an encounter maintain their individuality, their isolation is overcome. The one is fully known by the other, which gives the I-Thou relationship its fulfilling quality. Indeed, one does not exist in full selfhood outside such encounters. Rabbi Soloveitchik apparently takes a more atomistic, individualistic view of the self. Though he learns much from Buber about relatedness, he insists that isolation and loneliness are so basic to personhood they cannot be overcome, even momentarily.

Since Adam the first and Adam the second are ideal types, it should not surprise us that Rabbi Soloveitchik believes people actually must live in both realms. Religion suffers today because Adam the first is so dominant culturally that only his manipulative way of thinking is acceptable. We are interested in, even needful of, religion but we then insist that it be limited to cognitive, controllable structures. Anyone in whose soul Adam the second becomes preeminent will feel an extra measure of loneliness in contemporary society. Most people spurn the truth on which Adam the second's faithful existence is grounded. These sensitive spirits are driven back upon themselves socially even as they have always been existentially, and thus must live in two distinct dimensions of alienation.

How Shall We Evaluate Our Situation?

A major difference between Christian and Jewish existentialism emerges as this point. Christian theologians identify contemporary alienation with "the fall" of humankind. People need to be saved from their split and struggling condition. With inner division built into their humanhood, people cannot save themselves. Only God can redeem them—and, Christianity teaches, God has, through the Christ, belief in whom brings people to "new being," that is, a healing of the inner split that prevents them from being fully human.

Judaism apprizes the human situation far more positively. People are an integral element of creation. And the Torah characterizes this creation not as potentially good, but as actually very good. Rabbi Soloveitchik makes a powerful case for alienation being the source of human creativity. "Man is a great and creative being because he is torn by conflict and is always in a state of ontological tenseness and perplexity." Rabbi Soloveitchik maintains that people who refuse to utilize their capacities to relate to the world about them live in existential slavery. As troubled as our situation is, only in accepting it and bringing the resources of our spirit to bear on it do we become true persons. The greatness of the self lies in not denying either the conflicted or the creative aspect of our being but in being able to integrate ourselves ever more fully as persons. He sees the *halachah* as designed to keep the warring parts of our being in proper balance with one another so that we are not defeated in this unrelenting inner struggle.

By contrast to Christianity, Judaism may be called optimistic. It does not denigrate the human situation, despite its realism about our embattled nature. It requires no miraculous act of God to make it possible for us to be the persons we were created to be. Our condition is trying but it can be noble. In addition to the spiritual power God put within each of us, God gave us the Torah. It enables people, through human action, to fulfill the best in them.

This positive view, however, is not so rosy-hued as to assert that a complete resolution of our conflicts can be reached in our lifetime. Our struggle inheres in the human condition and any momentary victory is quickly succeeded by renewed tension. These teachings lay down a personal basis for interpretations of the doctrines of the Messiah, of redemption, and of the life of the world to come, but Rabbi Soloveitchik never published on these eschatological matters.

The careful student of modern Jewish thought will see in Rabbi Soloveitchik's positive approach to human alienation an existentialist transformation of Hermann Cohen's ethical rationalism. Both systems praise the creative possibilities life provides to human reason; both see a moral-personal task laid upon us for our human good; both define accepting that challenge as our unique human duty and glory; both insist it can be accomplished only in part but stretches out infintely before us; and both profess that only in God's End Time will humankind attain true being rather than exist in becoming.

Some Consequences of Our Conflicted Selfhood

The divided self provides the context for one of Rabbi Soloveitchik's discussion of the problem of evil. In a not unfamiliar way, he describes people as having two fundamental identities, the one conferred by destiny, the other arising out of relationship. The former type relies on cognitive efforts to comprehend a world it structures by cause and effect. By definition, such a person's search for a theodicy must end in despair, since only a fully rational solution would be acceptable. The second type of person breaks through notions of natural order to become a free, creative subject, "a partner of God in the work of creation." Loving God, one does not raise metaphysical questions but accepts what comes as God's beneficently ordained challenge. One only asks of God, "What is required of me?" Of course, real people are necessarily mixtures of both types. In the first mode, we can never be satisfied with theologies of suffering and must continually create better ones. As people of faith, we live content with God and unconcerned about answers. Perhaps this explains why Rabbi Soloveitchik did not write directly about the Holocaust.

He utilizes the same dichotomy in explaining the two varieties of ethics that vie for our allegiance. The one derives from what may be termed our "cosmic consciousness," our sense of the unlimited opportunities before us. On the simplest level, we encounter it in our geographic mobility: we might go and live anywhere. More expansively, our intellectual and emotional potentialities seem to make us creatures of universal proportions. Our "origin consciousness" is of another sort altogether. We know how limited we are. Born into a given time, rooted deeply in a certain place, habituated to a specific culture, we feel quite insignificant. The great world about us seems more than we can cope with. In the one mood we create philosophic ethics and glory in the challenge of our responsibilities. We seek success in life and mastery over ourselves and our situation. In the other mood, we practice the ethics of withdrawal. Retreat and resignation appear to be the best means of retaining our integrity.

Once again, neither mode is the only proper or true one. Both occur in any authentic human existence. Real people must utilize the ethics of activism and passivity, avoiding an exclusivity that contradicts their divided nature. And again, the *halachah* helps us to achieve a proper balance between them.

The Shifting Typological Structures

Rabbi Soloveitchik sometimes replaces this twofold understanding of the human being by analyses that utilize three or more aspects of the self. Thus, in arguing against Jewish–Christian theological dialogue, he speaks of three separate, progressive levels of humanhood. As in the typology of the two Adams, he derives these from the biblical account of creation. The earliest stage of humanhood is natural and hedonic, in which creatures are so much at home in the universe that they do not even see it as task or opportunity. In the second phase, they are conscious of nature confronting them and reach out to tame it with their cognitive and normative talents. Should they grow further, they confront other persons as subjects and not merely as other creatures. Despite the joys of companionship, they discover they cannot overcome the barrier that separates one true self from another. In this three-stage typology, a new level, the hedonic, has been introduced into the anthropology. Since the author connects it with much modern conduct, it would be of great interest to know its relation to the scheme of the two Adams. Then too, the third type differs somewhat from the description of Adam the second, further complicating our difficulties in integrating Rabbi Soloveitchik's views.

A somewhat similar tripartite pattern appears when Rabbi Soloveitchik discusses the levels of human relationship to God. At their most basic, people come to God in an oscillation of trust and dread, passive before nature and resigned to its laws. They relate to God essentially in dependency. Many people rise beyond this level to a relationship of love and fear of God. They are conscious of God's law and responsive to it. They serve God not without a certain sense of coercion but mainly out of an awareness that the law is God's good gift whose observance brings one reward. At its best, this religiosity aims at the imitation of God. For on the third level, that of desire and clinging, every element of compulsion disappears. People serve God out of complete freedom, their will fully identified with that of God.

These three phases of piety do not completely correlate with the previous tripartite scheme, even if we allow for the fact that any analysis of religiosity must be far more subjective than one made of ethical motives. Whatever the case here, Rabbi Soloveitchik does not make our task of comprehending him very easy, for elsewhere he refers to four aspects of "the total existential experience—the aesthetic-hedonic, the emotional, the intellectual, the moral-religious. . . ." Our desire to have a coherent understanding of Rabbi Soloveitchik's anthropology must therefore await access to his presently unpublished writings.

Human Beings Are Also Social Beings

Though Rabbi Soloveitchik gives to the individual a central place in his thought, he rejects radical individualism and strongly affirms social existence. Though he has only marginally alluded to his social theory, some of its principles can be set forth. These derive consistently from his interpretation of the two Adams. One form of social organization reflects the human needs to organize and use. We organize ourselves in terms of ethical norms and human responsibility. Another form results from the more directly personal aspect of our humanhood. We create covenantal association when we reach out to other people in freedom, accept them as persons, and recognize God as the third partner in our fellowship.

One cannot identify one or another historic religious community with the ideal, covenantal community of faith. All religions necessarily mix the two ideal modes of human existence, the natural and the covenantal. Only unreflective souls can expect that participating in a given religious institution will assure one of the covenantal experience that assuages existential loneliness. Again, Rabbi Soloveitchik insists on a sharp, conceptual distinction between pure types and historical reality.

He also uses this bipolar analysis to describe the people of Israel. He declares that God made two distinct covenants with Israel, one in Egypt and another at Mt. Sinai. He terms them, respectively, a covenant of destiny and a covenant of relationship. The former describes Jewishness as the situation into which one is born, thus linking one with others in a common past, common suffering, and a common responsibility. The latter covenant predicates Jewish identity as a matter of choice; the community may ignore or freely fulfill the Torah.

For Rabbi Soloveitchik, being a Jew is not merely a matter of fate, a less than human situation, but neither is it only a matter of choice, for that might permit one faithless generation to end four thousand years of steadfast service. Since no person is complete in solitariness, a Jew must move beyond individuality to participate in the Jewish community. Human existence has ineluctable structure. "The individual is bound to his nation by the bonds of fate and the ties of its unique national designation." He can ascribe metaphysical reality to *Knesset Yisrael*—the Jewish people as ideal—predicating its existence as independent of the aggregation of the wills of individual Jews. Speaking of the Land of Israel, he says it was "given to the community as an independent entity, as a distinct juridic metaphysical person."

Contrast Between Halachic and Experiential Piety

True communities of faith may best be distinguished from one another (though, theoretically, not evaluated) in terms of the sort of character they seek to include in their participants. Rabbi Soloveitchik carefully distinguishes the *halachic* response to the sacred from the type of piety found in more subjective forms of religiosity. In personalistic religiosity, faithfulness can be fulfilled in withdrawal from life. Its devotees see piety as a sanctuary from the difficulties of existence.

Rabbi Soloveitchik, refusing to deny the existential torment of the two Adams, cannot accept peace of mind as the goal of genuine religion. Observing the *halachah* can bring us much personal certainty and assurance but the law provides neither a magical resolution of our ontological problems nor an escape from them. Rather, the *halachah* gives proper balance to the inner tension of the two Adams. Its specification requires that Adam the second express his intimately felt relationship with God in deeds done in the objective order of existence. It also frustrates the designs of Adam the first, who is delighted with an objective religious realm he can use to aggrandize his self-image. The *halachah* continually reminds him that he is serving the One God of all creation. All his religious accomplishments are as nothing, for what does the creature not owe its Creator?

One cannot help but see Rabbi Soloveitchik taking great pains here to dissociate his thought from the common Protestant existentialism. Much of his attack on piety as an inner experience seems an implicit polemic against Christianity, if, as is easy, one takes the "religious" personality as the Christian *par excellence* and the *halachic* figure as the Jew. Yet that easy identification will not do. Rabbi Soloveitchik specifically indicates that he is speaking of pure types and that there are other types of Jews than "*halachic* man." Rabbi Soloveitchik also speaks quite favorably about the mystic personality and uses many citations from the literature of Chabad Hasidism to illustrate the nature and virtue of that type. At the same time he obviously believes "*halachic* man" is the superior type of Jew. Indeed, the essay "*Ish Hahalachah*" may be read as an anti-Hasidic tract that seeks to show, by a phenomenology of *mitnagdic* intellectuality, that legalistic rationality contains all the spiritual and emotional power of Hasidism but manages to correct its subjective excesses.

Toward a Rational Ground for Jewish Law

There are some hints in Rabbi Soloveitchik's writing of what may, with some liberties, be called his philosophic validation of the *halachah*. By that I do not mean an effort to argue for its Divine origins or establish its worth in general human terms. Such apologetics are foreign to his purpose. To borrow and reapply Heschel's happy phrase, Rabbi Soloveitchik believes in God's gift of the Torah to the people of Israel as an "ontological presupposition." One does not argue one's ultimate premises.

But Rabbi Soloveitchik does make an implicit response to those existentialists who insist that we are not truly human unless we can exercise personal autonomy. We can best appreciate his response to such a liberalistic view of the self by considering the strategy the Protestant theologian Paul Tillich created to meet this problem. To people who value *auto*nomy, God's law appears to be imposed on the free self and hence morally unacceptable—what Kant called *heter*onomy. For God's law to be acceptable to one whose dignity is tied to personal decision, it must be shown to be the fulfillment of the self and its freedom. This is possible, Tillich opined, precisely because God is the source of our being. God's law cannot be alien to us but is, in fact, our completion—*theo*nomy fulfills *auto*nomy.

In a number of places Rabbi Soloveitchik identifies the *halachah* as God's theonomic completion of our personal freedom. In commenting on the rabbinic comment that an embryo knows the entire Torah, he says, "By learning Torah man returns to his own self, man finds himself, and advances to a charted, illuminated and speaking I-existence. Once he finds himself, he finds redemption." He explicitly offers this sort of argument in clarifying what he considers the highest form of relationship to God. Then, "one lives according to the Torah and commandments with great joy. One desires to do the will of God as if the will of the Infinite One (*En Sof*) was also the will of the finite person. The wonder of the identification of wills, we see in the third stage." Obviously, the communion of purpose is possible for an authentic human being because one's personal will is perfected in the Divine will.

Then why does *halachah* occasionally demand acts we do not understand and, on our own, we would not legislate? Rabbi Soloveitchik answers by reference to the dialectic of the self. One aspect of human existence, we must remember, seeks acceptance and surrender. "Precisely because of the supremacy of the intellect in human life, the Torah requires, at times, the suspension of the authority logos. Man defeats himself by accepting norms that the intellect cannot assimilate into its normative system. The Judaic concept of *hok* [the inexplicable precept] represents human surrender and human defeat."

Problems of Typological Thinking

Rabbi Soloveitchik's unique contribution to the field of modern Jewish thought is not without its critics.

Regardless of one's position on Orthodox Judaism, the substance of his thought, the use of typology as a conceptual tool always raises difficulties for thoughtful readers. Typologies may illuminate, but it is never clear whence the types arise, why these and not others are selected, how the types used for various situations relate to one another, and what gives the total universe of types its integrity. A Christian might well ask, if the *ish hahalachah* is a pure type, must one be a Jew to be an *ish hahalachah*? If so, why do Jews have a separate ideal type? Moreover, not only are types usually universal, many of the characteristics of *halachic* man could easily be applied to personality types in other religions. In Roman Catholicism, one may point to the Jesuits, whose emphasis on intellectuality and observance is akin to *halachic* piety. If acceptable, this interpretation would change the way most Jews read Rabbi Soloveitchik's most famous essay—though he is not to blame for their conversion of typologies into value judgments or authorizations for Jewish practice.

The problem of applying a typology to reality is particularly difficult. Rabbi Soloveitchik used a tripartite analysis of the human situation to argue that Jews might join with Christians in working for common social welfare concerns. Level two, the cognitive-normative level, where these are worked out, is one where all mature people can meet. But the progress to level three, that of true faith, reduces us to utter individuality. Though we may then join in covenantal association with others of similar faith, our basic sense of certainty and the content of our belief remain ultimately incommunicable. Therefore, Rabbi Soloveitchik argues, Jews and Christians should not, because they cannot, discuss theology. But when is direct extrapolation from the realm of ideal types to the real mixed human situation proper and when is it not? To be sure, people have incredible difficulty in communicating with one another about their deepest beliefs, yet Rabbi Soloveitchik's own success in clarifying the nature of the life of faith belies the absolute futility of such efforts by others. Moreover, applied rigidly, this position would prevent our accepting converts to Judaism, an uncommon position in the *halachah*, since conversion involves our deepest beliefs.

The Virtues of Typology for Orthodoxy

If existentialist Jewish theologies suffer from their inability to mandate structured Jewish action, typological theology will not remedy the fault. The movement from pure types to our mixed reality is always open to ambiguity. Knowing that the ideal pattern of human existence must include appropriate authority does not logically lead to the content of that authority, to what a real person must do. Why should one be accepting rather than creative in the face of a *hok*, an inexplicable precept? Rabbi Soloveitchik is content with a typological framework for his thought because he does not require theology to authorize action. That matter is already settled in his faith. He can know— though this is neither as simple nor as free of anxiety as it often seems to the non-Orthodox—what God wants him to do. His theology follows upon that reality. It does not presume to substantiate it. Rabbi Soloveitchik seeks only to illumine the meaning of believing Jewish existence by exposing its universal human aspects.

Still, typology has a great virtue. It enables a believer to bring a cognitive pattern to bear on what one knows but simultaneously confesses cannot properly be expressed. Where Heschel uses style, shock, and the inversion of questions to awaken and evoke, Rabbi Soloveitchik utilizes typology and phenomenology to expose something of the depth of his faith. He is therefore in closer communication with the thoughtful, but uncommitted inquirer than is Heschel. Though his types hover in some abstract realm transcending reality, they provide cognitive structures for understanding the amorphous arena of faith. Occasionally, too, they are quite compelling when they cast new light on the concrete situations in which people find themselves. For a moment the life of faith as seen by faith stands open.

Typological theology can be particularly persuasive today. Modern intellectuality no longer receives automatic credence when it disagrees with Jewish tradition. Participation in modernity no longer implies the rejection of Orthodoxy. The quality of life engendered by contemporary society seems inferior to that nurtured by traditional Judaism, as influenced by the Emancipation. Many modern Jews consider that fact a sufficient reason for a return to a more thoroughgoing commitment to Orthodox Judaism. The theological awareness underlying that socially determined attitude is then easy to state and accept. A good God would not leave humankind bereft and unguided. Jewish life and history confirm what Jewish faith has proclaimed: God gave Israel the Torah and those who live by its laws are sanctified and sanctify their people. To those who by life and faith know the truth of traditional Judaism, Rabbi Soloveitchik's thought provides an invaluable interpretation of their most fundamental, if ineffable, intuition.

The Need for a Second Type of Jewish Theology

What remains missing in Rabbi Soloveitchik's thinking is the way by which searching, critical moderns might come to such faith. The traditional Jewish doctrine of revelation—that God revealed the oral as well as the written Torah, including the methods and therefore the conclusions reached by the sages of our time—may be axiomatic to Heschel and Rabbi Soloveitchik, but it powerfully troubles many modern Jews. Their most basic understanding of human dignity and the most important lessons of contemporary intellect, especially history, will not let them accept the notion that any person, code, or institution should have sway over their conscience. The traditionalist theologian needs either to establish the Torah's authority for them or to help them find a way to believe in it. Heschel speaks to that subject in his particular way. Rabbi Soloveitchik does not. From what he published, we may reasonably conclude that he did not. His typological method certainly is incapable of that task. Moreover, his effectiveness is limited by his heavy reliance on existentialist categories that he employs to argue that faith is ineffable. One cannot then argue over an orthodoxy. This device protects his premises but also limits the usefulness of his philosophy. Most Jews do not begin with his faith but might be open to argument seeking to demonstrate its reasonableness. If, inquiring about a belief they might like to hold but find they cannot, they are told it is beyond any sort of exploration, then this theology cannot speak to their questions.

An unexpected issue now provides the crux of the dispute between revelation and modernity, namely, the question of the equality of women in Judaism. Being *obligated* to do the *halachah* has been seen as the hallmark of Jewish responsibility. If so, the substantial difference Jewish law assigns to the duties of women and men seems to make women not only separate but also a religiously unequal group. Is God the ultimate source of these distinctions or are they essentially human enactments? For all its problems, Western civilization has claimed ethical attention by universalizing the biblical doctrine of the equality of all people—a matter of no small importance to a clan as despised and segregated as the Jews once were. Against apparently ethical social pressures, shall faithful Jews not stand firm behind the present interpreters of the unbroken chain of Sinaitic tradition and affirm that Jewish women, as such, must have a different standard of religious obligation? Or is the Torah, for all its sublimity, an expression of the human spirit responding to God, whose sanctifying teachings of one age may need to be rethought in radically changed social circumstances?

Questions such as these necessarily divide those who accept the classic understanding of the Sinaitic revelation from those who do not.

Hence there must be two basic types of Jewish theology today, the Orthodox and the liberal, a situation not uncommon in most faiths.

In the Orthodox community thinkers continue to wrestle with the issue of dealing intellectually with modernity—particularly its emphasis on personal autonomy. The variety of their approaches is well illustrated by the systematic statements of Michael Wyschogrod (*The Body of Faith*) and David Hartment (*A Living Covenant*).

Wyschogrod: Reversing the Thrust of Jewish Philosophy

Formerly chairman of the Department of Philosophy of Baruch College, City University of New York, Michael Wyschogrod has found a way to speak the language of contemporary culture without compromising his passionate Orthodoxy. A generation ago doing so generally meant giving a certain authority to what the university judged to be true and then rethinking Judaism in its terms. However, this avenue always created difficulties because academic thought was resolutely secular—making belief in God problematic—and was universalistic—thereby reducing Judaism to only another faith. For a devoted Orthodox Jew, that approach was "good" methodology dictating assimilation; hence it was utterly unacceptable. No wonder there has been so little systematic Orthodox theology. In more recent times, the result has been the rejection by the right-wing Orthodox of university education, including that offered by Orthodox institutions like Yeshiva University. Wyschogrod is convinced that he will not compromise his faith if he carefully utilizes only that kind of philosophy which is reasonably adaptable to Judaism's truth.

For his apologetic and communicative purposes, Wyschogrod early took up the thought of Martin Heidegger (whose Nazism he believes can be separated from his philosophical ideas). Its (secular) theory of Being often sounds like classic religious treatments of God. Thus Heidegger's notion of Being breaking through to human consciousness makes possible a strong sense of revelation. And Heidegger's commitment to particularity and historicity equally allows for a rich sense of the people of Israel's relationship with God. This notion allows Wyschogrod's thought to base itself on God's revelation even more centrally than that of that other great exponent of revelation, Abraham Heschel. Where Heschel says that the prophetic pathos indicates mainly God's feelings (and Buber says God never becomes an "It" for us), Wyschogrod argues that the Bible gives us quite explicit information about God's nature. It tells us God is a Person, One with a definite character and "psychology." Even more important, it discloses the Divine Person's name.

We therefore have a philosophical grounding for Judaism's teaching that the Bible tells us what God wants us to do. Most of the injunctions make immediate good sense but, knowing now something of God's greatness, we also realize we cannot hope to understand the reason for them all. Wyschogrod, describing our relationship to God, does not hesitate to use the famous Hegelian terms and say we are the Slaves of the Master. To be sure, God has made us free creatures but we must use our autonomy only within the area delineated by the Master and delimited by God's awesome presence. This view of God's exalted transcendence not only authorizes a rich life of Torah; it teaches us how we must face evil. God, not we, knows what is best, but only an understanding equivalent to God's could know why the righteous suffer. In contrast, modern questioning too easily passes over into presumption. Rather than overstepping our limits, we should do the commandments, accept sacrifice when it is unavoidable, and be grateful for every good the Master bestows on us.

This philosophy seems almost anti-modern, and some polemical intent clearly seems present. However, Wyschogrod's indebtedness to the culture is also plain. His work, for all its uncommon accents, is determinedly philosophical. It includes a striking defense of the rights of conscience once self-determination is founded on and respectful of biblical revelation. He thereby offers an Orthodox theology of democratic pluralism, something no other Orthodox thinker has done. And despite his acceptance of a strong, almost literalistic, theory of God's revelation, he is sufficiently troubled by the problem of evil that he makes no effort to restate the biblical view of God's retribution.

Though Wyschogrod's philosophy would seem to commend itself to the Orthodox who wish to keep culture at a certain distance, it has attracted only modest attention among his fellow believers. The ostensible reason is his resolute biblicism, a trait made particularly egregious by his principled refusal to let rabbinic teaching in any way infringe upon God's direct revelation. Some trace this unusual approach to Judaism to his long involvement in interfaith activity and a desire to demonstrate the close affinity between Christianity and Judaism. For these and other reasons it remains problematic how much his thought will influence Orthodoxy.

Hartman: How Modern Can Orthodoxy Be?

David Hartman's work has taken the more familiar road of an apologetic for Orthodoxy, a seeking to answer modernist charges of its legalism, passivity, rigidity, and impersonal focus. Acknowledging that his is but one way of understanding the rabbinic tradition, he wishes to show how it validates his appealingly personalistic, voluntaristic, and human-centered view.

His interpretation of Judaism largely in terms of what it does for humans rather than as a response to God's specific commands has a systematic basis. Hartman's Orthodoxy does not center about Sinai and a strong, God-dominated theory of revelation. Rather he sees Sinai, for all its importance and symbolic centrality, as the archetypal beginning, one that not only allows for but positively encourages individual initiative in responding to God. Thus his general apologetic stance strongly resembles that of religious liberals, and echoes of this position are heard in his entire reading of the Jewish tradition.

A significant example of this approach is Hartman's treatment of the central metaphor of his book, Covenant. He thinks of the Covenant between God and the people of Israel as a relationship of love, making little reference to it as contract (which would highlight its binding obligations). This view allows the relationship to have a mutuality of the partners that far exceeds the traditional sense of the human role in covenant making or keeping. The commandments now become the gifts of God's love that the community follows out of its love for God and its sense of their spiritual utility. They are not what we must do in return for God's saving us from slavery or out of fear of God's punishments or desire for God's rewards. Moreover, Hartman does not claim that they cement an utterly unique Jewish relationship with God, one more significant than that of any other faith. We know only that we are part of Israel and lovingly, beneficially share in its quite particular history and tradition.

Hartman's Orthodox revisionism leads him to respectful criticism of his teacher, Rabbi Soloveitchik, and the great intellectual maverick of Israeli Orthodoxy, Isaiah Leibowitz. He finds the thought of the former much too submissive. He considers Rabbi Soloveitchik's view that Jewish law sets proper bounds to the tempestuous human spirit insufficiently appreciative of human spirituality. For similar reasons he rejects Leibowitz's *halachic* positivism which denies human useful-ness as a motive for Jewish observance. The Israeli thinker asserts that we must follow the commandments because God commanded us to; it is that simple. No other reason is needed for observance or could be of equal weight.

Since this idea radically contradicts Hartman's personalism, he finds it unacceptable. But just how far Hartman takes his espousal of human initiative in Jewish practice is not clear, and we will learn its power only when we have some significant *halachic* rulings by him.

In his thoughtful, feelingly presented case Hartman makes telling use of Maimonides' thought, for that consummate rationalist often gives maximum play to human initiative in the life of Torah. But Mai-monides, following the Rabbis, believed that God had given both the Written and the Oral Law and that we were therefore bound to follow them. Moreover, in them God had given us the ultimate truth about God, humankind, and history. Therefore, the people of Israel, its only recipient, was "chosen from among all other peoples." Hartman denies the metaphysical singularity of Sinai and the prophetic tradition, reducing chosenness to a metaphor. It is a most daring, courageous vision of Orthodox Judaism and, perhaps as a result, it has not earned much acceptance in the Israeli or American Orthodox communities.

Despite their astuteness and appeal to different elements in Orthodoxy, neither Wyschogrod's nor Hartman's thought lies behind the recent resurgence of Orthodoxy. That has had largely a social basis, the desire to dissociate oneself from the evils of modernity. From this perspective thinkers like Wyschogrod and Hartman—and to some extent even Rabbi Soloveitchik—have been perceived as giving Gentile culture too much credence. Those passionate on this issue carry on Jewish thought in traditional fashion, by writing of commentaries on the Torah and other classic texts, by works of ethical exhortation, and by the *halachic* reasoning that seeks to determine what God wants of us today. These may not be the intellectual forms esteemed by the university, but centuries of Jewish reflection stand behind them. Momentarily, at least, the future of Orthodox Jewish philosophical speculation, by contrast, will remain clouded until contemporary rationality regains some of its old authority.

11

The Turn to Mysticism

WHILE the rise of a vigorous, culturally sophisticated Orthodoxy would have surprised the Jewish thinkers of mid-century, the parallel growth of a living Jewish mysticism would have astounded them. They thought it incontrovertible that being modern meant doing all our thinking and decision-making rationally, a process that took for granted the scientific understanding of the world. Orthodoxy had little future in this world view, and mysticism seemed medieval fantasy and superstition. The academic study of Judaism was similarly identified with strict rationality and so from its beginning it shunned the texts of Jewish mysticism, considering their content unworthy of a serious mind. Nonetheless, the emergence of Jewish mysticism as an academic discipline has had some bearing on the rebirth of this Jewish spirituality, making some comment about its scholarly career appropriate.

A specific cultural factor heavily influenced the prior deprecation of the kabbalistic tradition. ("*Kabbalah*" literally means "reception"; in rabbinic literature it figuratively became "tradition"; eventually it has become "the [whole] mystic tradition," though it more specifically refers to the Zoharic tradition, the *Zohar* being the late-thirteenth-century Spanish Jewish work basic to all later mystic speculation.) German culture—out of which modern Jewish scholarship and thought arose—esteemed philosophy as the summit of human rationality. Considering the towering philosophical figures eighteenth- and nineteenth-century Germany produced—Kant, Hegel, and Nietzsche, for example—the widespread academic contempt for the nonrational is understandable. Jews, eager to modernize, and utilizing the university to do so, shared this bias. It had at least two positive results: the vigorous academic study of medieval Jewish philosophy and the initial steps by creative minds to philosophize about Judaism.

Giving Mysticism Its Proper Place in Jewish History

All this changed with the pathbreaking work of one of the greatest Jewish scholars of the twentieth century, Gershom Scholem. Beginning just after World War I, his painstaking, resolutely cognitive study of the literature and history of Jewish mysticism clearly established it as a major strand in Jewish religiosity.

Scholem, an avid Zionist, immigrated to Palestine in 1923 and became an early staff member of the fledgling Hebrew University in Jerusalem. His steady output of studies employing the rigorous philological, critical method he had learned at the great German universities showed that the Jewish mystical tradition was older, more indigenous and, as the Middle Ages wore on, more widely significant than was philosophy. And in the widespread fervor that greeted the messianic pretensions of Sabbetai Zevi and then the Hasidic movement, mysticism became a mass movement, something Jewish philosophy never did. In all this work Scholem also exposed the coherent intellectual structure behind the imagistic texts that rationalistic modern Jewish intellectuals considered to be the bizarre fantasies of unsophisticated minds. In fact, he contended, Jewish mysticism was distinguished by its highly cognitive character and by its uncommon reinforcement of religious practice.

Scholem had no interest in reestablishing the practice of mysticism among Jews. His work was purely, some would say coldly, academic. So to speak, he validated Jewish mysticism to the rational intellectual world by revealing the unusual mental constructs that the mystic's experience found appropriate. Scholem died in 1982 but his influence remains great. Some of his students have suggested that his work needs to be supplemented to provide a greater place for the experiential aspects of Jewish mysticism but such an endeavor should be understood as a continuation of Scholem's own methods.

From the Academy Into People's Lives

In the 1960's an American cultural rebellion against a triumphant modernity took place for reasons historians have yet to clarify. A widespread mistrust of institutions and social conventions suddenly became manifest. Its positive result was a rejection of impersonal human processing in favor of a profound affirmation of individuality, selfhood, and caring interpersonal relationships. This shift from mind to whole person suggested the value of comprehending reality by more than the rigidities of science and logic, implying specifically that one might hope to learn far more by searching the depths of one's own self. (Critics have connected this turn to subjectivity with the then endemic disillusionment with social institutions.)

The new American Jewish mysticism arose from this seismic cultural shift. The adventurous turned to Asian or quasi-Asian religious teachers or communities, in itself a telling rejection of American culture. Others preferred psychologized movements that taught them how to find greater depths in their own being while remaining a participant in Western culture but at a certain distance. Through these movements and beyond them were the many searchers who turned to drugs to gain a new level of consciousness, with marijuana, considered the "safe" one, most widely used. As always, a disproportionate number of Jews joined the new cultural movements, and when the movements began to abate, a small but increasing number turned to their own tradition for guidance. They found that Scholem and his disciples had already charted the history and content of Jewish mysticism. But the searchers wanted something more, the contemporary practice of Jewish mysticism, and they discovered the teachers of Jewish mystical practice waiting for them. They soon found a place in ongoing Jewish community life, though the movement has, in many respects, been itself somewhat domesticated as a result. (One motive leading some Jews to Orthodoxy was their search for an authentic Jewish mysticism and a community in which to live it.)

The Mystic Life: Lived, Not Thought

We now confront a procedural difficulty: the contradiction between mysticism's central insight and our desire for clear explanation. World-wide, the great mystics teach about gaining access to a height of reality hidden from ordinary consciousness. They also say this takes one far beyond what the mind can envision or words express. The higher one ascends and the more refined one's insight, the more inexpressible it is; anything other than attentive silence verges on blasphemy. Yet, para-doxically, one can discover this personally if one learns and practices the teacher's way of delving into and beyond one's very self. The Bible refers to this strange nearness-farness of God when it says we cannot "see God's face" yet insists we live in intimate partnership with God. And the Rabbis capture this ambivalence in the rule that though we know God's personal, four-letter name, we may never say it (and so we say "Adonai" instead).

This duality of content and method led to mystic teaching's be-ing quite personal, imparted by a teacher to a worthy disciple only orally and in private. For a long time the esoteric tradition was not put in writing and so we have no biblical texts clearly alluding to Jewish mystical practice or experience, and only a tantalizing few references in the early rabbinic centuries. While such documents as surfaced later have increasingly been analyzed by academics, to this day the living practice of Jewish mysticism is communicated more in person by one's mentor—one's "rebbe"—than by any text, rite, or utterance. When compared with the living bond between the guide and the seeker, everything explicit seems trivial, per-haps even foolish. With this bond, the hidden meanings dawn and a growing insight opens up one's ability to perceive the truths being communicated.

Those to Whom the Searchers Turn Today

Mysticism would thus seem to be the enemy of thought, yet, as Scholem taught us, Jewish mysticism has been highly cognitive and we can therefore learn by studying its ideas. Nonetheless, we miss its own understanding of true religiosity if we do not first say something about those contemporary *rebbes* who have sought to communicate its truth to moderns.

Many of these spiritual guides are, as in the past, anonymous. They did not publish or have large numbers of disciples and yet, as people learned to seek, they found these mentors available. In most large cities in recent decades one could, with a bit of effort, learn by word-of-mouth who was teaching Jewish mysticism. Some have become widely known, influencing substantial numbers. Perhaps the mystic leader most widely identified with the religious transformation that began in the 1960's—the "Jewish renewal movement"—is Zalman Schachter-Shalomi. Now retired from Temple University, Zalman—or Reb Zalman, as his followers refer to him—was European born and was ordained in America at a Lubavitcher *yeshivah*. He soon became known for his unusual ability to reach many types of Jews. Part of his great appeal came from the embracing scope of his spirituality. He was unique among Hasidim in his passion to learn from the mystics of all religions, not only to study their texts but—knowing how much mystic insight depended on the personal—also to expose himself to the instruction of their contemporary saints. He also manifested an impressive Jewish erudition in his instruction, drawing as easily upon the mystic classics and esoterica as from the Rabbis. All this learning he blended with his rare ability to speak to people in their own idiom, accepting contemporary culture's truth while making it a vehicle for his own Jewish teaching. He left Lubavitch some years ago and now heads a community/organization called *P'nai Or*, literally "Faces of Light" but easily understood as "the enlightened."

Zalman's publications have been few, a testimony to the conflict that so overflowing a soul feels at the constriction of the printed page. From what he has written he seems less the creator of a new interpretation of the Jewish mystical experience than a master who has made the past his own, has refined it in the crucible of his soul, and thus, continually renewed and refreshed, makes it live again in new hearts. A better sense of Zalman's special power comes through the audio and video tapes made of his actual instruction. Yet his renowned effectiveness testifies to the mystics' truth that the *rebbe*'s person communicates far more than do the words. The sociologist Max Weber coined a term for the special gift some leaders have of communicating as much by their very being as by any direct teaching. He called it "charisma."

On the Variety of Jewish Mystical Experience

Some Jewish mystic teachers exhibit their charisma in quietude, others by their apparently unfailing effusion of spirit, some by uncanny personal insight, others by their depth of thought. Not uncommonly, spiritual seekers must spend time with several *rebbes* before they find one who illumines their soul.

Proof of the widespread recent appeal of Jewish mysticism is its appearance in the last decade or so in Reform Judaism, not so long ago the most rationalistic movement in our community. Perhaps the most visible of its charismatic mystic mentors is Lawrence Kushner, a congregational rabbi in Sudbury, Massachusetts. How a child of the American Middle West (Detroit), who grew up in a relatively classical Reform congregation and was ordained by the Reform seminary, spurned the rationalism of most of his teachers and developed a mystical spiritual life and a love of Hasidic-kabbalistic texts is a story yet to be told. In many ways Kushner mirrors the fundamental shift of caring Jews in the past half century, taking his quest more seriously than most of them care to do.

Kushner's great charisma is given a special sheen by his uncommon talent for homiletics, that is, public textual instruction. Often he exercises it by culling and restating the observations of classic mystic masters, retelling their tales and restating their homilies in a fashion all his own. This ingenious recycling has the effect of making them newly compelling, a style, incidentally, with solid rabbinic-Hasidic precedent.

Or he will open up a chosen text in his own fashion, utilizing whatever cultural trend—psychoanalysis, for example—attracts his fertile imagination and speaks to his listeners. He has also brought to his several books an aesthetic sensitivity that has enabled him to speak to his reader more than verbally. And he has a delicious sense of humor that somehow illuminates his quite serious point. Much of this comes easily off the page to his reader, giving one an indication of the exceptional impact personal study with him must engender.

Kushner's work remains too unsystematic for any good sense of its overall outlines or its special contribution to Jewish mystic thought. Still the possibilities remain intriguing. Scholem suggested that, unlike those faiths in which personal spirituality tended to oppose established tradition, Jewish mysticism has created especially observant Jews (a pattern that continues). Classic Reform Judaism overrode the authority of the law by making reason rather than revelation sovereign. If mysticism now replaces reason in Reform Judaism, on what basis does it maintain the right of dissent from the past? Perhaps this question, which transcends one movement and states the problem besetting all serious non-Orthodoxy today, may receive its answer from this charismatic rabbi.

These two well-received mystic masters must represent here the many other teachers, old and young, Orthodox and non-Orthodox, female and male, who quietly carry on the personal work of nurturing Jewish souls. We turn now from personalities to ideas, dividing our attention between those who seek essentially to communicate the received tradition and those who, consciously or unconsciously, have given it creative restatement.

Adin Steinsaltz: Our Generation's Great Commentator

One caveat must be entered before we turn to the traditionalists: this kind of presentation makes the idea-systems of traditional Jewish mysticism sound more fixed and static than they ever were. Even where one can identify a significant resemblance among mystic teachers—what we term a "school of thought"—differences generally abound. There is almost always a greater looseness of terminology and images (which proliferate grandly in *kabbalah*) than one finds even in the notoriously fluid midrashic literature. One must therefore always keep in mind the mystic's need to transcend the limitations of language.

Two teachers will serve as our representatives of those who seek to impart the message of *kabbalah*, Adin Steinsaltz and Aryeh Kaplan. Neither grew up as an observant Jew and both came to Judaism and its mysticism as a result of their inner growth. That fact makes their mastery of Jewish tradition, impressive on its own, even more extraordinary.

Steinsaltz is justly renowned for his project of issuing a new, contemporary reader's edition of the Talmud (the Talmud of the Land of Israel as well as that of Babylonia), seeking to make this classic available to people without *yeshivah* training. To that end he daringly provided its text with vowels and modern punctuation. More important, he provided a running commentary to the talmudic discussion, presenting its meaning in simple modern Hebrew as well as identifying (sometimes with drawings) various objects mentioned in the text. The erudition and skill required for this undertaking are staggering, particularly as Steinsaltz remains faithful to the traditional understanding of the text while communicating its meaning to the contemporary reader.

He has done something less textual and more general in his Jerusalem lectures on Jewish mysticism. Some of these have been transcribed and translated by his disciples but he himself presented a comprehensive statement of his view of *kabbalah* in a volume entitled *The Thirteen Petalled Rose* (a metaphor for the people of Israel, used in the opening lines of the Zohar).

In direct, simple language Steinsaltz sets before his readers a dazzling view of the structure of reality as he, in the tradition of later Hasidim, sees it. The world we humans know is but one part of an inconceivably vast system of worlds, most of which is utterly unknowable. But by God's revelation to the prophets and the insights of the mystic masters we have learned all we need to know to take our proper place in God's universe.

What Is the Kabbalistic World View?

There are four tightly related "worlds." These are, beginning with the most spiritual, the world of Emanation, *atzilut;* that of Creation, *beriah;* that of Formation, *yetzirah;* and the one in which we live, that of Action, *asiah.* The world of Emanation is one of utter clarity and transparency, so it is as good as identical with God. (One must always remember in these locutions about God that God, spoken of as the One related to and involved in the worlds, is/isn't somehow the En Sof, the One Without Bounds, about whom nothing at all can properly be said.) The world of Creation is less transparent to God and may be said to be the realm of spiritually perfected mind. Only the most exalted prophets and saints have attained it and gained its great prize: the most intimate possible human insight into God and the system of the four worlds. More opaque still is the world of Formation, which Steinsaltz uniquely describes as a realm of pure feeling, one whose constituents and patterns are determined by emotion. And most opaquely, we exist in the world of Action, the one where the physical appears to complement the spirit, though the distinction between them is essentially an illusion. (Thus, while the four "worlds" are quite "real," they are not so in a physical sense, in contrast to what seems common sense in our world.)

Steinsaltz says much more about the similarities in structure between the worlds but perhaps the most significant thing to remember is the dynamic character of this arrangement, with energies continually flowing back and forth between the worlds. The decisive factor in changing these energy flows is humans' willing and doing, for all the worlds are characterized by determinism, with one critical exception: human beings. We are created with free will, so what we do with our freedom has cosmic consequences, the four worlds being so thoroughly interrelated.

Thus only when Adam and Eve still dwelt in Eden was the structure of all reality fully harmonious. Once they sinned, our world and its three counterparts became disordered. Human sin throughout history has only further disturbed the worlds, impeding the flow of Divine goodness from above to below and transforming God's beneficent energy into an energy as harmful to the spiritual "creatures" of the universe as to human beings. Fortunately, the dynamic also works the other way; every act of human good—particularly the performance of the commandments, *mitzvot*—restores and perfects the broken universe, in a process called *tikkun*. Thus the classic Jewish process of turning from sin to righteousness, *teshuvah*, is as critical for the universe as it is for the human relationship with God.

The Subtleties of Divine–Human Interaction

Human beings are therefore very much at the center of this dynamic understanding of reality. But this point must not be overstated so as to deprive God of absolute sovereignty. Indeed, what gives humans their unparalleled role in existence is that in some obscure way they have a portion of God in them; Steinsaltz does not hesitate to say, metaphorically but truly, that in one sense they are God. To be sure, this may be said of everything, that if it were not for the power and presence of God in them they could not possibly exist. God is that Presence in all the worlds and their "creatures."

God becomes manifest everywhere through the ten *sefirot*, the nodes of Divine energy or "character," and the Divine-human closeness is worked out in a special way in the human form, with the human body corresponding to the configuration and interplay of the *sefirot*. This closeness of form makes it possible for anyone to undertake mystic ascent and achieve greater intimacy with God. At its highest, in the case of Moses, this process can result in unimpeded, fully realized communion with God.

Alas, there is a dark side to this multi-world universe, for though God is truly present in the worlds of ever lesser spirituality, God's hiddenness necessarily increases in them, and it is radically exacerbated by the record of unrelenting human sinfulness. *Kabbalah*, then, helps us understand the sorry record of human history and teaches us how we may rise above the threatening chaos to reverse it.

One effect of the opaqueness of God in our world is that *kabbalah* must be hidden in the Torah in all its many forms. Yet when one learns how to read it kabbalistically, the Torah provides us with the one sure understanding of how to repair this broken world. Actions are particularly powerful and thus the Torah's emphasis on deeds. Every *mitzvah* performed creates a good angel, a "creature" of the world of Formation, who accompanies one, with beneficent effect. But every sin creates a malevolent angel-companion who seeks to cause us harm. God's reward and punishment operate this way, and their obvious imperfections are traced, not to the system, but to our unfulfilled obligations in our prior lives—the transmigration of souls being affirmed—and our involvement with the guilt and merit of others in our time. The steady emphasis on Torah and *mitzvot* is climaxed in the kabbalistic view of the people of Israel. While all human beings have access to God via the cosmic scheme, the people of Israel concentrates holiness in itself through its way of life. It is "the heart of the nations."

What Steinsaltz Does for Us—and What He Doesn't Do

This sketch of Steinsaltz's understanding of "the essence of Jewish existence and belief," the subtitle of his book, provides a hint of how admirably he has summarized the vast kabbalistic tradition. Of course, he has given his own reading of it, but that too is part of the Jewish mystic's way.

In one respect his manner of presenting his *kabbalah* is quite modern. The standard kabbalistic rhetoric has eschewed making the "hidden" so public. It communicates merely by allusive hints amid midrashic interpretations of texts or through creative allegorical tales. But Steinsaltz lays out the doctrine before his reader as simply and directly as he can, often providing scientific or mathematical analogies to his ideas. He is also continually sensitive to the modern identification of "meaning" with relevance to one's personal life. He therefore often seeks to show how the individual self finds fulfillment through the mystic approach to living and the Jewish discipline that channels it. Yet in a critical move he sharply breaks with the rationalistic assumptions of modernity. First, he ignores its bedrock procedure:

Descartes' dictum that people should doubt every thought that they cannot turn into a clear and distinct idea, that is, one that rationalistically convinces them. Second, he pays no attention to our culture's naturalistic world view and refuses to explain "reality" in its scientific, secular terms. Instead, he states the truth he has "received" and only then shows its application to the readers' world.

A not insignificant number of contemporary Jews who read Steinsaltz, and read others who explicate the kabbalistic tradition, quickly respond to these mystics. Something in their souls that has not been touched by other modes of interpreting Judaism finds a spiritual home here. Many more may be touched by various aspects of what is said but find themselves troubled by a number of its aspects, ones that arise far more from the nature of *kabbalah* than from his interpretation of it.

Some Questions About Mysticism That Trouble Seeking Moderns

Consider the highly peripheral place of history, at least recent history, in this teaching. Steinsaltz and other mystics can discuss the basic nature of Judaism without significant reference to the Holocaust or the State of Israel. Obviously Steinsaltz is deeply affected by both but he is still more fundamentally touched by the kabbalistic understanding of the relationship between God and the worlds, and particularly by people's (specifically the Jewish people's) role as restorers of the lost perfection. Recent history changes only the specific backdrop against which we must act on our essential responsibility. The fundamental truth has not been altered by it—the reason mystics worldwide call their teaching the "perennial philosophy."

Note, too, the intense interiority of this Judaism. While it esteems action, the deeds are valuable not for what they do in the external world but for their effect on the four worlds. The intention that accompanies the deed, the proper mystic *kavannah*, not the actualities created by politics or community building, constitutes the most effective *tikkun*, the repair of the disordered cosmos.

A related problem arises in mysticism's response to the problem of evil. On one level, it seems simply to ignore it; thus it finds no important place in Steinsaltz's presentation. God is the one and only reality; how then can evil truly exist? Of course we claim we see evil around us but that is so because we do not have a proper understanding of God and God's relation to us. On this higher level of mystic understanding there "is" no evil, for only the abiding good, one God has and can confer reality. Even mystics cannot long live at that height of insight. So on the lesser level that we call existence, we find evils abound and we, through Torah, must do what we can to fight them. This "second best" attitude toward Jewish practice and Jewish ethics is quite different from the primacy given them in other interpretations of Judaism.

In some places the Zohar teaches that we must give evil far more reality than to call it, essentially, an illusion arising from faulty perception. In these comments it daringly suggests that four evil "worlds" exist as parallels to the four realms of goodness. The Sitra Achra, the Other Side, is almost as real and powerful as the realms of goodness, and its infernal "creatures" are responsible for much of our pain. Some of the late Hasidic mysticism has preferred to concentrate on God and God's good power, with the result that the problem of evil disappears when one properly communes with God.

The ultimate issue for the searching modern is how Steinsaltz or any mystic teacher knows such esoteric truth. And on what basis is it asserted with such certainty that others ought to live by its discipline?

An anecdote Gershom Scholem once related in my presence may clarify the two different kinds of mentality involved here. When Scholem first came to Palestine he sought out a highly regarded Jerusalem kabbalist and asked to study with him. The adept agreed to accept him as a student but said he must accept two absolute conditions. The first was that Scholem must never in any way try to pay or otherwise reward him, something Scholem quickly agreed to. The second was that no matter what the provocation, Scholem must never ask him a question, and this, Scholem said, was the end of their conversation.

In all the non-Orthodox thinkers we considered above, the issue of warrants, the grounds for believing a certain understanding of things, was critical. It caused the thinkers to move from one way of thinking about Judaism to another, hoping thereby to make their case more convincing, at least more reasonable. Moderns may have carried skepticism too far but most people believe it remains the individual's best safeguard against arbitrary and capricious teaching. Steinsaltz at least commands our respect by his extraordinary scholarship and his exemplary service to the Jewish people. But he and most other introductory teachers of *kabbalah* have not shared with us the personal mystic experience that has validated the kabbalistic tradition for them.

The Reader's Guide to Experiencing the Higher Realms

A few teachers, however, have been willing to provide some public insight into Jewish mystical meditation techniques, perhaps the most informative among them being Aryeh Kaplan. A nuclear physicist by training, Kaplan began dedicating his life to Jewish mysticism only as a mature adult. He was deeply troubled by the many Jews who disdained Judaism for not providing the spiritual experience they found in various Asian teachings like Transcendental Meditation. This concern moved him to recover Judaism's teaching about mystic meditation. He believed it had been the essence of Jewish practice in biblical and early talmudic times and he showed how texts from these periods could be read to demonstrate this fact.

Some of the earliest books of Jewish mysticism do describe the authors' supernal experiences but they are largely silent about the methods that led to these ascents. Scholars commonly consider Abraham Abulafia (late-thirteenth-century Spanish mystic) the first writer who explicitly described the methods used to ascend to the higher realms. Abulafia suggested some procedures already used by the German kabbalists: *tzeruf*, recombining various letters in Hebrew words to reveal their hidden meaning; *gematria*, utilizing the numerical value of a word (since the Hebrew letters also serve as numbers) to reveal its rich associations; and *notarikon*, treating words as acronyms that abbreviate phrases. He also discusses meditating on God's ineffable name and the various substitutes for it.

After Abulafia it became more acceptable for Jewish adepts to say something about the practices they found helpful. However, this always remained a minority practice, one considered troublesome by many of the great masters. Aryeh Kaplan became an indefatigable researcher of these materials, many of which exist only in manuscript in European libraries. He felt it his life's mission to teach others what he had discovered, and his primary method of doing so was teaching small groups. A number of his publications arose directly from this practice as he customarily prepared carefully for the sessions that were taped.

These edited lectures display Kaplan's exceptional gift for explanation. He does not minimize the abstruseness or the ineffability of much of what he wishes to convey and he responsibly emphasizes the severe limits to what can be conveyed publicly. Nonetheless, he then communicates his message with remarkably simple language. For example, he describes meditation as disciplined concentration, one that frees the spirit of the static of ordinary life and enables us to tune in to its spiritual depths. He has a talent for apt analogies and often clarifies his meaning with an example drawn from contemporary culture or science or, occasionally, by comparisons with the mystic practices of other faiths.

First Steps in Drawing Closer to Reality

Moreover, Kaplan's instruction is quite down to earth. Thus, he says that mantra meditation, an introductory technique, works by habituation so any word or even nonsense syllables can be one's mantra. But using a mantra with spiritual power brings one to a higher level of consciousness. Any charged Hebrew religious term might do for this purpose but he commends to the undecided the one suggested by the famous Hasidic *rebbe* Nachman of Bratzlav, namely, *ribbono shel olam*, "Master of the Universe." Kaplan prescribes thirty minutes a day be devoted to this method, also noting that it usually takes between thirty and forty days of this regimen for its results to become manifest.

Kaplan believes that the basic meditative practices of Judaism were largely the same as those in other faiths, but he contends that their use with Jewish content allowed them to yield the fullest truth. To begin with, the Jews have the Torah, which is an emanation of one of the Divine *sefirot* and thus provides an inexhaustible source of supernal secrets. More important, they have been given the supreme key to ultimate truth, God's very own name. Since one may never say it, he introduces this most potent symbol only after he has spoken about contemplation. In this technique one learns to fill the mind with a visual image, selected initially by simply sitting and looking. An advanced form of contemplation is based on a reference in the Zohar and involves discerning the five colors in a flame. The white, yellow, and red each convey their own meaning to the one attending to them. At a higher stage one begins to "see" the blackness around the flame and this yields an experience more profound than that of contemplating the light. But at the highest stage of this practice one becomes aware of an indescribably gorgeous blue surrounding the blackness.

One can apply this visual contemplation technique to God's ineffable four-letter name and elevate one's soul to an exalted level of mystic insight because the name gives us a direct link with God. To help the beginner Kaplan provides two mystic interpretations of the letters of God's name. One utilizes the motif of giving charity. The *yod* that begins the name is the smallest letter of the Hebrew alphabet and can be considered a coin. The second letter, *heh*, whose numerical equivalent is five, is a hand. The third letter, *vav*, with its long vertical stroke, which is the Hebrew conjunction "and," is the arm that reaches out to give. And the final *heh* is our hand, with which we receive what God gives. To say "Adonai" ("my Master," our standard euphemism for God's name) is thus to speak of the giving God and our need to receive what is offered. Thus far all we have is an interpretation of the name, but contemplation can turn ideas into intense personal experience.

As always in mysticism, symbols have many meanings, so Kaplan offers another approach to contemplating the name. Now one "sees" it as a combination of masculine and feminine elements. The *yod* is the seed of creation which must be placed in the womb of creativity, the *heh*, so that it may bear fruit. The *vav* then becomes the extended providence by which God orders creation, and the final *heh*, with its small opening at the top left, is the womb of reception while the large opening at the bottom is where the offspring, a purposeful natural order, emerges. In this reading human sexuality provides the metaphor for contemplating God's creative nature and appreciating how God's unity transcends and fulfills our divided masculinity and femininity.

The Heights and the Dangers Awaiting

Kaplan provides a glimpse of some advanced levels of mystic ascent, going as far as the visualization of pure nothingness. He consciously breaks off his introduction to Jewish meditation with only a mention of the nature of *yichudim*, the spiritual unifications that bring one into the Divine reality. They are, as Isaac Luria taught, our chief means of *tikkun*, of mending the ruptures history has brought into the God-creation harmony. Kaplan did provide some description of these mystic exercises in his historical exposition of *kabbalah* but enough has been said here to answer our prior question: How does the seeker know that the esoteric doctrine taught by the Jewish mystic is true? Kaplan's work indicates how it can be verified through compelling personal experience, one that he says accompanies insight with an infusion of energy greater than anything one has ever known.

If most mystic teachers in the past have been reluctant to share their techniques for attaining such certainty, the reason is that every step forward increases the potential danger to the soul. Kaplan continually warns his readers that the unwary neophyte can easily become lost in the pleasures or overwhelmed by the trials of mystic activity. He has overcome his strong inhibitions about this matter only because he considered it a calamity that so many Jews were mired in skepticism and desperate for spiritual nourishment. But he regularly repeats the admonitions of past teachers who are adamant that no one undertake the mystic way without proper preparation, and then only under a *rebbe*'s guidance and control.

We now turn to the teachings of two figures who may be taken as representatives of creative Jewish mysticism today. Their thought, while recognizably an outgrowth of their involvement with the Jewish mystical tradition, nonetheless has moved off in new directions. The earlier figure, whose significant activity took place in the first third of the twentieth century, was the first Ashkenazi chief rabbi of (then) Palestine, Abraham Yitzhak Hakohen Kook, commonly known as Rav Kook. The other is the contemporary non-Orthodox rabbi and academic Arthur Green.

The Extraordinary Independence of a Most Traditional Rav

Perhaps we should not call Rav Kook an innovator, for his most unusual creation was a personality that seamlessly combined interests others considered incompatible. A devout mystic, he was an effective man of affairs. Dedicated to personal spiritual experience, he studied the major secular philosophers. A committed kabbalist, he followed no school or *rebbe* but from his youth went his own spiritual way. An authoritative Jewish legal authority, he had an interest in the major European cultural currents. The leader of Orthodoxy in Palestine, he often criticized Jews so involved in minutiae that their religious life lacked personal illumination. His love of Torah made him an early Zionist, one who made *aliyah*, immigrating to Palestine in 1904. Yet zealous as he was for Jewish observance, he cherished the anti-religious pioneers whose activities were building Jewish national well-being.

The years since Rav Kook's death have softened the harshness of these earlier conflicts but his ability to rise above these polemics remains remarkable. Why he alone did this—and remains without a significant successor—can be ascribed only to "genius." Nonetheless we can, with some effort, connect much of Rav Kook's unique stance with his particular emphases on *kabbalah*.

The difficulties in the way of understanding his thought are notorious, he himself acknowledging that his prose was more like poetry than straightforward exposition. Moreover, he preferred short discussions of what was on his mind at the moment rather than extended treatments of his outlook as a whole. He published much in his lifetime but died leaving the apparent bulk of his work in manuscript. Several volumes of this material have appeared but, as long as access to his manuscripts was restricted, it was not been clear how much of the posthumous teaching was the editor's selection and arrangement and how much due to Rav Kook himself. Once the manuscripts were made available, one early conclusion was that though there is a certain integrity to the whole, his key terms and ideas have a fluidity that runs through his many writings. Still, we can now proceed with less trepidation to describe his central ideas.

Naturally, Rav Kook is in many respects a traditional kabbalist. God as the utterly Hidden One, the En Sof, creates and makes contact with the universe as we commonly know it through the system of the ten *sefirot*. With God being the only reality, there is a continual flow of creative energy down the sefirotic system into the world. Human sin sends a disruptive energy back up the path, disturbing the ideal harmony between God and creation. The flow back and forth is continual.

Envisioning Science Kabbalistically

Rav Kook accepts Darwinian evolution as a drive toward the increasing complexity of creatures—the accepted interpretation in his time—and grandly sees the theory grasping a kernel of the mystic truth. He holds to the Lurianic description of creation's having shattered the "vessels" prepared to hold the surging Divine creative power. Our world has been a mix of broken pieces and Divine sparks ever since—to this point Luria—with all things, from the tiniest inorganic bits of matter/energy to the galaxies, "yearning" to return to their primally destined integrity with God. Evolution is what a scientist can see of nature's movement toward this goal.

On the human level, where consciousness suddenly emerges full-blown, the moral and spiritual dimensions of this drive finally become manifest in all their centrality. *Teshuvah*, repentance, literally, "return," therefore cannot be limited simply to what individuals must do to repair their personal relationship with God. For Rav Kook, return also has supernal importance as the cosmic process by which creation carries out its ultimate task of restoring its integrity with God. So, too, repair, *tikkun*, now is the glorious upsurging of all creation whose greatest efficacy is reached in the pious Jew's mystic observance of Torah.

With the one God the only source of reality, Rav Kook is highly sensitive to the interrelatedness of all creation. No part of the world could have come into being or now exist without a "spark" of the Divine. All things are therefore united in their mutual dependence on God and in being bearers of a "spark" of the Divine reality. In a sense, they are all the same, a notion that should give humans a consciousness of their unity with all creation. The world being broken and humankind being sinful, one must carefully sift out the "sparks" from the shards, the holy from what contaminates. One does this with God's help and the teaching of *kabbalah*. The Jewish people have a unique role in this common task, as we will discuss.

Rav Kook's holism gives his teaching two special emphases. Jewish mystics in recent centuries substantially internalized their sense of the critical aspect of Jewish observance. Rav Kook does not belittle what must transpire in the soul but he insists interiority is only one part of our destined work. Nature and humankind in all their physicality must drive toward God in holiness. As the Torah indicates, God creates all the "tongues and nations" as well as individuals, so their corporate spark needs to "return" to its primal situation. He thus gives far more weight to the actions of human collectives and to their continuing sacred responsibilities than do most mystic authors.

The Mystic Who Read Western Philosophers

Holism also requires that intellect—but not dogmatic skepticism—accompany mystic insight. Consider the model God set for us in the "movement" from En Sof, God the Ultimate, to the very first of the *sefirot*, Keter (literally, "Crown"). Truthfully, we can't begin to understand why the Infinite should "want" to be related to the finite. As best we can imagine: the very first creation must have been the "will" to create—and this "act" necessarily involved "freedom," the liberty not to remain eternally self-contained in wholeness but to create the worlds. Thus the most intimate thing we can say of God's own "nature" is that it manifests this will/freedom.

All human beings, being created in God's image, have something of this mysterious talent at the core of their being. With it they can ascend the sefirotic system, ideally to the closest possible reidentification with God, the entry into Keter. But the second *sefirah* is Chochmah, "Wisdom," that special power or talent by which, as the Bible says (Prov. 3:19), God created all things. If, then, will/freedom is our closest Divine characteristic, then its nearest fellow attribute is wisdom. Hence, our intellect is our second most precious means of identifying with God.

Rav Kook transforms this vision of the highest *sefirot* into a dialectic of spirit and mind unparalleled among other Jewish mystics. For them, "wisdom" equals *kabbalah* while he, though giving *kabbalah* unequivocal priority in his teaching, is willing to see Divine "sparks" wherever intellect is at its best—and thus in the works of the great nineteenth-century philosophers. The liberal Jewish thinkers, knowing no truth higher than intellect, would modify or reshape traditional Jewish belief when it conflicted with the modern mind's conclusions. That is impossible for Rav Kook to do since kabbalistic wisdom, recognizing God, reaches infinitely higher than the secular intellect can. But that does not mean that the mind cannot sometimes be the means of stretching toward God's truth. Wherever people do so, Jews should acknowledge this wisdom, even if the source is quite distant from Judaism. Here, as elsewhere, sorting out the truth from the error is not easy but that very task itself refines one's intellect for those whose Jewish roots and piety are equal to it.

Rav Kook happily notes that Torah (*kabbalah*) and the modern intellect share a dynamic sense of reality. For *kabbalah* this means God's creative "movement" through the *sefirot* to give being to the created order, a wholly positive energy flow now disrupted and reversed by human sin. Rav Kook gives this "vertical" vision a "horizontal" extension. The swirl of spiritual energies aspiring to their ultimate goal, God, amid the historic conflicts of this world will one day find its social fulfillment among us with the coming of the Messiah. The Jewish people, with its singular role of loyalty and observance, is critical to this historic task.

Rav Kook was thus greatly taken with the emphasis of Kant and the Neo-Kantians on ethics as a partial but important means toward effectuating this historic task. He frequently gave the ethical—understood as a major aspect of Torah—independent emphasis in speaking of Jewish duty and he deemed it a proper criterion by which Jews should judge their faithful observance. This viewpoint enabled him to see signs of positive spirituality in the effort of nations to increase justice and enhance the well-being of their citizens.

The Particular Roots of This Expansive Universality

The embracing reach of Rav Kook's Judaism might have led others to play down their Jewish particularism, as the liberal thinkers clearly did. But two features of his thought anchored him firmly in the Jewish people and its way of life: his understanding of the Jewish nation's God-prescribed destiny (thus his Zionism) and his mystic view of Torah.

The origins of Rav Kook's Zionism are utterly unlike those of the secular leaders of the movement who learned of nationalism from nineteenth-century European secular politics. He was a kabbalist to his core and his mysticism's uncommon stress on collectives brought him to his unique religious Zionism.

With so divergent a premise to his nationalism, he often came into serious disagreement with most of the Zionist leaders. The followers of Herzl's political Zionism found his insistence on Jewish religiosity impractical or impolitic, as did some early Orthodox Zionists. Others in his community were appalled by his benign attitude toward the atheist-secularist Zionists. However, he refused to restrict to a pious enclave the fulfillment of the Jewish nation's messianic role. The entire folk was called to this historic task and it needed to be restored as a whole to carry out its God-given assignment. (Much of this understanding lay behind his own *aliyah*.) Rav Kook therefore had a positive appreciation of the Zionist pioneers seeking to rebuild the nation on its ancestral soil. He looked beyond their provocative anti-religious ideology and self-righteous nonobservance and saw them driven by the spark of Divinity that animates all Jews and keeps them messianically faithful. And he was forbearing of their disdain for the Torah, for he suffered over the spiritual depths into which the nation had fallen in its recent history.

Rav Kook's emphasis on the collective led him to another surprising concern: the role of the folk in shaping Jewish law in response to its changed social situation. He did not mean by this what non-Orthodox thinkers, such as Mordecai Kaplan, have spoken of as the legislative power of the ethnic group. For all his devotion to the nation as such, Rav Kook insisted on the observance of the *halachah* and the traditional leadership of the rabbis. Nonetheless, he alone saw them in a social context, as part of the Jewish collective moving along its messianic way.

This uncommon dialectic stemmed from his view of the sefirotic origin of the Torah. In some sense there is nothing new about this notion since it had long been Jewish teaching that God gave the Torah to Israel. The mystics, in characteristic fashion, had only clarified the sefirotic places where God's giving of the Torah originated. Rav Kook said that the Written Torah came from the sixth *sefirah*, Tiferet, "Beauty," while the Oral Torah came from the tenth *sefirah*, Malchut, "Kingdom." The tenth *sefirah* is also the source of the people of Israel's special attachment to God and in this sense the nation, in its ideal role, is a partner in the shaping of the Oral Torah.

There can thus be no question for Rav Kook of why, despite its appreciation of the spiritual-ethical striving of all human beings, the Jewish people must remain faithful to the *halachah* and its particular way of life. The law is God's special emanation to the Jewish people and only by observing it can the Jews be faithful to their true Malchut-originating self. Thus, though the nation must have a role in the shaping of the law in every age, that properly can take place only through the institutions God authorized.

Various aspects of Rav Kook's thought have been taken up by non-Orthodox thinkers to lend authenticity to their efforts to make Jewish law more flexible. However, they always end up giving the Jewish people far more authority in relationship to God than did classic Judaism. This position would have been unacceptable to Rav Kook, whose mysticism made him utterly God-centered though somewhat more appreciative of human initiative than most kabbalists. God made the Jewish people "Israel" and did so by giving them God's one and only Torah. They may have a role in its elaboration but only in uncompromising fealty to the one and only Reality and the authorities God had established.

Another extension of Rav Kook's thought has had contemporary political impact. He has been cited as a *halachic* authority for the Jewish duty to occupy the "whole" land of Israel, that is, the West Bank territories occupied by the State of Israel after the 1967 Six-Day War and traditionally called Samaria and Judea. It is not difficult to see how this principle flows from his thought even though he never said anything directly about it. He did say the Jewish National Fund's purchase of land for the nation fulfilled the commandment "to conquer [and occupy] the land." This conquest was so important that Joshua and the people were commanded to go to war and die for it. How doubly praiseworthy, then, for the Fund to find a way to fulfill it peacefully. Equally important is the inference from his teaching on redemption that the Jewish people is God's unique instrument for bringing holiness to the universe and that its national rehabilitation on its land was the critical prerequisite to that service. If so, Jewish settlement and rule in Judea and Samaria has messianic import and is not merely a matter of national security. While the Palestinian residents must be treated with the respect for "the stranger" required by Jewish law, God's authority cannot be negotiated or compromised. This involvement of traditional religious faith with politics has not been uncommon in Jewish history and in its own way mirrors the manner in which religious liberals brought their faith into the public arena.

The Reinterpreter of Kabbalah for the Non-Orthodox

In our own day Arthur Green has set forth his own creative depiction of Jewish mystic experience. An American, Green graduated from Brandeis University in 1961, was ordained by the Jewish Theological Seminary in 1967, and received his doctorate from Brandeis in 1975 (climaxing his many years of studying mysticism, with a dissertation on the singular Hasidic leader Reb Nachman of Bratzlav).

The chronology helps explain the cultural currents amid which Green's thought developed. The 1960's—with civil rights and then the Vietnam War increasingly creating moral problems—was a time in which many of the assumptions of modernity crumbled. A minority thought the Death-of-God movement the fulfillment of the modernist increase of human responsibility. A larger and more enduring group began reaching beyond scientized rationalism's constricted understanding of personal and interpersonal reality in a search for a more humane existence. Feeling reasserted its role in human wholeness, and mysticism reasserted its claim to give the fullest insight into ultimate truth and loving human relationships. Amid the social turmoil, the use of drugs became widespread. While the harder psychedelics attracted only a minority of the searching few, the recreational use of marijuana became relatively common and accepted. The positive reaction of many users to the heightened consciousness they experienced lent its own credibility to mystic spirituality.

Green's major response to the currents of the time was the founding in 1968 of the neo-Hasidic Havurat Shalom Community in one of Boston's urban neighborhoods, Somerville. The name indicates the new institutional concerns. The *havurah* was to be a moral "community," one in which an egalitarian, nonhierarchical Jewish life style might be lived. Thus Green was not its "founder" and certainly not its "rabbi" but only one of its "founding members." Still, by dint of learning and soul he emerged as its formative spirit. Note, too, its dedication to peace and its associated forms of social idealism. The community took its liturgical life very seriously but had no formal commitment to Jewish mysticism. Nonetheless, because of Green's involvement, a strong interest in intense spiritual experience characterized its life.

In 1973 Green became a full-scale academic with his move to the University of Pennsylvania, a position he left in 1984 to join the faculty of the Reconstructionist Rabbinical College. This move allowed him to work with students not only intellectually but as a spiritual guide. In 1987 he became president of the college, an appointment that signaled an important spiritual transition for the Reconstructionist movement. Founded to promote Mordecai Kaplan's philosophy of Judaism, it had until then emphasized his naturalistic, human-based theology. By the 1980's that stance no longer carried its old cultural conviction, while Green's more appealing mysticism could easily be reconciled with Kaplan's basic social theory. In 1993, Green relinquished his administrative and fund-raising activities and returned to academic life at Brandeis.

The Mature Vision of a Religious Visionary

All during this busy, useful career—another telling refutation of the image of the mystic as a self-contained recluse—Green spoke and wrote about his mystic understanding. He capped off his work in 1992 with the publication of a major statement, *Seek My Face, Speak My Name: A Contemporary Jewish Theology*, which allowed us to see where he continues the Jewish mystic tradition and where he transforms it.

On the surface, there is much in this book that sounds classic, for it is an extended series of meditations on the four letters of God's ineffable name. His treatment of these is reminiscent. The *yod*, the smallest of the Hebrew letters, is the primal point of all reality. The *heh*, with its small opening above and large one below, is the womb of cosmic birth. The *vav*, the common Hebrew conjunction, is the point drawn forth toward the final *heh*, the receiving point which, bearing the Divine energy, moves toward the work of *tikkun*, repair. Much else of Green's exposition takes the form of *derash*, of the (re)interpretation of biblical verses, and of familiar prayers and practices. To one who reads these for their mystic intent he gives the stuff of Jewish living fresh meaning. He makes little reference to the *sefirot*, but the distinction between the En Sof and the *sefirot* has major consequences for his view of reality.

Green's mystic experience has led him to proclaim union with God, even if only temporarily achieved, as the goal of spiritual striving. Academics remain divided over whether union with God has been central to *kabbalah* over the centuries. One group of scholars denies that Jewish mysticism generally has aimed at thoroughgoing communion with the Divine, usually referred to as the *unio mystica*. They contend that no matter how far we might climb the sefirotic ladder we would never reach the highest *sefirah*, Keter, the "Crown," that is En Sof's first and thus purest emanation. And, of course, one cannot go beyond that to the En Sof itself. Thus Rav Kook connects the highest *sefirot* with prophecy and we do not see any prophets among us, nor did Judaism recognize any after biblical times.

The other reading of the Jewish mystic tradition reminds us that union with God is a matter of the utmost inexpressibility. Hence we are not likely to find much literary evidence of it. Nonetheless, these scholars can cite texts in which identification with God is clearly the goal. Theoretically, this should be possible via any of the *sefirot* since each one, in the special "logic" of mystic theosophy, is not only a localized center of the Divine energy but equally a representative of the whole system.

In any case, Green unequivocally teaches the reality of the *unio mystica* and its resulting piety. He makes this plain by the example of sexual intercourse between husband and wife. He says its highest accomplishment is the ecstatic merging of the two selves into a higher unity and it is this transcendence of self in the coming-together that makes its human giving-receiving so fulfilling. (By contrast Martin Buber describes the I-thou relationship as an intimacy that preserves enough distance between the partners to allow them to become most fully themselves through their togetherness.)

The Spirituality of Joining the One

Green does not detail any special methods, as Aryeh Kaplan does, of how we may reach such ultimacy but, God being the reality behind everything, he finds means to God everywhere and particularly so in Jewish practices. Human beings, that special locus of Divine creativity, have only to plunge into themselves with requisite depth. Having done that, having linked up their spark of Divinity with the Divine, they transcend the limitations of human understanding and gain a vision of the cosmos from God's own perspective. They can now speak about reality as—if such a thing can be said—it appears to God.

The most critical insight to emerge from this exalted view is that God is the only true reality and by that standard all else is essentially illusion. Such reality as creation has—its "sparks"—comes from God's continuing creative power flowing into it, a mysterious condition that can be attributed only to God's love or "desire" for companionship. Thus for Green, as for much late Hasidic teaching, existence should be understood as a thoroughgoing duality. What is Real is God, su-premely one and undifferentiated. Our ordinary sense of "reality" as fragmented, beset by distinctions between self and others, between men and women, between nations and ideologies, even between what is holy and profane, is essentially unreal, the result of the brokenness of creation and not of the one God's integrated creation.

Logically, this two-level view of the universe devalues the worth of created things for they are ephemeral, unreal in their individuality and marred by the brokenness of nature. However, Green, like many mystics who build their lives on the *unio mystica*, does not wish to abandon the world and its creatures. So he meets this difficulty by pointing out that our two-level existence is God's dispensation for us, one that calls us to be active partners in completing creation and thus by action uniting us with the Fullest Reality.

Moreover, seeing everything from God's own perspective brings an uplifting, commanding sense of unity into our level of existence. All things are ultimately one in God, so life now needs to be lived with that sensibility.

Five commandments immediately suggest themselves. First, one must be aware of the wondrous duality of the "absolute" One who is also the Reality permeating that lesser level of mixed being-nonbeing called the creation. From it, as against all the false views of truth—the idolatries—all the other commandments flow. Second, one must treat all human beings, regardless of what they appear to be, as one's equals by virtue of creation in the Divine likeness. From this comes an imperative for realizing women's equality with men. Third, one must hold important a *shabbat*, more precisely, a sabbath, a day in which one stops exploiting creation and devotes oneself to reality itself via a communal or personal discipline. Fourth, since nature shares the basic unity of creation, ecological sensitivity becomes critical to one's living spirituality. Fifth, in keeping with this sense of basic natural harmony, a vegetarian *kashrut* seems mandated to acknowledge our root identity with the animals.

In these duties one sees the hope of God's name moving closer to the day when, as the Jewish liturgy intones, it will finally be One. For the primal point—the *yod*—must be completed in the three following letters, the ones that stand for creation, revelation, and, the climax, redemption. They are brought back into proper relationship by our great work of *tikkun*, of repairing the broken cosmic structure.

Everyone who has been inspired by an increasingly global vision of humankind's solidarity and its integrity with nature will be inspired by the embracing sweep of Green's spirituality. And everyone whose soul has been uplifted by efforts to rise above human division to a concern for all humankind's well-being will be inspired by its strong stress on ethics universally applied.

The Issues This View Has Raised for Some

Green's work has already drawn some significant criticism. For a book whose subtitle is *A Contemporary Jewish Theology*, it seems odd that it has no significant discussion of either the Holocaust or the State of Israel. The relative unconcern with the Holocaust may be related to the work's comparative silence about evil in general. This surely cannot be due to an insensitivity to suffering, for where Green does write of evil his compassion for what humans must often endure is evident. Rather, it must be ascribed to what we may call the classic "mystic theodicy." That is, knowing what is truly real, and what is not, evil is not "real." On God's level of Utterly Complete Oneness and Truth, there can be no evil. We, who must live on another level, can know pain so intolerable it makes the problem of evil overwhelming. But if we can remember or reexperience the other level, we will know that, in Truth, there is no evil and no "problem of evil."

Critics of mysticism have found all such theodicies unsatisfactory. For them, the Holocaust, for example, has too much "reality" to be "answered" by the statement that with the proper mystic awareness we would see its horrors as illusion. The classic kabbalists took evil far more seriously than this and posited four real worlds of evil paralleling the four worlds of goodness. They saw the Sitra Achra, the Other Side, impinging on our world of the lowest good with such perverted Divine energy that were it not for the good God's ultimate supremacy we would be lost. That concept, at least, gives mythic expression to the gruesomeness of much human existence and cannot be accused of deprecating the reality of evil. It does, however, envision our cosmos as radically dualistic, and it may be for that reason that Green gives this strand in kabbalism no place in his work.

And Are the Jews and Judaism Merely Incidental to God?

Green's thought, like much God-centered mysticism, is largely unconcerned with the reality of history and thus of the religiously significant events within it. The true happenings take place in the inner life of the soul, ascending to the One and merging with it. Sinai, in effect, becomes interiorized, at best Moses' work of reaching and uniting with God, with its resulting new vision of duty. The Diaspora becomes a metaphor for the alienation of human existence in the mixed realm of reality-illusion, and the State of Israel is transformed into a symbol of the ultimate homecoming in God that is redemption. How could history have any ultimate significance when one knows that in Truth, on God's level of Utter Oneness, there is no history?

As events are finally of no significance to God, the same may be said of all particulars, especially of institutions, movements, and ideologies.

Of course, it is only through these hybrids of Divinity and illusion that human beings can hope to commune with God for we too are hybrids of "sparks" and "shards." There is no way to avoid the paradox: anything might be a means to gain access to God but, from God's perspective, it is also an empty exercise, obscuring as much as it unveils. On either count, the grand sweep of Green's religiosity radically relativizes Torah and the Jewish people; for him, the Jews and their Torah are only another true-false spiritual possibility. They have no special place of origin in the sefirotic system as Rav Kook and the classic kabbalists believed. They are not unique centers of God's holiness deserving utter loyalty and requiring dedicated observance. His God-centeredness precludes any such real differentiation among the created things.

Green does not conceal his view about the ultimate dispensability of Israel and Torah, but he is too devoted and passionate a Jew not to make the best case he can for our people and tradition. At the simplest we are Jews because that is where we find ourselves. Then, too, the Jewish tradition is a wonderfully rich source of human and religious understanding and practice. We who have had the privilege of knowing it in depth find it an incalculably rich and rewarding medium for our spirituality and its social working out. Its wisdom often appears to illuminate our souls with insights unique to our people's experience, though that same possibility must also be extended to other peoples. Yet all this having been said, Green acknowledges that remaining a caring, observant Jew remains only a personal "choice."

Making Judaism merely another alternative mystic life style, though commending it as uncommonly rewarding, hardly seems to Green's critics to be an adequate response to our times. In the global marketplace of spiritual options and communities, there are many attractive candidates for our souls, in particular, groups that make mysticism central and not secondary to their religiosity. Yet how long can any minority without some special sense of itself hope to survive meaningfully in cultures that esteem tolerance and, while preaching pluralism, slowly homogenize their peoples? Moreover, there are special problems connected with being a Jew. Why should one burden oneself with them if other ways of life, unencumbered by our old or latent pariahhood, might equally be ways to know and serve God?

In Green's mystic vision as in the rationalistic universalisms treated in prior chapters, the classic problem of the Emancipation again finds expression: If truth is unremittingly universal, why should we long continue to be Jews?

This issue returns us to the pressing problem of non-Orthodox Jewish mysticism: How does it mandate deviation from the Torah while simultaneously calling for substantial observance? Once, the Jewish rationalists thought that reason, in one form or another, could be entrusted with the work of discrimination. But mystics, whose authority derives from a transrational level of experience, cannot reempower rationalism to do that work without stripping the mystical of its commanding role (as happened in Baeck's theology of "mystery"). Green's response is to follow the One Truth undeviatingly and lovingly transcend/recommend Judaism. Perhaps another non-Orthodox Jewish mystic teacher will explain in some modern sense our old belief that the One God of all the universe also has a special relationship with the people of Israel and the way of Torah. Such an explanation would be a valuable addition to the many spiritual benefits the resurgence of mystic teaching and practice has brought to contemporary Judaism.

PART V
Concluding
Reflections

12

Postmodern Judaism:
Eugene B. Borowitz

FOR MOST of two centuries almost all Jews who could modernize
did so. They knew that modernity was good for them, that the great
gains that equality and opportunity brought made the problems connected with modernization acceptable. But as the twentieth century
waned, doubts about modernity's beneficence arose throughout Western civilization. People were profoundly disturbed by the deterioration
of the quality of life. A great deal of their unhappiness was disappoint-
ment. The Enlightenment, the intellectual credo of modernity, had
promised that replacing tradition with rational skepticism, hierarchy
with democracy, and custom with freedom would bring messianic
benefits—and it certainly hasn't.

On a much deeper level, this loss of confidence in Enlightenment
values has come from the collapse of its philosophical foundations. All
the certainties about mind and self and human nature that once
powered the bold move into greater freedom now seem dubious. We
have had some hints of the Jewish manifestation of this general
Western mood in prior chapters. Reading Heschel today, we can see
him responding to this situation with his heartfelt argument for an
authoritative, God-centered revelation. Heschel's response also provides something of an explanation of modern Orthodoxy's evanescence into "centrism" while vitality grew in just those groups that
consciously distanced themselves from the modern. And in its turn to
mysticism, the Jewish community was moved by its strong reaction to
modern rationalism. These currents have, however, had only a limited

appeal even among those Jews deeply discontented with our civilization. I believe their search can now best be understood and responded to in terms of that broad-scale cultural movement that calls itself "postmodernism."

A *Phenomenon Eluding Definition and Lacking a Center*

The antagonism to modernity is manifest in many fields and, because it did not begin with an ideology or theoretician, it is best depicted as a moving cultural wave continually redirected by various people who apply its energy to their own fields. Architecture offers the most accessible examples, with the sleek, spare buildings of a modern master like Mies van der Rohe being succeeded by the imaginative, decorative structures of his former disciple Philip Johnson. In musical composition the tight rigidity of an earlier formalism now often relaxes into looser, more expressive creations. In academic and cultural circles these developments have been closely identified with literary criticism and the effort to refashion philosophy, and here we can point to a dominating influence in the work of the French thinker Jacques Derrida.

To keep Derrida's far-ranging, stimulating ideas within some bounds, it will help to focus on some earlier thinking about language. Our humanity is elementally shaped by our speech. Though many fleeting impressions float through our consciousness, it seems unreasonable to call any one of them a "thought" or "knowledge" until it has been put into words. How that happens is not easy to understand but two essential aspects of the process can be specified. First, naming or saying is substantially social. We do not invent our own language but learn it from our culture. Though we may be highly creative with our people's tongue, even adding to it, we are still limited by what, in largely unarticulated ways, it can allow. (Comparative linguistics often indicates how languages differ, each having some areas where it is rich and nuanced and others where it is less articulate.) Second, philosophically speaking, if "to know" is to put into words, then "to name" is to create the thing for us.

We construct our view of the world with language (whether the symbols of subatomic mathematics or the baby-talk of lovers). For example, you are reading the little black marks on the page before you. If you know how to read—in our culture from left to right, not from right to left or from top to bottom—you can make a "world" out of these marks. The Hellenistic philosophers called these procedures for interpreting texts—"reading" in the fullest sense—"hermeneutics." But if we get meaning only by turning signs into sensible language, then just about everything we do—science, religion, art—depends upon how we go about "reading," that is, interpreting what confronts us. And our readings depend on our hermeneutic rules.

The Great Master of Contemporary Hermeneutics

Jacques Derrida has been a most acute and imaginative "reader" not only of texts but of our use of language. Against the French structuralists (who discerned the same bipolar logic operating in all human language—jungle myths and university philosophy), Derrida argued that language not only creates but tends to destroy logic; no wonder this theory is called "deconstructionism." If one reads texts with great care, as he has demonstrated, one regularly finds them subtly "doubling" back and negating their positive statements. Therefore our hope of convincing others by being ever more precise and logical will always be subverted by our putting thoughts into language, for our thought is essentially structured by our language. Another aspect of deconstructionism is its polemic against our thinking that "good" language describes real things when all its usefulness merely depends on properly following the rules of usage. In sum: words are all we have. There is no way, as philosophers long dreamed, of starting our thought with notions that are simply "given" or "self-evident" and thus uncontestable foundations for knowledge. That being so, thinking and writing should best be understood, not as unmasking reality, but simply as elegant word play.

This attack and others like it have as good as destroyed modernism's supreme confidence in the human mind. But in the process they have also deconstructed ethics, turning moral imperatives into merely words about words. No Jewish thinker, no sensitive human being, could fail to be appalled by this nihilism, particularly when we have been witness to one ethical outrage after another. With the memory of the Hitler occupation still alive in France, the Derrideans have not been blind to this problem and their writing is often touched by a strong moral passion. But none has yet clarified how a deconstructionist could have a commanding ethics that carries the urgency of biblical commands. An American philosopher, Edith Wyschogrod, has made a notable effort in this direction by her study of a number of female moral exemplars, but the distance between good models and compelling norms remains great.

Two Non-Derridean Philosophic Jewish Paths

Some Jewish philosophers, conscious of the clash between deconstruction and their commitment to ethics or *halachah*, Jewish law, have sought new postmodern ways of proceeding. Peter Ochs, a leader in the development of postmodern Jewish philosophy, has identified two intriguing non-Derridean possibilities.

The more reminiscent of these is to explicate one's thought in the traditional fashion of commentary on classic Jewish texts. Moderns did this with a philological, historical hermeneutic that called for an "objective," critical attitude toward the text; reading the tendentious scholarship of, say, two generations ago makes this claim ludicrous. But if all reading is largely the creative work of someone necessarily reading as one of a community, then why not come to the texts as a committed Jew? Why not do one's commentary fully conscious of one's indebtedness to the tradition of Jewish interpretation and particularly alive now to all readings' delicate interplay of reading out (exegesis) and reading in (eisegesis)?

Some venturesome thinkers have suggested pursuing this hermeneutic opening in a second direction. Postmodernism recognizes that the reader is as much a part of the reading as are the text and the community, so why not make the reader the "text" and proceed by spiritual autobiography? This is not to suggest another modernistic wallowing in one's self and its travails, thereby recapitulating modernity's much criticized radical individualism. Rather it is the situated self, the person as the child-then-member of a community and the product of its "texts"—interpersonal and folk as well as verbal—who spurs the reflection. Explicating what interactions brought the thinkers to their special Jewish faithfulness, and which possibilities they rejected, might clarify for others what it is to be a believing Jew today.

The Theological Non-Derridean Approach

My own postmodernism has taken a third direction: an explication and development of my Jewish faith. Against Derrida's confident assertion that it is no longer possible to have any foundations for our thought, I come to the work of intellect as a Jew first and as a reflective thinker second. What I believe may be obscure, wavering, and difficult to put into words. But to deny it would be false to who I truly am, for despite its hiddenness it is real—real enough that despite my secularization and skeptical intellectualization I try to base my life on it.

So I seek to interpret and communicate "my" experienced life of Jewish belief, hastily adding (in typical postmodern consciousness of the circularity of all thought) that this "my" does not refer to individual, interior religious experience as in modern thought. Rather (in typical postmodern particularity), I read the Jewish people's experience in recent decades. Most of the Jewish community is too highly secularized or academicized to scrutinize its corporate spiritual subtext. I seek to do this in my book *Renewing the Covenant: A Theology for the Postmodern Jew* and then educe its latent affirmations and subject them to theological analysis and development. I shall shortly review this argument. But since mine is the first full-scale postmodern theory of Judaism—and a non-Derridean, theological one at that—I want to explain why I consider it "postmodern."

My working from my inchoate Jewish faith admittedly conflicts with Derrida's central charge that we postmoderns can no longer claim foundations for our thinking. This position runs afoul of some Derridean enthusiasts who say that those of us who do not carry on the master's significant emphases should not call ourselves postmoderns. Their assertion strikes me as self-contradictory. If all thought should be deconstructed, so must that of Derrida. A Derridean orthodoxy is an oxymoron. I find the cultural climate—postmodernism—created by his work congenial because it allows me to express my intuition of Jewish truth with less distortion than does any other language of our time. Let me explain.

Postmodernism's rejection of foundations ends secularism's gagging of religiosity, linear logic's claim to exclusive value, and "clear and distinct ideas" as one's required style of exposition. It allows for the "thick" writing that anthropologists have found helpful in describing a culture's many layers, validating its use in theology. With "objectivity" unattainable, the religious thinker's particularity now has a proper role in thinking, a shift that speaks to one certainty of Jewish religiosity. All thinking being circular—its conclusions prefigured in its chosen focus and method of procedure—it comes as no disgrace to find this phenomenon in theology. Lazy, self-indulgent, or anti-intellectual writers can, of course, exploit this postmodern linguistic openness to produce works that seem less "thought" than effusion. But I trust the Jewish community to determine in due course which statements of its corporate faith have value.

The Postmodern Difference: My Three Assertions

I can epitomize my understanding of religious postmodernity as three revisions of the modern views of people and God, of self and community, and, as a result, of personal autonomy.

First, modern religiosity, including the Jewish, is more certain of people than of God. Thus its typical procedure is to move from some certainty about human beings toward what people can on that basis reasonably call God. (In modern Judaism Hermann Cohen's foundation was rationality, Mordecai Kaplan's the experience of growth and development [in a culture], and Buber's the I-thou experience [though his God has some independence].) Religion has thus always been a personal spiritual search or quest, as secure or as ambivalent as its human base allowed. This definition had the virtue of encouraging people to use their power, individual and communal, to do the good, a liberation that contributed in countless ways to the betterment of human lives.

This reliance on human knowledge and activism came in conscious rejection of that "premodern" religiosity dominated by God. Thus in Judaism, God descends on Mount Sinai, gives the Torah, and thereby transforms an aggregate of slaves into the people of Israel. So in the Bible and prayer book God speaks, commands, listens, answers, observes, judges, rewards, punishes, forgives, helps, saves, and much else. These events had the great virtue of bringing stability and security into Jewish lives and investing them with an admirable holiness. But they tended to make Jews so dependent on God that, by modern standards, they seemed passive. This perspective made the new freedom a means to fuller humanhood and thus highly attractive. But we can now see that modernity's self-confident activism tended to have human judgment fully replace God as the ground and guide of human value, a gross overestimation of human goodness and discernment.

For some postmoderns the disillusion with messianic modernism validates a return to classic religiosity with God at its center, powering the recent rise of fundamentalism. But most postmoderns intuit something different: a relationship between God and people that is less God-dominated than the traditional religions taught but also less people-centered than the moderns claimed. They sense the reality of a God who grounds our values yet makes room for human independence and calls human beings into an active partnership.

How Independent, How Universal a Self?

Second, moderns thought truth to be fundamentally universal, that is, applying to everyone, everywhere even as gravity applied in the farthest reaches of the universe. Therefore defining something meant relating it to the class in which it fit, and explaining something meant showing how it operated in terms of a broad-scale natural process. This system had the exhilarating effect of showing how everything could, in theory, be related to everything else and giving new breadth of vision to every field of endeavor. It led Kant to insist that only when moral imperatives applied universally—to everyone, everywhere in the same situation—should they be called "ethical," an idea that still powers efforts to include "outsiders" in our communities. Modernizing Jews have had good reason to love this liberating vision and enshrine it in their intense commitment to ethics as the essence of religion.

Again, this notion reversed the premodern religious view in which God's revelation came to a particular group and not to anyone else. In classic Judaism only the people of Israel received the Torah, Written and Oral, and by its standards the people of Israel understands itself and all other peoples, "the nations." The chosen people have duties incumbent on them alone, and when they are observant they receive God's special favor. This faith makes them impervious to their difference from other peoples and enables them to survive history, confident that they are God's favorites.

In contrast to the premodern judgment of others by (God-given) group criteria, modern Jews first determine what is true universally and then investigate how Judaism exemplifies it. Thus Cohen, Kaplan, and Buber first determine what is true for everyone—rationality, sociology, or the I-thou experience—and then create a theory of Judaism to conform with it. When the Jewish agenda focused on modernization and on demonstration of Jewish humanhood, this method was invaluable, for the universalistic hermeneutic revealed a dimension of Judaism not previously so evident.

Today a changed Jewish and human agenda has made two flaws in the priority of the universal painfully evident. After the Holocaust, Jewish survival could no longer be subordinated to achieving acceptance in society (mostly by diminishing one's Jewish particularity). Many Jews gradually realized that being and staying a Jew was elementally right, and therefore unbridled universalism was wrong. Moreover, if truth is fundamentally universal, then all particular forms of its expression, including Judaism, are in principle expendable. With the Jews a tiny minority everywhere and one subject to special disabilities, emphasizing universalism made it easy to rationalize giving up or drifting out of Judaism. For those whose Jewishness was too elemental for them to do that, it was clear that the supremacy of the universal was a faulty standard.

Many groups in Western civilization had come to a similar conclusion. People of diverse races and cultures began protesting the moral arrogance of an ideal that said, in effect, that they would be more fully human if they became more like the cultured Western, white man. Another blow against the universality of the universal came from feminists, who rebelled against the subordination of their gender to male criteria claiming to be correct for everybody, everywhere. Intellectually, these groups had been preceded by Marxism, psychoanalysis, anthropology, and more recently, deconstructionism. They denied that anyone who was necessarily speaking out of a given class, a given self, a given culture, and a given language could enunciate something true about everyone, everywhere.

If human beings are quite particular and everything we posit arises from our specific situation, then the particular inevitably precedes the universal. Should one affirm the commanding truth of universalism—as most Jews, out of folk experience and faith, do—then it arises out of being part of a certain community, in our case our being modernized Jews. And this priority of the particular to the universal is thus the second trait of my postmodernity.

Retaining but Rethinking Autonomy

With regard to the first two matters—greater involvement with God and with Jewish particularity—postmodern Orthodoxy and non-Orthodoxy largely agree. They disagree over my third affirmation: the need to keep (but reinterpret) modernity's notion of personal autonomy. Orthodoxy can permit individual self-determination only where the Torah, God's revelation, permits it. Though caricatures of Orthodoxy ignore it, the Torah does provide substantial areas for personal decision in the observant life. But to stretch these to the point of dissenting from the Law is a sin and leads to all those human tragedies wildly abetted by the rampant individualism of the modern ethos. Therefore many Jews, like people of the other great Western faiths, have turned their back on anarchical modernity and its degraded life styles and have chosen to be Orthodox.

Despite the appeal of this reasoning, the masses of the three widespread faiths have rejected orthodoxy. Many do so out of self-indulgence; they want to do whatever gives them pleasure to the extent that they can. But more reflective types, though they agree with some of the criticism of liberalism, have not been convinced that it was fundamentally in error. Their strong sense of responsibility and their resulting perception of their personal dignity have come from thinking for themselves and deciding just what they truly believe and what they ought to do. With a certain humility they seek guidance from their religious leaders and traditions but then insist upon making up their own minds about what they have been taught.

In the postmodern context, however, "making up their own minds" cannot mean a return to the self-confident heyday of modernity. Then autonomy assumed that individuals had (or could have) in their minds, experience, and learning all the resources they needed to determine what they and society should do. In the postmodern situation, God and particularity set the context within which people go about "making up their own minds." In my postmodern theology, personal autonomy has validity only when exercised in intimate involvement with God as part of one's community relationship with God. For Jews that means as part of the people of Israel's historic relationship with God, the *brit*, or Covenant.

These three affirmations structure my non-Derridean postmodern understanding of Judaism. I could not have expressed them so abstractly before writing *Renewing the Covenant*, but authors too learn from what they write.

In the review of the book's argument that follows it will help to keep several other things in mind. The presentation is systematic and holistic, which means that each of its four major sections is not independent but tightly bound to the others. It is also what is technically called an "apology," a believer's effort to make sense of his or her faith in response to modern semi-believers, would-be believers, and non-dogmatic skeptics. It tries to meet them on common ground by beginning with our experience in the past half century. But instead of focusing on what individuals have undergone, my postmodern particularity (thesis two) demands a communal focus, what happened to the Jews as a people. This account, the first major section of the book, yields the affirmations that are then subjected to intensive theological analysis.

Modernization, the Messianic Redeemer

Modern Jewish thought is a response to the radical social and cultural upheaval the Emancipation brought to Jewish life, particularly because it involved secularization. With science as the model, natural law, not God's rule, now explained the orderliness of things; human will, particularly as expressed through politics, replaced God's providence as the shaper of history; and rational ethics, not the Torah's commandments, now defined duty. Animating the modernized societies was an optimistic hope that as knowledge succeeded superstition and reshaped old institutions, a time of justice, peace, and human flourishing would begin.

No group in society more enthusiastically embraced secularization than did the Jews. Only in secularized states could they be equals and, by redefining duty as ethics, modernizing Jews were free of the Jewish practices they saw keeping them from full participation in society.

The sorry record of the beneficiaries of modernity in the past few generations has destroyed that early optimism, for those who claimed to be bringing messianic redemption have often done startling evil. All across Western civilization a backlash against modernity's moral pretentiousness and ethical incompetence has made itself felt. With human reason itself also suspect, our civilization has lost its once rock-solid ground of value. This process, I suggest, has had deep spiritual resonance and has powered the utterly unexpected major religious phenomenon of the past generation: the rise of fundamentalism in the three great Western faiths.

The Jews, who so avidly reoriented themselves to Western culture, have not escaped this civilizational shift. For us the Holocaust has been the awesome lens we have used to look anew at our relationship to modernity. By contextualizing our response to the Holocaust, I do not mean to argue that it has no qualitative uniqueness. Nevertheless, we shall not plumb the depths of our present religious situation without clarifying how our integration into Western culture helps us understand our unanticipated reaction to our agonizingly particular suffering.

The Contradictions of the Common Holocaust Wisdom

Much of what is commonly said about the Holocaust ignores the contrary evidence. For example, Why did the issue of God's rewards and punishments never become central to the debates? Why did the years of talking about God yield no ideas about God not well-known before Hitler? If modernized Jewry was largely agnostic before the Holocaust, how could God have "died" among us as a result of it? Why did sizable minorities of our community, instead of turning to greater secularity, develop an interest in greater Jewish spirituality, indeed, in the practice of Jewish mysticism? Why did Orthodoxy, the doctrine supposedly most decisively refuted by the Holocaust, undergo a vigorous resurgence? And why do the non-Orthodox Judaisms, all tarred by modernity's failures, retain the spiritual allegiance of most modernized Jews?

My theological Holocaust "revisionism" has a simple premise: as long as we continue to think of "Holocaust theology" as an argument about what kind of God Jews might continue to believe in, we shall repeatedly clash with the realities of Jewish life and not understand their true import.

To begin with, the post-Holocaust theological discussions could not be about God's retribution, for no modern Jewish leader or thinker of the past two hundred years taught that God regularly rewarded the good and punished the bad as the Bible, the Rabbis, and the prayer book said. The new, scientific view of nature and the secular view of history as well as simple human experience made that doctrine unten-able. The distancing of God's governance was already deeply en-trenched in the modern Jewish consciousness when the Kishinev pogroms outraged the civilized world in 1903. It engendered no la-ments that God was punishing the Jews for their faithlessness. Instead the response was thoroughly secular and activist: the use of political pressure, the organization of international Jewish protest groups, and the formation of Zionist self-defense forces.

The "outcome" of the debates is another such anomaly. Already in the 1920's and 1930's, rabbis and educators at non-Orthodox American seminaries were regularly taught the two theological positions about God that would find the greatest acceptance after all the Holocaust theologizing. The modern response has been that the reality of evil despite a good God indicates that we cannot any longer sensibly think of God as having unlimited power. Rather, God, like everything else, has limits even though God is the greatest of all realities. The other view is the traditional one, that though we can understand why the good God allows evil (so as never to infringe on human freedom), still we cannot understand why there is so much other evil, but we trust God nonetheless. Once this fact has been made clear, a question forces itself upon us. It arises from the historical fact that both ideas about God, particularly the modern one, were widely taught in the Jewish community—that is, when anyone cared to talk about God. Why, then, hadn't they made the theological discussions about the Holocaust less intense?

This anomaly points us to a deeper truth that realism must now insist upon. Most modern Jews at mid-century were agnostic, content to let metaphysical notions drift out to the margin of their conscious-ness if not entirely out of it. Their social goals were integration and economic security. At their best their spirits were buoyed by a strong secular sense of ethics and the pleasures of Jewish ethnicity. Having a meaningful life, they perceived God to be superfluous. That mood still dominated when the Holocaust debates began in the mid-1960's. Confident agnosticism began fading about a decade later as the faith in modernity eroded—a process that continues—and now it remains the stance only of those who still think secularity sufficient.

If, then, most Jews in the 1960's didn't take God very seriously to begin with, how could the Holocaust theological debates truly be about God?

The "God" Who Really Died in the Holocaust

Ironically, the Holocaust argument that initially appeared to reinforce modern Jewry's covert agnosticism then turned into its refutation. Moderns had long assumed that the certainty of ethics—the basis for denying or limiting God—was given by human reason or human nature. But experience kept sundering those intimate bonds between values and mind or personality. Practically, the Holocaust and countless other evidences of human perversity—by educated, cultured, advantaged people—made faith in the natural goodness of all human beings unbelievable. Theoretically, science showed itself value-free in technology that hurt people, and philosophy, applying methodical doubt to reason, itself began denying that its rigorous exercise necessarily mandated ethical responsibility. The ground of secular ethics slowly collapsed. Worse, modern thought has shown itself incapable of generating a normative ethics, or, as it applies to this discussion, of clarifying a commanding, qualitative difference between the SS death camp operators and their Jewish and other victims.

On what secular basis, then, must there be an enduring protest against the Holocaust? And on what basis and with what insistence ought we resist the inhumane trends in our society today?

A deconstructive reading of death-of-God theology is therefore in order. I based mine on Feuerbach's famous nineteenth-century thesis that human assertions about God are really affirmations about people's view of themselves. (Secularists once loved this idea, for it justified their converting God-talk into statements about humankind.) In that light, the death-of-God discussions may (with some liberty) be said to double back on themselves. What "died" was not the biblical-rabbinic God moderns did not largely believe in or teach but the one they did: humankind, themselves. Moderns had, as it were, thought humanity could be "God," and now events and ideas radically undermined that faith. But the loss of this "God" was too great a psychic trauma to face directly, so they found a safe substitute: the God they didn't much believe in anyway.

This interpretation not only clarifies the Jewish aspect of a general Western cultural development; it also explains some paradoxical results of the discussion of the "death of God." Instead of widespread atheism, our community has shown increased interest in Jewish spirituality, that is, in the kind of Jewish practice that gives people a personal experience of God's presence. It has even taken the form of a revival of Jewish mysticism. And in direct contradiction to all the insistence that the Holocaust made traditional Jewish belief untenable, it is Orthodoxy that has in recent years demonstrated the greatest religious vitality. All this testifies to the Jewish version of the postmodern turn to religion for a commanding ground of value.

The Rise of Particularism—and Its Limits

The response to the Holocaust produced a second, more evident change among world Jewry: a substantial identification with the State of Israel and the creation of an identifiably Jewish Diaspora way of life (thus the experiential basis for my second postmodern affirmation). Emil Fackenheim early captured this sense of post-Holocaust Jewish duty in his now classic formulation of a 614th commandment. He said the Jewish people had heard itself enjoined by an anonymous but commanding Voice from Auschwitz: do not give Hitler posthumous victories. Some decades before, when universal concerns dominated the modern Jewish psyche, the proud self-assertion by Jews of their Jewishness would have seemed "too Jewish." Today that negativity seems self-hating and servile, a typical excess of the optimism modernization engendered.

However, the Jewish community remains split over just how much weight to attach to this intensified Jewish identification. Many see their Jewishness as a great treasure and resource, something they love and would be pained to see die out in their family. Yet for all this deep sentiment they cannot say that there is anything compelling or obligatory about Jewish identity. They could, with some sadness, see the reasonableness of another generation's moving on to a broader form of ethical, humane existence. Others have discovered that they do not believe the Jewish people is dispensable. For them Jewish continuity is not merely a matter of human satisfaction but, as difficult as this is to assert, a response to a Divine imperative. As a result, the threats to the State of Israel and to the meaningful survival of the American Jewish community affect them to the very depths of their being.

The centrifugal push to assimilate has been a significant factor in Jewish life ever since the Emancipation. What is not clear is how much the new centripetal motivation among modern Jews will offset the steadily shrinking barriers to their drifting away from Judaism.

Yet despite the new postmodern openness to God and the affirmation of one's Jewish particularity, a certain qualification of both has also been broadly visible. Most Jews are unwilling to follow that path into Orthodoxy. In fact, though they identify with the Jewish people, particularly with the State of Israel, they have not been willing to follow its leadership without occasional significant dissent. Two examples quickly come to mind: Diaspora Jewry's refusal to stop welcoming Russian Jews who wished to go elsewhere than the State of Israel, and the unprecedented, near unanimous American Jewish uproar over possible Israeli legislation to constrict the definition of "Who is a Jew?" In both cases, going against what Israeli leaders claimed was in the best interests of the Jewish people as a whole, world Jewry insisted that pluralism be honored in contemporary Judaism. And pluralism, like democracy itself, is a modern notion, one based on the dignity of each single self.

With regard both to God and to our particularity, most Jews still insist on exercising some self-determination (thus the experiential basis for my third postmodern affirmation). In my postmodern Jewish ideal one would exercise one's freedom fully conscious of one's normative membership in the Jewish people and as a participant in its historic relationship with God. Nonetheless, this postmodern reinterpretation of autonomy affirms something of the modern insight that individual human dignity is premised on reasonably significant self-legislation.

This reading of the religious substrate of recent Jewish history sets the agenda for contemporary Jewish theology. First, it should tell us about the God who both grounds our values yet grants us a measure of independence in our relationship with God. Second, it should then clarify our people's relationship with that God. To make sense to moderns, it must explain why particularity necessarily precedes universalism. But in emphasizing Jewish particularity, it must nonetheless indicate how the established virtues of universalism are now mandated. Third, it should then indicate how the living relationship between God and the people of Israel—and thus with individual Jews as part of that relationship—yields Jewish obligation, a contemporary meta-*halachah*, if you will.

These three issues structure the bulk of *Renewing the Covenant*, the entire exposition directed toward, as the subtitle indicates, *A Postliberal Theology of Jewish Duty*.

Whence the Commandingness of the Postmodern God?

Before beginning the direct discussion of God, I will discuss two uncommon characteristics of the theological analysis to follow: its criterion of judgment is *covenant-functionality*, that is, how well a proposed idea would work within the experientially intuited God-Israel-self frame; and it is *holistic*, that is, how any conception of one aspect of the God-Israel-Torah triad (around which the book is organized) would affect the nature of the others or their interaction.

The substantive statement about God begins by asking, in an intellectual-religious sense, "where" (to dare a troubled but instructive spatial metaphor helpful with issues of authority) we might "locate" the God we intuit. Somehow we must try to understand how God can at the same time be the One who commandingly opposes a nihilistic existence yet who "grants" and "respects" human freedom. Some religious believers envision God utterly above and beyond us as the commanding Absolute that negates all relativism and properly calls for our obedience. By contrast, traditional Judaism, despite its emphasis on God's beyond-ness—"high and lifted up," "exalted," "the Highest"—incessantly affirmed God's involvement with human beings and nature. The Absolute of some world religions, like Vedanta Hinduism, or of Western philosophers, like F. H. Bradley, is too "absolute" and self-contained for such outreach. The biblical-rabbinic God, however, is sufficiently beyond us to rightly command our action and expect a reverent response—yet by that very act is near us.

Many modern believers want God intimately close to them and everyone and have creatively explored the possibilities of God's immanence. Examining those aspects of life that "exalt" and refine people, like nature or art, non-Orthodox religious leaders have found such experiences to be the modern equivalent of the traditional presence of God. This view certainly makes us more aware of the spiritual possibilities around us. Yet if we sense that our God rightly engenders our compelling sense of values, then ascribing that authority to something entirely immanent runs into a logical difficulty. Why should any one aspect of our experience—like beauty, or ethnic loyalty, or love—be granted dominance over our contrary experiences, some of them quite strong indeed? Aesthetic appreciation does not debar cruelty, ethnicity does not explain why sometimes we must radically dissociate ourselves from a stand of our community, love has shown itself quite fallible.

In each of our immanent surrogates for God we are already operating with an independent standard of quality. We shall best find it and identify God's unique commandingness by ascribing transcendence to our God. By employing this language, I wish to highlight three aspects of our religious experience.

Describing a Transcendence True to Our Ethical Intuitions

First, our religiosity testifies to the supreme value of a "dimension" of reality other than that we commonly sense. In some mysterious way, "it" is fully independent of us; it "made" us, not we it, and though we are ephemeral, it is permanent. Yet we also sense an ennobling sameness about us and it. This odd mix of farness amid nearness (and vice versa) produces the widespread phenomenon of religious awe.

Second, this numinous transcendence confronts us not only with rightful authority but with exalted quality. What we sense as best in us is manifest mostly in fragmentary, conflicted, and unrealized fashion, but is perfected in "it." And this fullness of goodness—more precisely, holiness—in "it" draws us compellingly to perfect ourselves.

Third, the integrity of its supremacy and its quality indicates why "it" is the bedrock of our values, demanding not only a good life but a holy life from us—and guiding us in how to live it.

An aside is of some importance. Transcendence can be described in impersonal terms, but there is a contradiction in giving central significance to values and making their source impersonal. By definition the impersonal is value-free, and only on the human level does valuation become characteristic. That paradox suggests itself as the reason our tradition freely utilized personal metaphors when speaking of God. These cause us gender difficulties but make plain that God rightly commands us because God is Creator, Ruler, and Holy One. In either case, God's incomparable commandingness arises from being the Transcendent One who is also the Immanent One.

Feminist thinkers have criticized the notion of Divine transcendence as providing too easy a justification for some people to subordinate others, specifically men to dominate women. I fully agree with the ethics of that stand but dissent from its usual conclusion that feminist theology must therefore be radically immanentist. I do not see how anything but arbitrary choice can justify exalting one aspect of nature as a quality control over its other aspects, such as demanding that we radically reject sexism for egalitarianism. We can reach the ethical goal of transcendence without dominance by abandoning any sense of transcendence as absoluteness and rather understand it, in Buber's terms, as relationship. God is sufficiently distant to make "space" for us yet to make us sufficiently God-like that we can be in a significant relationship with God. In the Buberian metaphor, God remains on one side of the I-thou hyphen—remaining the Transcendent Other—and we, on the other side, remain independent persons. Yet the hyphen also links this God and us humans in that astonishing, transforming intimacy that the Torah calls "love."

Intimations of God, the Far-Near One, are not difficult to come by if we are not dogmatically secular. No special preparation is required and no resulting emotional high should be expected. As the classic system of Jewish blessings indicates, we might well brush up against God, or vice versa, when we sit down to eat or after having been to the toilet. Moderns often find this concept difficult because they have been taught to filter out any "signals of transcendence" and explain them in social scientific or emotional terms. Developing an openness to the Immanent-and-Transcendent One is a critical postmodern act of "return."

Of God's "Nature" and God's "Acting"

The postmodern situation suggests two further issues about God. What may we say about God's "nature," evil being freshly real to us? And with the current demythologization of science, what can we now say God does?

A few Jewish thinkers have argued that after the Holocaust logic and human feeling require us to say that such a "God" as there is must be value-neutral and not good or holy. That idea refutes itself for most Jews, for it negates any utterly fundamental qualitative difference between the Nazis and their victims, an absurd consequence of "explaining" where God was during the horror. At the other extreme, some thinkers contend that God so transcends our comprehension that we should not question God's absence; we could not hope to understand the answer even should one be forthcoming. That conclusion seems quite traditional but generally a certain modern modification accompanies it: its advocates do not also assert that the strong biblical view of God's reward and punishment explains the Holocaust.

The idea that God is limited in power preserves God's goodness yet explains why God does not stop evil. However, it creates as many problems as it resolves. It effectively limits God's unity by opening the question of who or what stands behind that part of creation where God does not. God's power now being limited, our hope for the

Messianic Time now cannot be so confidently asserted. Without God's ultimately efficacious power behind us, can we still believe after the Holocaust that humans are good enough to supplement God's power so substantially that our effort will do what God alone cannot? And do we want a piety that makes it unreasonable to argue about evil with God—who simply can't do more than God is doing—and thus makes the book of Job essentially irrelevant?

Despite its awesome difficulties, I affirm a Buberian view of God as the One who relates to us (and our people). I do not know how one would get the distance to be able to say that God is infinite or all-powerful (the Bible says neither), but God's unity seems ultimate and thus the source and orderer of everything. It is our sad but true human experience that sometimes those we love most hurt us terribly—yet inexplicably we often find we can still love them, even if we don't understand them. That fact says more about our living relationship to God than any intellectually more coherent theodicy.

Postmodernity's creative possibilities become more apparent when we ask what God actually does. When a deterministic science was the necessary way of thinking about natural processes, God was banished from active involvement in the universe (and life after death became simply unimaginable). But with science now increasingly viewed as only one possible way of constructing an integrated view of the natural order, we may find other, better ways to envision reality as a whole. Science still has too efficacious and integrated a view of things for us to spurn it for the cosmologies and superstitions of prior ages or for the unverifiable speculations of contemporary anti-scientific visionaries. Nevertheless, a breach needs to be made in the dogmatic naturalism of modernity and I have therefore made an effort to defend the operation of a rough and limited but real pattern of God's justice in the world.

Can We Say God Has a Particular Relationship with the Jews?

Turning now to the people Israel presents special problems. Speaking to moderns about particularism remains more difficult than speaking positively about God. Methodical skepticism having overreached it-self, a new openness to religious experience has provided a basis for meaningful God-talk. But the universalistic premises that led mod-erns to denigrate particularism have not been similarly discredited. As a result there is still no way to move logically from modernity's assumption that truth is fundamentally universal to the postmodern insistence that the particular always precedes the universal.

Therefore my views about the people of Israel are presented as two separate but related sets of arguments. Before specifying these, let me present an overview of the strategy. The first cluster attacks the three most tenacious modern reasons for devaluing particularity: confidence in all humankind's spiritual competence; radical individualism; and the priority of universalism. Once these have been negated, I can hope to win a hearing for my postmodern view of Jewish particularity. In this second group of expositions, I first point to some remnants of chosen-ness in contemporary Jewish experience; then I explain why covenant (a two-sided relationship with God) is the best way of describing this; and, having strongly emphasized particularism, I suggest how universalism and particularism might now be kept in proper dialectical tension.

The polemical side of this presentation begins with an attack on modernity's utter human self-reliance. If education, politics, culture, and therapy were truly transforming enough to bring the Messianic Age, why has the late twentieth century been characterized by a shocking amount of evil? One need not be a sophisticated social critic to have lost confidence in a prior generation's optimistic liberalism. Some Jewish thinkers have therefore turned back to the kabbalistic notion that evil is built into the very framework of reality and we are constantly beset by the evil power of the Sitra Achra, the Other Side of the good creation. That idea at least indicates realism about evil and the unlikelihood of even the best of people escaping sin. However, for all their chastened liberalism, most moderns have found that bleak mystical vision of the divided nature of things insufficiently apprecia-tive of the good that people can do.

Our tradition has another, earlier insight into the source of human evil-doing, one that ascribes it to both God and humankind yet also sees them working together to overcome it. The Rabbis of the Talmud say that God has set two urges within human beings, leaving us fundamentally conflicted. Primarily we are beset by a wily, treacherous, implacable will-to-do-evil. Alas our will-to-do-good is always stretched to the breaking point in order to win its temporary victories over the will-to-do-evil and it is only with God's help that we momentarily succeed. To postmodern realism this view seems truer to human nature than either modernity's optimism or the *kabbalah*'s mystic salvation. But it involves acknowledging that the self, even at its best, is far less spiritually competent than we once thought.

Selfhood's Social Side and Universalism's Particularity

Moderns have always found it easy to disparage particularity by insisting the self was utterly superior to its social situation and granting it supreme authority. Yet most people did not personally create that notion of the primacy of the individual but learned it from their culture. Western thought's self-centeredness since the nineteenth century was long mitigated by the strong sense of conformity and respectability that permeated society. But the increasing distrust of convention and the breaching of barriers in the twentieth century have threatened to turn individualism into narcissism. If responsibility to others is fundamental to humanity, then people must be social as they are individual, as much shaped by their communal situation as by their unique selves. For caring Jews, then, that means their very selfhood is as likely to have been formed by their Jewishness as by their particular personality.

The other classic modern evasion of particularity has been to spurn its parochiality and identify with humankind as a whole, a dream arising from believing that the mind enabled one to transcend time, place, and personality and attain universal truth. For some time that assumption managed to survive the challenges of Marx—that ideas were expressions of class interest—and of Freud—that they arose from a given psyche's structure—and of the anthropologists—who showed how greatly ideas varied by culture. But it has now been mortally hurt by the attacks of people of color—denying that the white race's ideas are necessarily everyone's—and of feminists—indignant that males set themselves up as the standard for both sexes. If we are inevitably bound to the countless particularities of our time, then we humans are more fundamentally social than moderns had dreamed.

What then remains of the ennobling vision of a humankind working together for its common good? And what becomes of that moral sense of humanity that mandated outreach to everyone, including that pariah caste, the Jews? Our community can continue championing universalism because our tradition, refined by the experience of emancipation, promotes it. Other groups that affirm God's unity and thus humanity's solidarity, particularly as refined in the Enlightenment's humanitarian vision, will have their own particular reasons for doing so. But if universalism arises from a particularistic foundation, then Jews turn their backs on Jewishness at the risk of rooting themselves in a new community less centrally dedicated to human betterment than the Jews are.

Particularity Without Chosenness

Despite their desire to be like, not different from, others around them, modern Jews still evidence a vestigial sense of the specialness of being Jewish. One sees it most clearly when their high human standards clash with their particularity, especially as manifest in its central focus, the State of Israel. Many Zionists had seen the normalization of the Jews as their national goal, that is, that Jews should finally be allowed to live like all other nations. Yet when Israeli acts are perceived as exceeding the exigencies of political realism and become morally offensive—such as the 1982 incursion into Lebanon, the tactical support provided for the Sabra and Shatila massacres, and then the readiness to take Beirut—such acts seem unworthy of a "Jewish State." Large numbers of Israeli and Diaspora Jews set aside their discipline of uncritical support of the State of Israel to protest. If the State of Israel merely lived up to the human standards of its neighbors, like Syria, Iraq, and Iran, most Jews would be heartsick.

Something of that attitude also attaches to individual behavior. In the United States when Supreme Court Justice Abe Fortas was forced from the bench for doubtful morality, caring Jews considered our whole community disgraced. But let the current year's list of Nobel Prize winners again include a disproportionate number of Jews, and Jews everywhere will rejoice in another proper expression of Jewish character.

Modernized Jews, however, recoil at affirming that we are God's chosen people. Practically, this assertion flouts the democratic equality we cherish. Theoretically, it ascribes a specific action to God—itself a troubling notion to moderns—and an arbitrary one at that. The efforts to humanize this doctrine by proclaiming the Jews have a mission to all humankind or by calling our people to assume voluntarily a national moral "vocation" have so little substance today that they have faded out of our communal rhetoric. But with God and particularity having greater significance in postmodern Judaism a new possibility suggests itself. We can affirm both our sense of intimate Jewish involvement with God and our tradition's teaching about God's closeness to all humankind by speaking of our belief as covenant rather than as chosenness.

Relationship, the New Leading Metaphor

Covenant implies a two-sided partnership, the involvement both of God and of people. Our tradition understood this agreement to be dominated by God's authority and structured through God's law; it was regularly spoken of as if it were a legal contract. For postmoderns that balance of the partners gives too little scope for human religious responsiveness and creativity. Drawing on Buber, I understand the Covenant between God and the people of Israel on the model of personal relationships. These are inevitably particular; one connects with just this person but not in the same way with that one. Relationships have a certain commanding power, for the more significant a relationship is the more we avoid acts that might damage it and seek acts that fulfill it. And we build our lives on our most important relationships. In all of this, our actions remain our own responsibility but we now do them out of our concern for the one we love. We do not deny that others also have such true relationships—thus our universalism—but knowing that ours too is a true one, we hold on to it tenaciously despite many trials and temptations. This is, I am convinced, our best metaphor for pointing to our sense of Jewish particularity.

The Covenant is, of course, not primarily a matter between individuals and God but one between God and the Jewish people, the particularity we share. Hence it immediately involves us modernized individualists in our people's historic, ongoing relationship with God. Postmodern particularity is therefore personal in a way quite different from that of modern Judaism. For the latter, Jewishness is secondary to humanness and the human-God bond. My covenantal view instead sees our personal singularity situated unreservedly within this particular community, still very much as oneself but now also equally constituted by one's Jewish particularity—ideally, what I envision as "the Jewish self."

As sharers in the Covenant, we have responsibilities not only to God but to the Jewish people (and ourselves, but more of that shortly). With Jewishness now fundamental to our being, our duties as one of our people must have considerable priority in our lives. Our non-Orthodox religious Zionism grows out of this faith. Every believing Jew should give the most serious consideration to the possibility of living in the State of Israel. Doing so will allow them to participate in the fullest life of covenant our people now knows because it gives our Judaism its most social expression.

But the Covenant can be lived anywhere, though Diaspora existence imposes special burdens on the serious-minded Jew. Wherever it is lived, Jewish folk existence must be understood in covenant context, which requires that our people be true to its partnership with God— surely a criterion no "normal" people applies to itself. Covenantal living requires seeking a balance between the realism that group existence demands and the holiness that God requires. No rule can be given for doing this, so covenanted Jews must live with the tension of occasionally conflicting commitments. The openness of history derives from this situation, as does the measure of our responsibility for our actions.

The Five Aspects of Postmodern Jewish Duty

This theological analysis now reaches its goal with a statement of a theology of Jewish duty. Whenever a serious decision needs to be made, living in covenant involves a responsible Jew in five holistically integrated operations.

First and foremost, we seek to discover what God wants of us as, in all our individuality, we seek to live a life with God among the people covenanted with God. Often this will best be discerned through the next three means of deciding what we must do (the communal ones), but these can never supplant the priority of what we conscientiously believe to be God's will. Sometimes, in Buberian fashion, we know this out of the general sense of our relationship with God. Sometimes, standing in God's presence, we know more directly what to do.

More commonly we learn what God wants through participation in our people's covenant life or some particular aspect of it. Three facets of this process can usefully if artificially be separated out.

Our individuality being social, we acquire our sense of who God is and what God wants largely from our *community*, that is, from how Jews live and think today. (On general human issues, that often has considerable overlap with much of the ethical thrust of Western civilization.) Our people's ongoing practice of our traditions, as limited as it is, can still powerfully impart the reality of covenant obligation. And despite all their secularization, Jews remain the people of the Covenant and often approach the troublesome new issues of life with a religious sensitivity that derives from their ancient pledge to God. A Jewish self will therefore want to learn what caring Jews today have to say about a given issue, and that is the second of the five decision-making operations.

Third, our people's relationship with God now has the experience of more than three millennia behind it. Most of what happens to people today has in one fashion or another already occurred to Jews in the past. Sages then often reacted to events out of their dedication to the Covenant and its tradition. Naturally, their judgments sought to create covenant holiness amid the particularities of their specific socio-historic situation, and we must translate those judgments into our own. Nonetheless, their religious insight often transcends their own day to instruct us powerfully today about our covenant duty to God.

Fourth, for all its concern with the living past, the Covenant directs Jews to the future. It calls us to hope and work for *messianic fulfillment* for ourselves and all humankind. We cannot then be satisfied with determining what, primarily, will keep us faithful Jews in the present, no matter how richly grounded we are in the past. Every Jewish generation has a messianic responsibility to every prior generation as well as to all the Jews yet to come to empower the long-range continuity of the Covenant. Hence every decision requires us to consider whether a given action lends endurance to our people for its long redemptive trek.

In all this attention to our covenant partners we must not forget, fifth, that it is just each particular Jew—you, me, this or that one—who now must make a decision and do an act. Sharing our humanness in covenant, we will most often know we are right in doing what other caring Jews are doing to serve God's purposes. Yet sometimes we must find our own way. Then, to some extent, we need to explain to our community why we have chosen this uncommon way. For even in the postmodern vision of covenant with its strongly contextualized view of personal individuality, each Jewish self ultimately stands alone before God.

My theology therefore emphasizes process over product, caring more about the covenant-faithfulness shown in determining our Jewish duty than about how carefully we observe a specified inventory of Jewish obligations. This conclusion supports the community's overwhelming abandonment of the binding quality of Jewish law. It has the further problem of reinforcing the indeterminacy that characterizes much of our community's practice. But, as against the Jewish left, it safeguards against anarchy by constituting the Jewish self as intimately involved with God and people, and, against the Jewish right, it legitimates Jewish pluralism in ways classic Jewish law cannot. Were our community to accept and live by this postmodern vision of its faith, then a living community of covenant-faithful individuals would likely create new, compelling communal patterns of covenant existence.

The Critical Response

This interpretation of Judaism has, of course, received its share of criticism.

From the right, the central objection has been that it does not provide a rationale for Jewish law. This flaw is devastating for any group for, it is charged, no substantial community can long hope to exist without a legal structure. The matter is particularly significant for Judaism since law and commandment have been so significant a part of Jewish religiosity. Worse, by seeking to validate the individual choice, which has been so deleterious a feature of modern existence, this approach weakens the central structure that keeps Judaism strong and it does nothing to remedy the problems created by modern individualism.

One philosophic complaint about this theology focuses on its attack on philosophic rationalism. The critics suggest that philosophers as well have seen many of these problems and moved on to other positions. Stimulated by science, it is argued, contemporary rationalism fully reflects the truth of relatedness rather than affirming detached, objective, Cartesian reflection. If this new pattern of reasoning were employed, most of my critique of philosophy would be irrelevant and an academic model would be available for the exposition of a (postmodern?) rationalistic covenant theology.

This criticism is related to the more general one, that by rejecting philosophy for theology, I severely limit the audience to whom this vision of Judaism can be addressed. Moreover, by consciously starting from a Jewish base and speaking to the modernized Jewish community, I have further limited the group likely to find meaning here. This approach clashes with my commitment to the continuing participation of postmodern Jews in our civilization. Were I to speak philosophically, starting from a universal base and developing my case in its idiom, I might better hope to reach that large number of Jews whose primary frame of reference is the general culture.

Another academic critique spurns such a resolutely modern stance and suggests that I would more likely speak to the culturally alert and be a more authentic postmodern if I identified my thinking more closely with that of Jacques Derrida. Currently, by affirming God's reality and referring to "the self" with similar assurance, I contradict the anti-foundationalism Derrida and his disciples have seen as the heart of postmodernity. Moreover, my thinking rarely displays the characteristic "doubling" so typical of Derridean exposition. I should then not identify my thought with a movement some of whose central themes I reject.

Other self-proclaimed postmoderns, doubting that any abstract statement about Judaism might mandate robust Jewish practice, prefer to proceed by the traditional path of commenting on a classic Jewish text. In opposition to the moderns' detached, historical-philological concentration, they utilize modern methods of study in the context of self-conscious engagement with the text as part of the believing community that has studied it over the centuries. My work does not, however, display the same rootedness in tradition nor evidence its continuity with classic Judaism.

Perhaps, then, the most general if essentially unstated criticism has been that my vision of postmodernity, founded as it is on an interpretation of what Jewry has recently experienced, will not long be relevant. Modern Judaism may simply have more vitality and staying power than I give it credit for. Or some other interpretation of these events, one less theological and more humanistic, may soon surface and appeal more directly to the secularized contemporary Jewish psyche. In any case, a theological interpretation of recent Jewish history seems a highly speculative basis on which to erect so demanding a religious theory.

So go the major objections and, like all thinkers, I believe I can answer them. But having tried to present myself and them fairly, I leave them with the conscientious reader, with whom, as my theology indicates, I believe the responsible choice lies.

13

Jewish Feminist Theology
by Ellen M. Umansky

A note to the reader from Eugene B. Borowitz: In the past decade or so Jewish feminist theology has brought a vibrant new religious awareness to Jewish intellectual life. Primarily, it has been notable for giving voice to the inner life of those many women seeking a fuller expression of their Jewish piety. But no less significantly, it has challenged those Jewish men who recognize the truth of Jewish feminist claims and wish themselves to participate in a more just and inclusive expression of their religious tradition.

A central motif in Jewish feminist thought asserts that women's religious experience has somewhat different contours than that of men. Thus as long as men continue exclusively to set the rules for acceptable statements of Judaism women are effectively disenfranchised. In simple self-respect, therefore, women are now insisting upon the right to speak for themselves, expressing in their own ways the fullness of Jewish women's religious experience.

Ellen M. Umansky, Carl and Dorothy Bennett Professor of Judaic Studies at Fairfield University, has been at the forefront of this intellectual activity, writing and teaching widely about it. She is uncommonly well qualified to provide us with a broad perspective of the paths that Jewish feminist thinkers are pursuing and it is with great pleasure that I welcome her to these pages to share her views of this exciting development.

ATTEMPTS to create a Jewish feminist theology—or Jewish feminist theologies—have been fairly recent. Most of these attempts have been articulated in articles and public addresses rather than in full-length books. Thus, a summary of the published writings of Jewish feminist theologians is limited by the fact that, with the exception of Judith Plaskow, none has yet written a major theological work. What's more, some of those currently engaged in writing Jewish feminist theology are graduate students whose doctoral work has been presented at academic conferences but has not yet been published. The reader, then, needs to keep in mind the following: Jewish feminist theology is not only a new field but also a growing one. New articles are continually being published and one can hope that a number of book-length theological works soon will appear. This chapter therefore represents an early step in the delineation of both the nature and content of Jewish feminist theological thought.

Jewish Feminist Theology as Responsive and Contextual

While, as we shall see, the specific theological concerns articulated by Jewish feminist theologians differ from one another, all seem to share an understanding of theology as rooted in personal experience. All, in other words, recognize that theologians have always drawn on their experiences in developing both a theological language and a theological system. What differentiates feminist theology from many theologies of the past, and some of the present, is both a willingness to acknowledge openly the autobiographical nature of theology and a consequent reluctance if not refusal either to assert universal truths or to make universal claims. The goal of feminist theology is not to persuade others to share any one feminist vision. Rather, its goal is to articulate the theologian's own understanding of the self, God, and the world and, within a Jewish context, to view these realities through the lens of Jewish feminist experience.

This does not mean that all Jewish feminists share the same experiences of the self, God, and the world. What it does mean is that Jewish feminists approach theology with an *a priori* commitment to writing a theology that is both feminist and Jewish. By feminist, I mean that which is consciously rooted in the theologian's own experiences of self. These experiences, not limited to those of gender, are shaped by specific cultural, historical, and economic factors. As a perspective, feminist theology calls into question any theology that views male experience as universal. It begins with the presupposition that traditional Jewish theology—like traditional Christian theology—has been androcentric. That is, it has placed men in the center, using the experiences of Jewish men as a lens through which the world is viewed. Thus, one still finds some Jewish theologians referring to the "613 commandments that Jews traditionally are obligated to perform" even though it is only men who are obligated to perform 613, while other theologians refer to "the study of religious texts and participation in regularly scheduled public worship" as *the* central expressions of Jewish piety when in fact only men have been obligated to study and to participate in public worship. Consequently, in the writings of such theologians, the ways in which the piety of Jewish women traditionally gained expression are minimized if not ignored.

Jewish feminist theology, *as feminist theology*, thus begins with what the Christian feminist theologian Elisabeth Schüssler Fiorenza, in her work on the New Testament, has labeled a feminist hermeneutics of suspicion. As Schüssler Fiorenza has written, the feminist theologian begins her study of biblical texts and their interpretations with the assumption that they are androcentric and also serve patriarchal functions. The Jewish feminist theologian, then, like the Christian feminist theologian, approaches traditional texts suspecting that the experiences of women will either be peripheral to the text or simply will not be recorded. When they are recorded, such experiences are most likely described in such a way as to reinforce male power or to justify the traditional roles to which women have been assigned by men. While Jewish feminist theologians, then, may advocate making such liturgical changes as *"Elohei avoteinu v'imoteinu"* ("God of our fathers and mothers") to replace the traditional *"Elohei avoteinu"* ("God of our fathers"), there is still the recognition of how difficult it is to talk of God as the God of our fathers *and* mothers when the only known stories are male stories and the Jewish experiences read about have been solely the experiences of men.

Having recognized that sources of Jewish theology, including the Written and Oral Torah, philosophical and mystical texts, and traditional liturgy, were largely (if not exclusively) created by and for men, the first task of the Jewish feminist theologian is thus to recognize that the visions we have received are incomplete. Before the feminist theologian can reform or transmit Judaism's traditional visions, she needs to receive these visions herself. She needs to hear her own voice and feel her own presence within the sources of Jewish tradition. Before she can shape the content of religious expression, she must discover what women's religious experiences have been. To do so may require reading between the lines, filling in stories, writing new ones, making guesses. Consequently, Jewish feminist theology, *as Jewish theology*, can be described as a theology that by definition is "responsive."

As defined by Daniel Breslauer in an essay entitled "Alternatives in Jewish Theology" (1981), responsive theology is that which emerges out of an encounter with "images and narrative from the Jewish past" and from the experiences of the theologian. Unlike normative theology, responsive theology does not begin with a set of norms delineating what is authentically Jewish. Rather, it begins with the "subjective response of the theologian to a set of experiences," encouraging, therefore, a "more fluid view of Judaism and the Judaic experience itself."

If Jewish feminist theology is responsive theology, its *a priori* commitment to Jewish tradition need not be a commitment either to the past norms of that tradition or to the current articulations of those norms as expressed by Judaism's major religious movements. Rather, its commitment is to the sources and fundamental categories of God, Torah, and Israel. Jewish feminist theology, then, is a theology that emerges *in response to* Jewish sources and Jewish beliefs. These responses are shaped by the experiences of the theologian as woman and as Jew. What may emerge is a transformation not only of Jewish theology but of the sources the feminist uses in transmitting her visions.

What's more, because Jewish feminist theology is rooted in the experiences of the theologian, it can also be understood as contextual theology, that is, a theology self-consciously rooted in the context of the theologian's own life. Rather than attempting to create theological systems that transcend personal experience, feminist theologians have firmly grounded their theologies in the realities of their own lives. The similar concerns and at times the similar visions of many contemporary Jewish feminist theologians can thus be attributed not to their having arrived at some universally attainable ontological truth but rather to their writing in a similar context—for example, as white, middle-class, religiously liberal, university-educated, U.S. feminists writing during the last three decades of the twentieth century. This does not mean, however, that feminist theological claims have relevance only for the theologian herself. On the contrary, it is the hope of the feminist theologian that by drawing on her experiences and sharing her stories, she will encourage others to draw on their experiences as well. In so doing, the feminist theologian offers women and men a means of formulating their own articulated and unarticulated responses to the categories of God, Torah, and Israel. She also offers women and men a means of viewing their own experience as Jewish experience, enabling them to recognize, as Rabbi Laura Geller has written, "that to be a Jew means to tell my story within the Jewish story." Acknowledging the importance of personal experience as a source of wisdom and truth, the feminist theologian leads others to discover, sharing Laura Geller's sentiments if not her terminology, that there is a "Torah of our lives as well as the Torah that was written down. Both need to be listened to and wrestled with: both unfold through interactive commentary."

Judith Plaskow: Toward a Hermeneutics of Remembrance

Judith Plaskow's ground-breaking *Standing Again at Sinai: Judaism from a Feminist Perspective* deserves recognition as the first major attempt to provide a coherent vision of a Judaism that incorporates women's experiences into its understanding of Jewish history and Jewish self-identity. Plaskow's work is methodologically grounded in feminist analysis and interpretation and has been greatly influenced by such (non-Jewish) feminist thinkers as Mary Daly, Audre Lorde, Elisabeth Schüssler Fiorenza, and Carol Christ, with whom she co-edited the highly acclaimed *Womanspirit Rising: A Feminist Reader in Religion* and its sequel, *Weaving the Visions: New Patterns in Feminist Spirituality.*

Plaskow studied philosophical theology at Yale University, where she received her Ph.D., and her first major theological work did not focus either on Jewish thinkers or on Jewish thought. Rather, her dissertation, later published as a book, was a feminist critique of the twentieth-century Christian theologians Reinhold Niebuhr and Paul Tillich. While in graduate school, however, Plaskow developed a strong interest in the role of women in Jewish life, and in February 1973 she delivered a paper on "The Jewish Feminist: Conflict in Identities" at the first National Jewish Women's Conference, held in New York City. Her paper, later published and widely read, concluded with the reading of a *midrash*, or more properly, a *midrash* on a *midrash*, that she wrote in 1972 entitled "Applesource." A retelling and reappropriation of the biblical story of Eve and the rabbinic tale of Lilith, Plaskow's piece marked an early, and perhaps the first published attempt by any U.S. feminist to create a Jewish feminist theology.

Midrash, an explication of a biblical text, often told in story form, has been an important source of Jewish theology for the past two thousand years. While one can justifiably argue that the radical theological directions taken by some feminist *midrashim* stand in sharp contrast to those commonly identified as classical, rabbinic *midrashim*, feminist theologians, including Plaskow, have maintained that the intent of feminist and rabbinic *midrashim* are in fact one and the same. As she has written, ancient rabbis, like contemporary feminists, "expanded Scripture to make it relevant to their own times," clothing later traditions with authority and connecting them to the original revelation at Sinai, thus bringing their own questions to the biblical text.

In her story of Eve and Lilith (first identified in medieval rabbinic literature as Adam's first wife), Plaskow retains much of the traditional content of their stories filtered through her own experiences of self and sisterhood with other women. In so doing, she transforms—at first subtly, then radically—the relationship of Eve and Lilith to Adam and God. She describes the ways in which each woman views herself and the world around her. She also imagines what it might have been like had Eve and Lilith met and shared their experiences with one another. Finally, she envisions a powerful Eve and Lilith returning to the garden in order to rebuild it together. Plaskow's retelling of these stories clearly emerges out of her own response to the traditional narrative. Thus, while she accepts the rabbinic image of Lilith as she who claimed equality with Adam (an image that speaks to her own experience of selfhood), she rejects the portrayal of Lilith as night demon, imaginatively suggesting that Adam created this falsehood to enlist Eve's aid in the battle against Lilith and to make sure that the two women would not become friends. Similarly, she accepts the traditional image of Eve as created from Adam's rib to be his wife and helper but rejects the traditional assumption that Eve remained satisfied with her role. Moreover, by joining the Lilith and Eve narratives together, Plaskow is able to move beyond the biblical and rabbinic materials completely. Her new ending helps make her story compelling, not just to herself but to those whose experience of sisterhood has been as powerful as her own.

Since the publication of "Applesource" (since anthologized in numerous publications), Plaskow's own theological work has moved away from *midrash* toward a more systematic exposition of what she and others have come to identify as a feminist Judaism. This exposition is most clearly and forcefully articulated in *Standing Again at Sinai*, published in 1990. Methodologically drawing upon the work of Elisabeth Schüssler Fiorenza, she utilizes both a feminist hermeneutics of suspicion and a feminist hermeneutics of remembrance. Viewing androcentric texts with suspicion, she reconstructs such texts to include women's real or imagined voices. The recognition that women's experiences are nowhere recorded in traditional Jewish texts leads Plaskow to label "scandalous" the claim that the Torah represents Jewish teachings as a whole. In truth, she argues, it "speaks in the voice of only half the Jewish people." What's more, the omission of women's voices seems to be neither mourned, regretted, nor even noticed. Women, she concludes, are not only peripheral to biblical and rabbinic texts; they are in fact "other" than normative Jews.

Drawing upon Simone de Beauvoir's classic work *The Second Sex*, Plaskow concludes that while women are Jews, "we do not define Jewishness. We live, work, and struggle, but our experiences are not recorded, and what is recorded formulates our experiences in male terms." Recognizing, then, that the central Jewish categories of God, Torah, and Israel have all been constructed from male perspectives, Plaskow focuses her work on reconstructing Jewish memory through the deliberate recovery of women's previously hidden voices and the conscious discovery and creation of that which she identifies as women's Torah. Plaskow's radical theological agenda is clear: it is to overcome what she perceives to be the injustice of Torah by breaking with Jewish tradition and creating a feminist Judaism that insists upon the full humanity of women. The theological tools that she uses are those of suspicion and remembrance as well as critical method and religious unity. Critical method, she tells us, is important in enabling us to see sources within their patriarchal contexts. At the same time, however, we need to recognize that we have received many of these sources as stories whose context is irrelevant to the meaning Jewish communities have assigned to them. She thus suggests that we read Jewish texts through a multilayered consciousness not only to become aware of women's silence but also to envision a means of restoring their voices, thus connecting to the text in new ways. The question she asks throughout her work is this: How might the categories of Torah, God, and Israel change as women appropriate them through the lens of their own experience? How, in other words, might Judaism be transformed?

Plaskow maintains that to reenvision Torah is to reshape Jewish memory so as to include women's lives and visions. Summarizing some of the work that other feminists have taken in this direction, she includes writing *midrash*, recovering women's history, and creating new rituals and liturgies. While in defining Torah as "living Jewish teaching" she does not suggest that all of these teachings will be new (or that all of them will be rooted in the experiences of women), she does question whether there is any place for *halachah* within a feminist Judaism. First, she points to specific laws within the *halachic* system that discriminate against women, rendering them legally and religiously subordinate to men. Second, and even more important, she maintains that because the assumption of women's Otherness underlies these laws, merely ameliorating or changing particular legislation is insufficient. By itself it cannot alleviate women's Otherness, for piecemeal change can do little if anything to remove male concerns and questions from the center of the *halachic* system. Finally, she asks whether a feminist Judaism has any place for law *as* law. Drawing on recent feminist work both on women's moral development and on women's spirituality, she suggests that law may be a male form that by definition excludes women's voices and concerns. She thus leaves open the possibility that a Judaism that begins with feminist experience would be one based not on laws (*halachic* or otherwise) but rather on fluidity and relationship—two values that seem to shape women's lives. At the same time, however, she insists that she is not advocating anarchy. Rather, she envisions rule-making through communal process, a process that in and of itself will always be subject to change.

Plaskow's revisioning of Israel as religious community includes a call to incorporate the reality of women's presence into the understanding and practices of the Jewish people. Going well beyond equal access, she insists that Jewish institutions must be transformed not only to include women at every level of participation and leadership but also to reflect feminist values. One of those values that she discusses at length is that of honoring difference. According to Plaskow, Judaism's hierarchical understanding of difference, and more specifically of separation as leading to holiness, represents the greatest barrier to the feminist reconceptualization of Jewish community. Jewish feminists, she insists, "cannot transform the place of women's difference within the people of Israel without addressing the larger system of separations in which it is embedded."

The most problematic concept within this system, she believes, is that of chosenness. Unlike Mordecai Kaplan, who also rejected chosenness, Plaskow does not seek to replace it with *any* concept (including Kaplan's concept of vocation) that inevitably leads to a sense of self-identity through separation. While acknowledging that all religious communities have distinct stories, rituals, histories, and the like, she nevertheless believes that chosenness creates hierarchical distinctions not only between Jews and other people but also among Jews themselves. Linking chosenness to women's subordination, she writes:

> It is not that one can draw a direct line from the idea of chosenness to the creation of Others within the Jewish community or that the former provides an explicit model for the latter. But both are part of a cluster of important ideas that make graded differentiation a central model for understanding difference, and the two are also linked to each other both historically and psychologically.

Plaskow's chapter in *Standing Again at Sinai* on revisioning the concept of Jewish community is an important one for an under-standing of her theology. Her rejection of chosenness and subsequent critique of the State of Israel as maintaining hierarchical distinctions among Jews, and even more so between Israeli Jews and Palestinians, reveal the great extent to which Plaskow's revisioned Jewish commu-nity not only reflects but also is given shape and nurtured by feminist values. It is this community too, as Plaskow here makes clear, in which she is willing to locate religious authority. While some Jewish commu-nities have appealed to divine revelation, others to *halachah*, and still others to some romanticized notion of tradition as sources of author-ity, in fact, she maintains, religious authority has always been located in specific communities of interpreters who have decided for them-selves and others that which is authoritative in sacred texts. Thus in claiming the Jewish feminist community as the primary community not only in which she invests authority but also to which she sees herself as accountable, Plaskow maintains that feminists are claiming authority for their own communities in much the same way that rabbinic communities have done in the past and continue to do in the present.

Finally, she maintains that it is out of one's vision of Torah and Israel that one's vision of God emerges. Rejecting the traditional under-standing of God as giver of Torah while retaining that of God and

Israel as covenantal partners, she insists that as our understanding of Jewish community is reconstructed to include women as normative Jews—that is, as full covenantal partners—so our images of God will begin to reflect not only the experiences of men but also the experiences of women. Among the images she explores are female images of Divinity (including that of Goddess), nonhierarchical anthropomorphic imagery, and nonanthropomorphic images of God as dynamic source or process.

Many of these images have been written about by other Jewish feminist theologians: God as mother, source of life, Shechinah, teacher, friend, and others. She also points to the ways in which exclusively masculine images of God continue to legitimate male political, social, and economic power while at the same time emphasizing that as important as it may be to reimage the Divine as female, a larger, more important issue has to do with the nature of Divinity itself. Thus in reimaging the Divine as female, she cautions against perpetuating images of hierarchical domination. Imaging God as Queen of the universe, in other words, may be no better than (or no different from) imaging God as King.

One issue that seems to be sidestepped in *Standing Again at Sinai* is that of revelation. In a 1983 essay on "Language, God, and Liturgy" Plaskow similarly does not explicitly discuss revelation yet takes a theological stance that more recently has led her to affirm that she does not believe in a God who acts in history. In her 1983 essay she maintains that undergirding dominance of any kind appears to be an image of God as Supreme Other. Once God is imagined as a Being who remains other than that which we are, God can all too easily become "the head of a vast hierarchy ... who puts his stamp of approval on the many schemes of dominance, including war, that human beings concoct for themselves." While this is not a theme to which she returns in *Standing Again at Sinai*, in a theological conversation published in *The Reconstructionist*, Plaskow not only rejects God as Other but also rejects God as separable Being. To return to the issue of revelation, then, because the God of her theology is not a Being, supernatural or otherwise, it is not a God who can reveal teachings either through commandment or through the kind of dialogical relationship that Martin Buber and others have envisioned. Rather, she writes, God is the "energy of the physical universe" and the sustaining and containing ground of the human community with which (in the words of feminist theologian Catherine Keller) we are in touch "through the depths of our own interpretative system." For Plaskow, it is when we experience our own power that we feel God's power. God, in other words, is for her the ground of being rather than *a* Being and thus, for her, the experience of acting in and attempting to transform the social order is not one of *working with* but rather *participating in* God.

In the final two sections of *Standing Again at Sinai* Plaskow examines ways in which a feminist Judaism might reconstruct Jewish understandings of sexuality and politics. Both of these reconstructions lead her to a life-affirming vision that, in rejecting previous paradigms that either suppress our emotions or lead to the domination of one group over another, seeks to draw upon human potential and the interconnectedness of all reality. While insisting that we must take responsibility for our actions, she nevertheless advocates "living dangerously" rather than repressing either sexual feelings or feelings in general. She also envisions a model of sexuality freed from the framework of heterosexual marriage and describes feminist political efforts as "an ingredient in the repair and transformation of the world that is part of its redemption." In light of the fact that the overwhelming emphasis in the last two sections of *Standing Again at Sinai* is on the positive values and visions of a feminist Judaism, her 1991 essay on "The Ambiguity of God" can be seen as a necessary corrective to what some have viewed, not just in Plaskow's works but in feminist theology generally, as a romanticization of feminist experience.

Recognizing that feminist reimaging of the Divine has emerged largely out of women's coming to self-awareness in community with other women and their asserting women's healing power of connection to the natural world, she writes that, these images have necessarily been partial. They have all been positive, empowering images, that while significant, have failed to name that aspect of life that is destructive, frightening, and divisive. Again drawing on her understanding of God as power or process, she focuses not on God as good or evil but rather on the irrationality and ambiguity of the sacred and of human experience. Thus, she admits, just as liberating movements often generate new forms of infighting and tyranny, so "many women have been hurt in the name of feminism." How, then, she asks do we name that power that terrifies us and makes us know that we are vulnerable? Can this power be named without our resorting to images of Otherness? Can one "jettison the Lord of history without also losing the Lord of contradictory life"? Can this ambiguous God be named without our invoking those "traditional metaphors that have rationalized oppression and denied the humanity of women"? Or, perhaps, can the image of God as Lord be used to invoke those forces in the world that we can neither control nor contain? While Plaskow does not provide answers to these questions, her conclusion brings her back from the "boundary of Judaism" in which she situates herself in *Standing Again at Sinai* to a "new place of wrestling with [her] tradition."

Rachel Adler: Toward a Theology of Justice

While the works of Rachel Adler have been less exclusively theological than those of Judith Plaskow, Adler deserves recognition as a Jewish feminist theologian whose writings have exerted a great influence on many within the American Jewish community. Trained as a literature instructor and psychotherapist, she did her doctoral work in social ethics at the University of Southern California and Hebrew Union College–Jewish Institute of Religion in Los Angeles. Adler's work reflects her own spiritual journey from Reform Judaism to Orthodoxy and back to Reform. Her early work, published in the 1970's, focused on the need for *halachic* change; her recent work has focused on spiritual transformation outside of the classical *halachic* system. What all of her works share, however, is an interest in law and traditional texts, and a passionate concern for justice.

In one of her earliest essays, published in 1973, Adler introduced the historical and theological category of women as peripheral Jews. Concluding that because women are seen as peripheral within the *halachic* system (or what Plaskow and later Adler herself have identified as Other than normative Jews), so women not only are legally subordinate to men but also have less access to the sacred. Her essay "*Tum'ah* and *Toharah*: Ends and Beginnings," also published in 1973, represented an attempt to emphasize the ways in which the laws of *niddah* (biblically based, rabbinic laws concerning menstruation) can spiritually enrich women's lives. Without denying that the chief *halachic* significance of these laws has to do with the regulation of ritual purity and impurity, Adler viewed them from the perspective of the observant, married, menstruating woman (i.e., the *niddah* herself). Perceiving the *niddah*, in other words, as subject rather than object, Adler envisioned immersion in the *mikveh* (stream of natural water) as a confrontation with mortality and re-emergence as a form of rebirth. While the *halachic* system may view women as peripheral, women themselves, she seemed to be saying, need not perceive themselves as peripheral Jews. Rather, she maintained, it is possible for women to discover religious significance within the context of classical *halachah* by reenvisioning or personally transforming the meaning of religious obligations.

By the early 1980s, however, Adler's growing sense of otherness, alienation, and exclusion from traditional Jewish texts led to her ideological and communal break from Orthodoxy. At the same time, she realized that the problem of women's otherness was not confined to Orthodoxy but was rooted in the texts themselves. She noted that in sharp contrast to her own, internal sense of being fully Jewish, biblical and rabbinic texts often address the Jewish people as a community of men (perhaps the clearest example that she offers is Exodus 19:15, which reads: "And [Moses] said to the people, 'Be ready for the third day; do not go near a woman' "). For Adler, then, the issue was no longer: How can observant Jewish women find personal meaning in the commandments? but rather: If the texts address only Jewish men, how are women to discover what God wants us to do, as Jews and as women? Or, put in more legal terms: "If the normative contractor of the covenant is the Jewish male . . . [how can] the Jewish female . . . be other than a partial and diminished participant?"

Whereas in 1973 Adler's interest (as seen in her essay on *niddah*) was in creating a theology of purity, she now believes that her essay did little more than create a "theology for the despised." Indeed, in some of her more recent writings Adler has asked whether the injustice of the *halachic* system (and, more generally, of Jewish tradition) is so great that for women to feel fully Jewish or feel close to God they must in fact imagine themselves as men. She asks, in other words, whether the exclusion of women's feelings and experiences from Jewish texts, rituals, and liturgy precludes women's *ever* feeling fully Jewish as women or whether it is only when women forget that they are women (and thus cut themselves off from who they really are) that they can experience themselves as normative Jews.

While the specific questions that Adler raises are different from those of Plaskow, the nature of their critiques have a great deal in common. Where their theologies differ is not so much in their understanding of what it means to be a woman within the classical *halachic* system as in their experience of God, Torah, and Israel. Because their experience of each is so different, the directions that their theologies have taken bear only a superficial resemblance to one another.

Like Plaskow, for example, Adler underscores the importance of reimaging the Divine. She shares Plaskow's belief that envisioning God as exclusively male has important political and social as well as theological implications, and she believes, as Plaskow does, that for women to feel that they too have been created in God's image, it is essential that God-language be expanded. Because, however, the community in which Adler situates herself is not a contemporary feminist community composed exclusively of women but rather a progressive Jewish community made up of women and men, the "we" to whom she refers in her writings explicitly refers to men and women. Thus, for example, in discussing the language of theology and prayer she asks: How can we, as Jewish men and women, expand our God-language to include masculine and feminine metaphors and words? Moreover, if the injustice of the tradition calls its content into question, "How will we retain our sense of commandedness, and how will we determine what we have been commanded?"

For Adler, the words and metaphors that Jews use to lead them toward God need not be anthropomorphic. At the same time, however, the God that she envisions is very much a personal Being rather than a process, One who is capable of commanding and of revealing religious teachings. Because Adler believes that Jewish teachings can be revealed, her source of authority does not derive exclusively from the community of which she sees herself as a member. Nor, for that matter, does it derive from a sense of autonomous selfhood. Rather, as she recently has written, authority is covenantal, reflecting an ongoing human-Divine relationship that is rooted in personal and communal experience as well as in sacred texts. It is by virtue of this covenantal authority, she believes, that the Jewish people are able to translate the teachings of the Torah into communal praxis.

Without calling for a complete revisioning of what Jews traditionally have identified as Torah, Adler insists that feminist Jews (men as well as women) must tell their own stories, "reinterpreting narratives the tradition believes it owns and understands." In so doing, she writes, we can create a new vision of what *halachah* can and should be. Drawing on Robert Cover's understanding of law as that which is generated by a *nomos* or universe of values, rules, and meanings embedded in stories, she exhorts progressive Jews to work with her in revisioning *halachah* from source of power to source of meaning grounded in communal praxis. She advocates retaining those laws that remain grounded in the practice of the progressive Jewish community while adding new laws, grounded in new stories, that reflect new communal practices.

While Adler's aim is to create a vision of liberal or progressive Judaism that maintains a sense of legal integrity, her understanding of law, again drawing upon the work of Robert Cover, is that which is constantly vulnerable to revisioning and reinterpretation. Adler insists that liberal Judaism needs *halachah* in order to embody its sacred stories and values in communal praxis. Yet in order to serve as a source of meaning, it must be dynamic rather than static, "visionary rather than conservative," arising cooperatively, communally, and covenantally rather than being externally imposed and passively obeyed.

Adler identifies the theologically based legal project in which she currently sees herself engaged as redemptive, for its aim, she writes, is "the moral transformation of the law and the social world in which it is practiced." Believing that a liberal *halachah* can ground beliefs and actions that are just, Adler believes that God, as covenantal partner, is also just, even though we do not always experience God as either just or loving. Indeed, she admits, the question of why we often experience a just God as unjust may never be resolved without our either falsifying our experience or absolving God of that for which God in fact may be responsible. Rather than attempting to find a resolution to what she believes may well be an insoluble theological dilemma, Adler focuses on ways in which Jews themselves can create *tzeddik* (justice by righteousness) and, in so doing, embody within the context of a just society a Torah that views human beings as ever-changing subjects in relationship to one another. In a 1991 essay on "Breaking Boundaries," Adler identifies this Torah as the Torah of self and other.

Marcia Falk: Beyond Anthropocentrism

Marcia Falk has long achieved scholarly and popular recognition as a poet and Hebrew and Yiddish translator. Since 1985, with the publication of her essay "What About God?" in *Moment* magazine, she has also gained recognition as a theologian working to create what she (like Judith Plaskow and others) has identified as a feminist Judaism. To date, most of her theological work has focused on the creation of new blessings. Some have argued that writing blessings is not the same as writing theology, and indeed, Falk's blessings may more properly be described as *expressions* of her theology rather than theological works per se. Yet those who dismiss Falk as a theologian on the basis of literary form miss the important theological statements that her blessings make. Responding to the three central categories of God, Torah, and Israel, Falk has created new Hebrew blessings (with English translations) that give voice to what she has identified as a theology of immanence.

Like other Jewish feminist theologians, Falk has insisted that in order for Jewish women to see themselves and to be considered by others as normative Jews, the names by which Jews address God must be reexamined. She too has maintained that exclusively male images of Deity not only reinforce male power but also suggest that there is an essential kinship between men and God that women simply do not share. Yet for Falk, the insistence that God no longer be addressed as exclusively male does not lead her to affirm, as other Jewish feminist theologians have, that God therefore should be addressed as male and female (Father and Mother, He and She, etc.). While affirming the importance of multiple images of Deity, Falk nevertheless believes that all personal images of God are limited, both because they can be only partial images of our experience and because favoring particular images over others inevitably sets up hierarchical dualisms leading either to the domination of one group of people over another or to the domination of humanity over the rest of creation. Believing in God as Process rather than as Being, Falk thus attempts to move beyond *all* anthropomorphic images of Deity. To her, one can affirm that all of us, male and female, have been created in the image of God without conjuring up images that are male or female (though given the structure of the Hebrew language, they cannot be grammatically neutral). Rather, she insists, to be created in God's image means that God is part of all of us just as all of us are part of God.

Yet Falk's vision of an all-inclusive Deity goes beyond what she has identified as anthropocentrism. Cautioning us against taking too literally the idea of *tzelem elohim* (humanity being created in God's image), she maintains that all of creation is part of God just as God is part of (or within) all of creation. While some undoubtedly would label Falk's theological vision pantheistic or pagan, she herself identifies it as authentically monotheistic. Attempting to reconstruct monotheism rather than reject it, she defines authentic monotheism as that which affirms the unity of all creation and believes that embracing a multiplicity of Divine images not only helps celebrate diversity and pluralism but also "diminishes the likelihood of unconscious forms of idolatry, such as 'speciesism,'" that is, the valuing of one group of human beings over another and the domination of the human species over other forms of life.

In composing new blessings, Falk thus turns to a variety of metaphors, many of which are drawn from nature. Whether imaging God as "Source of Life," "Flow of Life," or "Breath of All Living Things," Falk underscores her theological conviction that monotheism means that if all of life is created in the image of Divinity, then the "images with which we point towards divinity must reflect us all." Moving beyond anthropomorphic images enables Falk to envision God in ways that reflect the Divine as equally within women and men, while drawing on images that are nonanthropocentric enables her to name the Divine as that which exists, and flows through, all of creation. Falk's vision of God, then, is of an immanent force or power that is neither apart from nor above the world. Unlike classical Jewish sources, which, she believes, conceptually affirm immanence yet posit images of God that are overwhelmingly transcendent, particularly in worship, her blessings envision God as permeating the world. God is that which ripens fruit on the vine, revives and sustains us, and nourishes us and the earth. She rejects transcendence for many of the same reasons she rejects anthropomorphic images of Deity. Transcendent images, she believes, posit God as Other, creating a series of dualisms (God and humanity, God and nature, God and the world, etc.), and all dualisms lead to the hierarchical domination of God over humanity and of humanity over the earth. These in turn, she maintains, prevent us from embracing our commitment as Jews to *tikkun olam*, that is, to the repair of a world that is still fragmented.

The communities to which Falk addresses her work are both the liberal Jewish and feminist communities. Though the publication of her *Book of Blessings* will undoubtedly bring her work to a larger audience, increasing numbers of feminist prayer groups all over the United States already have begun to incorporate her blessings into their worship, and the Reconstructionist movement has included some in its new prayer book for Sabbath Eve. Among those aspects of her blessings that are most appealing to those who use them is Falk's replacing the formulaic "*Baruch Ata Adonai Eloheinu Melech Ha'Olam*" (Blessed are You, Lord our God, King of the Universe) with "*N'varech*" (Let us bless). In one stroke she both eliminates images of God as male and as the One who hierarchically dominates creation and also claims for the community the power to bless. In so doing, Falk transforms traditional blessings, which invoke God's blessedness, to those that assert for the Jewish community a more active role in the creation and redemption of the world.

Although to date the focus of her writings has been elsewhere, Falk's understanding of Torah is of that which is both ideal and process. Presumably created by the Jewish people (since she does not believe in a God who reveals teachings, values, or a divine presence apart from us and the world), Torah as she views it has at its core a passion and commitment to justice that can be found in a "central and significant body of teachings that have been inspirational for many feminist Jews, and that have even, for some of us, parented our feminist concerns." Falk's vision of a feminist Judaism is one based on empathy and a sense of connectedness to others (leading her, for example, to reject chosenness as "anti-Gentilism") and to the world in which we live. At the same time, however, she wishes to retain Judaism's recognition that separateness can lead to holiness (and thus her Havdalah blessing begins "Let us distinguish parts within the whole and bless their differences"). Without negating the importance of distinctness, then, Falk seems to be saying that Torah as process and ideal needs to underscore the unity of all existence while honoring the differences among us. Perhaps in the future Falk will discuss in greater detail specific teachings through which this goal might be achieved.

Drorah Setel: Feminist Theory and Religious Transformation

Biblical scholar and feminist theologian Drorah Setel has attempted to use feminist theory as a framework in which to view both women in the Bible and the more general world view espoused in Jewish tradition. The assumption underlying her work is that "feminism is a distinct perspective which, although emerging from the experience of women, is applicable to human experience as a whole." Most of her theological work, therefore, does not begin with Setel's personal responses to the categories of God, Torah, and Israel. Nor does it begin with the responses of other Jewish feminists. Rather, it begins by laying bare the comprehensive world view traditionally espoused by Judaism and then contrasting that world view to the one that underlies and gives shape to feminist values. It is Setel's contention that these world views not only are different but in some respects are antithetical to one another.

Beginning with the Bible (and making reference to later rabbinic texts), Setel maintains, as have other Jewish feminist theologians, that Judaism traditionally has viewed men as subjects and women as objects, or, drawing on the work of Simone de Beauvoir, as Other. At the same time, Setel insists that the objectification of women needs to be seen as part of a more general tendency to divide all of human experience into dualistic categories. Thus, for example, the categorization of feminine versus masculine needs to be placed alongside such polarizations as material and spiritual, emotional and rational, bad and good, passive and aggressive. Viewed from a feminist perspective, which values connectedness and relation, these dualisms, she writes, are inextricably linked with oppression. More specifically, she argues that once one affirms an essential separateness between men and women, so one inevitably is led to affirm an essential separateness among races, ethnic groups, and socioeconomic classes.

While Setel acknowledges the pervasiveness of this kind of polarized thinking within the Jewish tradition, she refuses to view it as inevitable. Arguing that the feminist transformation of Judaism is not only possible but imperative, she maintains that all of us—women and men—have a responsibility to fight oppression in whatever form it takes and to create a Judaism, and a world, that affirms the full humanity of all people. Setel's consistency in her claims that dualisms lead to the oppression of one group over another causes her to reject Judaism's traditional understanding of separation as leading to holiness. While acknowledging how deeply entrenched this view remains, she nevertheless insists that new forms of Jewish practice must be developed or old ones transformed. Those that cannot be transformed, she suggests, should be abandoned. Among them is male circumcision, which she believes theologically perpetuates the physical and spiritual separation of Jewish men from Jewish women in an all-male Covenant while at the same time hierarchically setting Jewish and non-Jewish men apart from one another.

It is clear that the feminist Jewish community envisioned by Setel is very much a community composed of men and women. Believing that the oppression not only of women but of other ethnicities, races, and classes will continue as long as polarized thinking persists, she has focused her interest on transforming the ways in which *all* Jews perceive the world. Emphasizing the fact that despite its underlying framework of separation, Judaism has always maintained such relational concerns as those tied to social justice, Setel insists that *tikkun olam* (repairing the world) is a task that requires all of our efforts.

While Setel places her visions of the transformation of Jewish practice and Jewish world view within the framework of feminist theory, she theologically grounds these visions in an understanding of Divinity that in many ways shares a great deal with that articulated by Marcia Falk. Falk's notion of authentic monotheism as affirming the unity of creation is similar to what Setel identifies as monotheism (in contrast to that which she labels "vulgar monotheism"). Both stress the immanence of Divinity as a process or force that pervades all creation, and both include images drawn from nature in invoking the Divine. Setel, however, drawing on as many images as possible that affirm the values of unity, diversity, and connectedness, retains such anthropomorphic (immanent) images as companion and friend. She also identifies Divinity as Shechinah ("She Who Dwells Among Us"), which she points out is one female metaphor preserved in the Jewish tradition that describes the Divine in relationship, and as God(dess), an image that underscores her belief in the unity of creation while making explicit the potential and validity of Divine images that are feminine or female. Affirming that despite all of its dualisms, Judaism, like feminism, has always valued relationship and has recognized that there is a link between personal liberation and social change, Setel invites women and men to work with her in creating a nondualistic Judaism whose theological beliefs, sense of community, and everyday practice truly reflect values that are not just fully feminist but fully Jewish as well.

A Personal Assessment

Much of the constructive theological work in which I myself have been engaged owes a great deal to the Jewish feminist theologians whose writings have been discussed. I have learned a great deal from reading their works and have been spiritually challenged by the many theological debates and discussions that we have had with one another. While not identifying my objective as the creation of a feminist Judaism, this demurral may be less ideological than communal, stemming from the fact that the Jewish community with which I most strongly identify is the liberal Jewish community, and even more specifically the Reform movement, of which I have been a member my entire life.

It is primarily with other liberal Jews, both laity and clergy, that I am most actively engaged in working toward the kinds of feminist transformations that I shall in a moment detail. My goal is not some universal transformation of Judaism nor is it the creation of a new religious movement or denomination. Rather, it is the transformation of Reform Judaism in ways that reflect feminist insights and values while at the same time honoring and maintaining the insights and values of Reform. While many, if not most, of my concerns share many commonalities with those articulated by other liberal Jews, including Reconstructionists, many within the Conservative movement, and those who identify themselves as New Age, *havurah*, or feminist Jews, the religious language that I speak is very much the language of Reform Judaism. It includes such phrases as "ethical monotheism" and "ongoing revelation," the belief that "one serves God best by serving others" (a phrase rooted in nineteenth-century Classical Reform taken from the writings of George Eliot), and the conviction that observance in and of itself does not make one holy. Perhaps the reason I most often identify myself as a liberal Jewish theologian (and not a Reform theologian) is that I recognize the great extent to which my religious language is also indebted to Mordecai Kaplan, whose understanding of Judaism as a civilization, call for "unity in diversity," allowing *halachah* a "vote but not veto," great commitment to change, and love for *klal Yisrael* (i.e., the Jewish community and all that has shaped and nurtured it in the past, as well as that which shapes and nurtures it in the present) have greatly influenced my understanding both of what Judaism is and of what it might be.

Torah, as I understand it, refers to Jewish teachings and values that reflect the ongoing covenantal relationship between God and the Jewish people. Like Rachel Adler, with whom my theology has a great deal in common, I envision God as a personal Being capable of commanding and of revealing religious teachings. Similarly, my source of authority is rooted in both personal and communal experience as well as in sacred texts. While applauding Adler's efforts to revision *halachah*, I question whether progressive Jews (and Reform Jews in particular) can be persuaded to forfeit their autonomy even for the best of causes, that is, for a *halachah* that gives meaning to their actions and helps transform Reform Judaism from a way of thinking into a way of life. Indeed, because autonomy has been so central to Reform Judaism, talking about a Reform *halachah* may well be premature.

Drawing on the values of relationship and connectedness, my interest is in creating a theology of peoplehood that is rooted in the experiences of American Reform Jews. In the recognition that feminism as a philosophical perspective has already had a great impact on the liberal Jewish community and that the Reform commitment to social action has long underscored relationship and connection as Jewish values (a point that Drorah Setel also makes in her writings), this theology begins with the rejection of classical Reform's identification of Judaism with personal religion. It suggests that the Jewish self exists in covenant not as a "single soul in its full individuality" (to quote Eugene Borowitz) but as a relational soul in community with others. Rather than beginning with the autonomous self who chooses to become a Jewish self, my theology, deeply infused with Jewish and feminist values, begins with the recognition that no self is fully autonomous. As Martin Buber wrote long ago, we always exist in relationship to others and to the world in which we live.

To date, most of my own theological writings have focused on my relationship to God and on God's relationship with all creation. Essays written in the early 1980's focused on the importance of reimaging the Divine as male and female, both to underscore the Jewish conviction that all of us—men and women—have been created in the image of God, and to eliminate the theological justification for male political and social power that exclusively masculine images of Deity provide. These essays also suggested, though these views have yet to be developed at length, that one possible solution to the problem of theodicy (the existence of evil in light of God's being all-knowing, all-powerful, and all-good) may be that God is neither all-powerful nor all-good but in fact has both an evil and a good nature, as do we, those beings created in the Divine image. God therefore cannot always prevent human tragedy because God is not only strong but also weak. Drawing on Heinrich Zimmer's study of Indian myths and symbols which suggests that a deity is great only if that deity can display "mutually antagonistic attitudes and activities," one essay concludes that Zimmer may well be right; by limiting God, we have in fact limited God's greatness.

More recent theological works have emphasized that God's metaphorical gender is less important that the kinds of images through which God is envisioned. Insisting that there is a direct connection between the ways in which we envision the Divine relationship and the ways in which we actually relate to the world and its creations, they maintain that using images of hierarchical domination in imaging the Divine—such as King, Lord, Queen—encourages an envisioning of the human-Divine relationship as one of domination and submission. It establishes this relationship as a model of how things really are, encouraging us, even if unintentionally, to set ourselves over and against both the earth and other people—especially over those to whom we may feel superior by virtue of our gender, race, socioeconomic class, age, religious affiliation, nationality, or other qualities. Believing that God is both immanent and transcendent, I am at present working to create new images of Divinity that will encourage myself and others to work with God rather than under God's authority.

At the same time, I am continuing to create *midrashim* that give expression to my theological visions. Like the intent of those Rabbis who created classical *midrashim*, my intention is to enable biblical texts to speak to me, that is, meaningfully to ground and give expression to my own understanding of Judaism. Such *midrashim* begin with a feminist hermeneutics of suspicion. Focusing on biblical women whose actions the text minimizes or ignores, they then attempt to view biblical texts through the lens of feminist experience (in this case, my own). *Midrash* clearly is an important resource for Jewish feminist theology, for if, as Laura Geller has written, to be a Jew means to tell one's story within the Jewish story, then *midrashim* written in story form (as mine and those recently created by other feminists have been) are particularly effective means of seeing women not as objectified Others but as normative Jews whose experiences of God, Torah, and Israel can add to, challenge, and transform previously held theological convictions.

But Is It Jewish?

Jewish feminist theology may be described as a contextual theology that responds to Judaism's fundamental categories of God, Torah, and Israel. Nonetheless, one may ask—as some critics have already—whether this theology is in fact Jewish. To this non-Orthodox Jew who believes in the authenticity of liberal Judaism, the answer is clearly yes. As this chapter has indicated, the sources on which Jewish feminist theologians have drawn and continue to draw are Jewish ones (though not exclusively so), as are the religious communities out of which each sees her theology emerging. At the same time, most Jewish feminist theologians, including those referred to in this chapter, acknowledge that there may be personal or communal boundaries beyond which they as Jews cannot go.

Though some Jewish feminist theologians (myself among them) seem to be more concerned with boundaries than others, even Judith Plaskow, who has maintained that an insistence on predetermined boundaries may confine the creativity and resources of Jewish feminists, admits that monotheism *is* a boundary for her. Indeed, it seems to be a crucial boundary for all of the Jewish feminist theologians whose works have been mentioned here. Other boundaries that emerge in the work of Jewish feminist theologians include the following: an *a priori* commitment to placing one's experiences of the Divine within a specifically Jewish framework; an understanding of Judaism that retains a sense of legal integrity; and a refraining from using names for Divinity (such as Elilah) that in the biblical text not only are names for a deity other than the Hebrew God but also, in Hebrew, equate such worship with idolatry.

For Women Only?

To the extent that Jewish feminist theology is grounded in the experiences of Jewish women, it is by definition a theology that can be created by women only. At the same time, however, because Jewish feminist theology can also be seen as a theology rooted in feminist and Jewish values, so its insights can be reflected upon and shared by women and men. Indeed, there are a growing number of male rabbis and academics—among them Daniel Boyarin, Howard Eilberg-Schwartz, David Ellenson, Lawrence Hoffman, Lawrence Kushner, Zalman Schachter-Shalomi, and Arthur Waskow—who have openly acknowledged their indebtedness to feminist theology. Just as many Jewish feminists have drawn on their work, so in their writings and teachings have they drawn on the works of Jewish feminists. At the same time, they have understood the importance of speaking with and to feminist theologians rather than speaking for them.

Contributions of Feminist Theology

Undoubtedly, one of the greatest contributions that Jewish feminist theology has already made has been to demonstrate that it is possible for diverse groups of people to talk seriously about Jewish theology outside of a *halachic* framework. While religiously liberal rabbis have long discussed the creation of a non-*halachic* Jewish self-identity, they have not taken the theological basis for this identity seriously enough. Certainly, in the twentieth century there have been a handful of liberal Jewish theologians who have taken the Jewish theological enterprise seriously, Eugene Borowitz among them, but feminist theologians have been the first to create, however loosely, a network of religiously liberal theologians who have seriously examined together, both formally and informally, traditional and liberal Jewish theological claims.

Further, in attempting to ground this theology in their experience as women, feminist theologians have called into question not only traditional theological language (for example, the concept of a Father, rather than a Mother, God, who gives birth to creation), but also the ways in which theology is done. Through the creation of new blessings, *midrashim*, poems, rituals, and the like, feminist theologians have added a vibrancy to the liberal Jewish theological enterprise. While it is hoped that more fully developed Jewish feminist theologies will be written in the future, the many questions raised and the many theological directions pursued have already awakened in a significant number of American Jews both an intellectual and a personal interest in theological exploration.

It is too early to identify, much less assess, all of the lasting contributions of Jewish feminist theology. It is hoped that among them will be the encouragement of growing numbers of Jewish women to reclaim the power of naming themselves, the world, and God. In so doing, it will have helped to create a more inclusive Judaism, for as Judith Plaskow has written, "Only when those who have had the power of naming stolen from us find our voices and begin to speak will Judaism become a religion that includes all Jews—will it truly be a Judaism of women and men."

14

Looking Ahead

IF WESTERN CULTURE today were dominated by several identifiable intellectual currents, one might hope to know in which directions Jewish thought is likely to develop. However, since fragmentariness best characterizes our inner life, any kind of extrapolation to the future appears particularly foolhardy.

Something similar may be said of Jewish practice, the living stream from which Jewish thought has often grown. One can identify two broad currents. One is spreading out in ever greater integration within the general society, a flow most unlikely to motivate concern with Judaism and its intellectual exposition. The other stream has channeled its energy into intensive Jewish living or practice. But contemporary Jewish spiritual activity is thoroughly diverse and frequently displays clashing emphases, all of which gives our Jewish religiosity much of its special fascination. Where this activity has taken the intense form of European-style *yeshivah* or Hasidic life, its concern with Jewish thought is quite traditional, the reinterpretation of or commentary on classic texts in styles that customarily eschew university methodologies. Where, in contrast, it has been religiously innovative, intellectuality has manifested itself mostly in seeking freshly expressive rites and liturgies.

In between these movements we see an astonishing diversity of efforts to reach out to Jews and make Judaism come alive for them. Who knows what theories of Judaism may yet be stimulated by one or another of these activities? Surely the twentieth century was full of surprising twists and turns of Jewish life and thought. The biggest shock would be if the twenty-first century turned out to be culturally stable and intellectually secure; stranger shifts have happened in that openness of activity we call human history.

In tribute to the many promising possibilities of Jewish thought that cannot be treated here, we might note two contrasting approaches taken by contemporary thinkers of rather different interests. Some people find themselves most comfortable taking an eclectic stance, from which they might have access to the best of all reinterpretations of Judaism. Others, believing anything less than rigorous cognition is a betrayal of the unique human capacity to think, seek a revival of Jewish philosophy.

The Beauty of the Parts Rather Than the Beauty of the System

The eclectic approach takes many forms, since there seem to be no limits to what people can find attractive in their understanding of Judaism. In the more philosophic utilization of this method—seen, for example, in the work of Neil Gillman and Elliot Dorff—the issues raised by specific intellectual systems are confronted and, where possible, their responses adopted. Thus with regard to God, the skeptical questions of the rationalists mean that doubt will be given considerable respect, but the greater latitude accorded religious experience by the nonrationalists will finally decide the issue for God's reality. The great advantage of such an approach is that one can be open to every stimulating intellectual movement and indicate how one's Judaism can be hospitable to each. To a considerable extent, eclecticism is what we see in most classic Jewish texts. They are far more likely to feature a summoning of views than a rigorously worked out systematic intellectual structure.

Eclecticism, however, suffers from an amiability that evades the logical clash between some of its affirmations, such as in wanting to employ both rationalist and nonrationalist modes of speaking about God. Where other thinkers seriously debate how to decide between the alternatives, the eclectics simply include both views, a move that causes many academics to denigrate eclecticism.

The more common variety of eclecticism prefers to explain Judaism by copious citation from our traditional literature. In its naive form, writers treat major themes of Jewish belief by presenting a series of texts that, as they read them, reach a certain theological conclusion, which they then assert is "the" Jewish view. Two fundamental problems beset this procedure. First, by what criteria are these particular texts presented and others, often of quite divergent views, not adduced? An unwillingness to face this vital methodological issue generally vitiates a writer's claim to serious attention. However, yet a second problem arises: On what basis do thinkers assert that their reading of the texts is reasonably faithful to these texts so as to vouch for a view's authenticity? While all interpretations of texts are necessarily somewhat personal, claims to classic Jewish continuity should be as laden with history and our reading tradition as with the scholar's personal preferences.

The most sophisticated and accomplished theological reader of the Jewish tradition is Louis Jacobs. He has given a lucid, erudite reading of the corpus of Jewish religious experience in his book *A Jewish Theology*. In response to the challenge of indicating his criteria, he suggests that his study of our tradition over the years has led him to the conclusion that certain religious positions constitute the enduring core of Jewish belief. He is bolstered in this claim by the breadth and depth of his publications over the years. Thus he is at home not only in the medieval Jewish philosophic texts—regularly cited by thinkers adducing Jewish predecessors—but in those of Jewish mystics. He has full command of Rabbinic literature and its *halachic* development. He has pioneered the study of theological topics in the *teshuvot*, the literature of legal *responsa* that remains authoritative for traditional Jews to this day. Almost alone, he has not evaded the dialectic of opinion and approaches of Jewish thinkers in any given age but has sought to expose the unity he sees underlying them. And he comes to his traditionalism with a thoroughgoing knowledge of contemporary findings in the history and philosophy of religion. Should further defense of his position be required, Jacobs can argue that his stance is fundamentally that of a Jewish believer and he therefore operates in this area as Jews have done in prior ages.

Jacobs' critics remain respectful but unconvinced. While his learning is exemplary, we still do not know the hermeneutical assumptions that control his reading of Judaism. Therefore we cannot give them the critical evaluation that responsible involvement in Jewish theology would seem to require. Let us consider a not insignificant issue: God's revelation. Biblical-rabbinic doctrine down to the present affirms God's authorship of the Written Torah (narrowly, the first five books of the Bible; broadly, the entire Bible). Jacobs rejects this doctrine on the basis of the critical study of the Torah text. But he does not similarly rely on modern study when assessing the tenability of the rest of traditional Jewish belief. He does not clarify the limits he would set on the use of so humanistic a criterion, one liberals would apply more broadly.

David Novak's work promises to overcome this difficulty. While most of his writing has been on *halachic* and ethical issues, he has infused these with a theological concern rare among experts in this area. On occasion, as in his impressive study of the image of the non-Jew in Jewish literature, he has indicated his belief that, the fundamentals of Jewish faith aside, rationalism best explains intellectually the development of Jewish law. His later work has increasingly turned to theoretical questions, with a rational explication of chosenness high on his agenda. Since his interpretation of Judaism may be located between modern Orthodoxy and Louis Jacobs' traditionalism, his systematic fusion of faith and reason would be of particular interest.

Rosenzweig: Unexpected Patron of Jewish Philosophy's Revival

Moving now to the other current, several factors have come together to make possible a rebirth of philosophical thinking about Judaism. The recent decades have been so dominated by nonrationalist approaches to Jewish thought that a reaction to them has almost seemed overdue. In this period, too, a significant number of young Jews have dedicated their lives to academic philosophy while maintaining a deep devotion to Judaism. Not so long ago colleagues would have sneered at proposals for courses in medieval Jewish philosophy or contemporary Jewish thought as being insufferably parochial. In recent, more pluralistic days, such courses, while not abundant, are offered in many places. Equally important, young academics interested in how philosophy and Judaism might live together harmoniously will not find their careers mortally wounded by devoting themselves to contemporary Jewish philosophic figures.

The posthumous publication of many of the Jewish writings of Steven S. Schwarzschild, the preeminent standard-bearer of Cohenian neo-Kantianism in the past generation, has reawakened interest in this stimulating point of view. Kenneth Seeskin's work has taken up this challenge with good effect. The difficulties lying in the way of a full-scale employment of this approach are immense, for it can gain credence only with the thoroughgoing rehabilitation of general Neo-Kantianism, a prospect that presently seems most unlikely.

The most lively philosophic prospects currently stem from post-modernism (briefly introduced in Chapter 12) and the thought of Emmanuel Levinas. A Lithuanian Jew whose life has been spent in France as an academic and a Jewish community professional. He survived the Holocaust years as a French soldier captured and interned in a prisoner of war camp. His thought, for all its difficulty and unfamiliar style of arguing, is especially attractive to philosophers interested in constructive Jewish thinking because he not only presents a commanding ethics but makes ethics central to his system. (For my view of the philosophical postmodernists' problem with ethics see Chapter 12.) And the unlikely, acknowledged pathfinder for this new wave of philosophic thinking is Franz Rosenzweig.

The strictly philosophic aspect of Rosenzweig's thought had little influence on Jewish thinkers until recently. Rather, the community has taken his intellectual eminence for granted and esteemed him for affirming Jewish law despite a nonverbal theory of revelation (see Chapter 6). But first in Germany and then in France thinkers of the past two decades have turned to him as one who saw the coming philosophic difficulties and responded to them.

With Marxism dead, the Germans wanted to rethink Hegel so as to create a nontotalitarian theory of the state, an interest that led to the republication of Rosenzweig's revised doctoral dissertation, *Hegel and the State*, more than half a century after its issuance. The French interest has been more generally philosophic. Many academic thinkers, particularly in continental Europe, have wondered how to reinvigorate Greek philosophy after Heidegger's telling attack on its historic development. With his own effort to reconstruct thought a shambles, how was it possible to refashion philosophy and thus avoid giving up on the mind's creative power?

Rosenzweig was one of those who foresaw this problem about a decade before Heidegger, but, unlike most others, he found a way to respond to it. Application of his method yielded *The Star of Redemption* but that work, paradoxically, led him away from philosophizing "into life" (*The Star*'s famous concluding words). He did once return to the abstract issue of philosophic method, in his essay "The New Thinking," but until recently most readers have not found the restatement much clearer than the opaque formulations of *The Star*.

Rosenzweig began his magnum opus with an argument rejecting traditional philosophy. He did so by contrasting the sense of reality brought on by the threat of one's own death with the anesthetizing of that feeling brought on by the standard philosophic project of explaining reality as the All (or as Levinas prefers to call it, Totality). Rosenzweig then proceeds by thinking about what the living-dying single self encounters as it goes into life. This exploration yields his well-known three realities—"Man," the World, and God—and then, in turn, a philosophy that tries to understand the relations among them. Rosenzweig called this new thinking "absolute empiricism." By this he meant that its fundamentals were not posited or freely created by the mind. In living, one simply found them before one, so thought ought to concern itself with them.

The French interest in this method arose largely, but not entirely, as part of the aftermath of Derrida's deconstruction of Western thought, that is, of its linguistic basis. Rosenzweig suddenly had relevance as one who had been in a similar situation but overcame it. All this describes the general intellectual situation. Levinas, however, had long found Rosenzweig significant for reasons related to his own view of the relation between Judaism and philosophy.

Can Levinas' Phenomenology Now Revitalize
Jewish Philosophy?

Levinas had begun his own philosophy long before the emergence of French structuralism and the deconstruction that then toppled it. He did so as part of that stream of French thought that derives from the work of Edmund Husserl. Born into a Jewish family, Husserl converted to Christianity to pursue an academic career and founded a philosophic method he called "phenomenology." His international reputation kept him and his Jewish wife safe from the Nazis. In 1939 he died and his wife was spirited out of Germany and hidden in Belgium by a Christian disciple. His philosophic method—to investigate internally the rational structures involved in our consciousness of anything—had its greatest acceptance through its application by Sartre and other atheistic existentialists. Levinas became one of the leading French exponents of Husserlian phenomenology.

Having survived Hitler, Levinas could not shake the horror of what the Nazis had done. Ethics had to be the central task of philosophy, in fact its fundamental premise and guiding principle. It also could not be the tepid liberal ethics that had failed so miserably to remind "good people" of what they must do in the face of evil, nor the old-style philosophy that reduced living persons to abstract categories. But with the standard rationalisms unable to generate a commanding, substantive ethics, philosophy seemed incapable of responding to this immediate, historic need.

It was just here that Levinas' phenomenological approach proved helpful, for he identified "the face" of the other as the source of a radical ethical claim on oneself. Consider what a "face" implies: another person, utterly not myself, with complete individuality that I do not control or even comprehend, who stands over against me and, by that very being there, demands to be treated differently from any object. This is the womb of responsibility.

A number of these themes are reminiscent of Buber, but Levinas rejects his notion of the I-thou encounter both methodologically and substantively. In regard to method, Buber reserves the ethical for a special realm, the I-thou, one inaccessible to ordinary careful thinking and therefore beyond the realm of examination and argument. Levinas demands the greater responsibility that intensive reflection can awaken even though he recognizes the need to refashion how philosophy is done. As to substance, Buber sees the I-thou as fully mutual but Levinas insists that in the presence of "a face" an unconditional demand is made upon oneself for the other. He will not soften this ethical imperative by limiting its extent. I must take full responsibility for the other, including what the other does, as hateful as that may be. And I must do this without any thought of reciprocity. I will compromise my ethic duty if I do it hoping that as I am unconditionally committed to the other, so the other person will now be to me. The ethical situation, Levinas contends, is that unqualified; and with similar intensity, it is utterly fundamental to one's humanhood.

The Rich Jewishness of the Philosopher

This philosophical side of Levinas quickly found expression in what he considers the other side to his mature thought, his explication of Jewish texts. In his many lectures to an annual meeting of French Jewish intellectuals, Levinas gave his contemporary interpretation of selected passages from the Talmud. His reading of these texts was based on the distinction he made between "Greek" and "Hebrew." "Greek" is the language of philosophy, the humanly valuable kind of abstract thinking that is the crown of our culture and hence the necessary language of anyone who proposes to live in it. But the "Greek" does not radiate from a passionate commitment to the rigorously demanding ethics that Levinas knows to be central to human existence. "Hebrew," the discourse of biblical-Rabbinic Judaism, may be weak in extended abstract reflection but it is utterly centered about ethical duty. Therefore only a continual dialectic between "Greek" and "Hebrew" can give us our full humanity. In the process, both "Greek" and "Hebrew" as we normally know them become more fully what they might be, and so do we.

One of the many things that Levinas admires in Rabbinic literature is the continual over-againstness of the thought. That is, what one sage proposes another disagrees with, a living example of thinking done in the presence of "the face." Moreover, as one reads and expounds these texts today, one not only joins in their discussion as a new "other" but does so as part of a long tradition of other expounders of the text. Since Levinas is much concerned with bringing out the social implications of his ethics, this sense of Jewish community means much to him. This particularity to his thought, among other themes, is the reason some observers have identified him with the postmodern movement.

Levinas found in Rosenzweig his model for a Jewish thinker who refused to give up on philosophy but sought in his "absolute empiricism" to turn it from abstraction to life. In Rosenzweig's positing of "the world" as independent of "man," he sees the seeds of his own view of "the face." Note that the fundamental action that devolves upon "man" in relation to the world is redemption, that kind of sanctifying action that will bring forth the fullest possibilities of life. Levinas' own less transcendent focus will not allow him to posit God as the third independent given of reality. Rather, speaking more phenomenologically, he calls attention to the radical otherness of the other I encounter—what now is termed in a key phrase of this thinking, the "radical alterity" that strikes me. In its radicality and in the absoluteness of the ethical command that arises from each "face," I find a "trace" of the transcendent. This experience, it seems clear to him, lies behind the Bible's rule that we cannot see God's face, and its awesome story that Moses was once allowed to see God's back—the "trace" that accompanies the command—as God, passing by Moses, proclaimed God's ethical character.

A Living Tradition, Ever Old, Ever Made New

Levinas' thought has found only a few followers thus far, perhaps because of the time it has taken to translate his works into English and because of his somewhat uncommon philosophical method. However, substantive considerations are also involved. Phenomenological analysis remains suspect among many philosophers who fear that what it deems the objective results of rational analysis are too private, personal, and subjective to be worthy of the title "philosophy." In Levinas' case this critique of the phenomenological view is exemplified by the question of just how real for most of us is his analysis of "the face." Even when we are open to the individuality of the other we meet, it is not clear that this "alterity," as such, generates an unconditional, binding ethical command in us. Moreover, Levinas' contention that the "face" not only commands us but bind us in one-sided obligation seems contrary to common experience and utterly impractical. To some extent Levinas has acknowledged the validity of this charge by indicating that the utter one-sidedness of the command is more an ideal than an immediate charge. In any case, Jewish law has taken the opposite stand, for the *halachah* significantly limits our responsibility to the other, a view based on its principle that the Torah's behests must be livable. In that spirit, critics charge that Levinas' reading of Rabbinic texts tell us more about Levinas' own ethical passion than about the core concerns of Rabbinic literature. His supporters believe they can answer all these charges and so his thought may well stimulate a new philosophic Judaism.

In sum, inquiring Jews do not lack today for guides to help them think through being a loving inheritor of this great tradition and a person substantially formed by contemporary culture. There is very much more of great interest going on among seriously reflective Jews than has been compassed in these pages, and many other interesting possibilities will surely come along. Yet even this record of intellectual and religious vitality among us gives one confidence that the chain of our tradition will yet have many firm links.

Appendix
Why Spinoza Is Not in This Book

Baruch Spinoza (1632–1677) is undoubtedly the Jewish thinker who has had the greatest impact on Western philosophy. Why then have I not given his thought the same attention I gave to the many other thinkers treated in this book? Certainly not because the Amsterdam rabbinate excommunicated him over three centuries ago or from any lingering belief that "Spinozism," as once widely thought, perniciously undermines true religion and thus the social order. Rather his exclusion was dictated by my specific focus: the major intellectual systems combining Judaism and modernity that still influence contemporary discussions of that issue. Spinoza's thought has no place among them even though his ideas once had a considerable influence on Jews thinking about Jewish modernity. Two aspects are worth mentioning.

Early on, it was not his philosophical system but rather his political thought that had a great impact on Jewish thinkers (though the two are clearly related). He elaborated this in his *Theologico-Political Treatise* (1670), a work so radical in its day that he could never again publish anything in his lifetime. Taking human reason as the one reliable source of truth, Spinoza argued that the state should not be grounded in a given religion. Rather it should give its citizens freedom to think for themselves, including making the choice of what religious beliefs they wished to hold, as long as these required them to be good neighbors and useful to society.

That early statement of what Americans have called "separation of church and state"—a doctrine critical to the possibility of Jews having equal political rights—would have been enough to ensure Spinoza a considerable influence on later Jewish political thought. But Spinoza did much more: he gave a modern explanation of why Jewish law appeared to mandate a way of life that separated Jews from non-Jews (thus preventing their full participation in a modern, nonreligious state). He argued that in ancient, pre-philosophic times, God's revelation was needed to give the masses an authoritative way of life. Hence Hebrew Scripture spoke of many matters unrelated to the ethical precepts and Divine reality that reason later showed to be universally required. The Bible should therefore best be understood as the Hebrews' social constitution when they lived as a nation on their own land. Now, people who could think philosophically, like Spinoza, no longer needed any part of this old theological-political thinking since worthy political and religious ideas could be independently, rationally derived. It was this thinking that brought on his estrangement from the Jewish community.

A century later, when the French Revolution made emancipation a genuine possibility, the leaders of the Jewish community there adapted Spinoza's ideas in order to explain how faithful adherence to Judaism could still allow them to be responsible French citizens. Many of the Torah's separatistic laws, they said, applied only to their long-ended national existence or had survived it in their subsequent dispersion only because of segregation and oppression. But, given equality of treatment, then, as the sages had taught, "the law of the land was (Torah) law" for them.

The Later Influence of Spinoza

The political aspects of Spinoza's thought faded from the Jewish community as the Emancipation became established. It was then that a curious adaptation of Spinoza's thought gained a certain prominence among Jewish secularists.

Philosophers esteem Spinoza as the first fully consistent modern mind. Unlike Descartes, he forthrightly rejected religion's claims to possessing eternal truths binding on all; he insisted on finding truth only through the use of reason applied after the model of mathematical proof. This reasoning led him to identify God with nature—more precisely, he said that what we can know of God is natural law, physical and moral. Late nineteenth-century Jewish secularists took Spinoza as their model, using him to justify their break with traditional Jewish observance and belief. However, although Spinoza created an intellectual system infused by what he still called God, the secularists more directly made the scientific view of the universe the foundation of their thought. Oddly enough, though they adulated Spinoza, they also generally advocated education and political activism as the means to transform society ethically. But Spinoza's ethics, grounded in scientific determinism and rational necessity, are essentially intellectual and remain externally passive toward the world's reality. Indeed, his ethical quietism has probably been the major reason that only an occasional thinker has tried to reestablish some form of Spinozism as a significant contemporary reading of Judaism.

In sum, Spinoza is breathtakingly modern in method, content, and the courage to see his assumptions through to their tradition-breaking consequences. But this very resoluteness about reason makes Judaism an anachronism he is content to leave behind. In this he presages the question that modern Jewish rationalists still must face: If truth is universal, is not Judaism dispensable? In any case, though he is one of the first truly modern Western thinkers, he has no direct relevance to the ongoing discussion of theories of how to be both truly modern and robustly Jewish. Therefore he has no place in this book—except, of course, that in a poor imitation of postmodern "doubling," I have, by asserting that thesis, given him one.

A Basic Reading List

This brief bibliography focuses mainly on those works my students have found useful. Since books go out of print quickly but may then later be reissued by other publishers, some diligence may be required in finding a particular title.

Comprehensive works continue to appear in this area. Eliezer Schweid's *Jewish Thought in the Twentieth Century* (Scholars Press, 1992) is written from a Zionist-nationalist perspective. Hence it covers mostly other thinkers than those dealt with in this volume. Norbert Samuelson's *An Introduction to Modern Jewish Philosophy* (SUNY, 1989) treats many of the figures discussed in these pages but does so with a special interest in their philosophic concerns. The last, modern section of Julius Guttmann's *Philosophies of Judaism* (Schocken, 1974) and all of Natan Rotenstreich's *Jewish Philosophy in Modern Times* (Holt, 1968) have a similar focus. William Kaufman takes a less technical approach in *Contemporary Jewish Philosophy* (reissued by Wayne State, 1993) in keeping with his naturalism. Eliezer Berkovits provides Orthodox critiques of the liberals in *Major Themes in Modern Philosophies of Judaism* (Ktav, 1984) as Steven Katz does more broadly and rationalistically in *Post-Holocaust Dialogues* (NYU, 1983). *Contemporary Jewish Religious Thought*, ed. Arthur A. Cohen and Paul Mendes-Flohr (Scribners, 1987) presents 140 short articles on various themes and of varying value. Michael L. Morgan, in *Dilemmas in Modern Jewish Thought*, brings an acute philosophic perspective to bear on many critical issues (Indiana University Press, 1994).

355

1. The Challenge of Modernity to Judaism

In "Part Four, The Modern Period" of *Jewish People, Jewish Thought* (Macmillan, 1980), Robert M. Seltzer provides a sweeping perspective on the turmoil of the Emancipation era. *The Jew in the Modern World*, ed. Paul R. Mendes-Flohr and Jehuda Reinharz (Oxford, 1980), presents a splendid collection of documents relative to this period. Michael Meyer clarifies the early problems of social and intellectual adjustment in *The Origins of the Modern Jew* (Wayne State, 1967). Moses Mendelssohn's small classic *Jerusalem, or On Religious Power and Judaism* has most recently been translated by Allan Arkush (University Press of New England, 1983).

2. Neo-Kantianism: Hermann Cohen

The easiest access is through the shorter writings, and Eva Jospe has selected and thoughtfully introduced a number of these in *Reason and Hope* (Norton, 1971). Cohen's classic, *Religion of Reason out of the Sources of Judaism* (Ungar, 1972) is only occasionally easy to read. The work of Cohen's most sophisticated recent disciple, Steven S. Schwarzschild, has now been gathered by Menachem Kellner as *The Pursuit of the Ideal* (SUNY, 1990). For the position in continuing evolution see Kenneth Seeskin, *Jewish Philosophy in a Secular Age* (SUNY, 1990).

3. Religious Consciousness: Leo Baeck

The Essence of Judaism (Schocken, 1948) is the indispensable guide to Baeck's thought. His later *This People Israel* (Holt, 1965) only continues the earlier book's line of reasoning. The important essays "Mystery and Commandment" and "Romantic Religion" are found in the collection *Judaism and Christianity* (Jewish Publication Society, 1964). The standard study of Baeck's thought is Albert Friedlander, *Leo Baeck: Teacher of Theresienstadt* (Holt, 1968).

4. Nationalism: The Zionist Interpretation of Judaism

Arthur Hertzberg, *The Zionist Idea* (Doubleday, 1959), has gathered key passages from the writings of the major Zionist thinkers and supplied the whole with a searching introduction. Shlomo Avineri discusses many of the thinkers individually in *The Making of Modern Zionism* (Basic Books, 1981). In English, one may find *The Selected Essays of Ahad Ha-Am* (Jewish Publication Society, 1912) and significant *Essays, Letters, Memoirs* (East and West, 1946). More contemporary are: Hillel Halkin, *Letters to an American Friend* (Jewish Publication Society, 1977); Harold Fisch, *The Zionist Revolution* (St. Martin's, 1978); A(vraham) B. Yehoshuah, *Between Right and Right* (Doubleday, 1981); Eliezer Schweid, *The Land of Israel* (Fairleigh Dickinson, 1985); and Arnold Eisen, *Galut* (Indiana University Press, 1986).

5. Naturalism: Mordecai Kaplan

None of his many later books usurped the classic status of *Judaism as a Civilization* (somewhat enlarged edition, Reconstructionist Press, 1957). Kaplan's position on specific issues is often most easily found by consulting *Questions Jews Ask: Reconstructionist Answers* (Reconstructionist Press, 1966). In lieu of a good critical study of Kaplan's thought, one may profitably consult the following: his biography by Mel Scult, *Jewish Thought Faces the 20th Century* (Wayne State, 1993); an anthology of his writings edited by Emanuel S. Goldsmith and Mel Scult, *Dynamic Judaism* (Schocken, 1985); and Arnold Eisen's *The Chosen People* (Indiana University Press, 1983), which trenchantly treats his rejection of this doctrine.

6. The Pioneer Existentialist: Franz Rosenzweig

The standard introduction to this difficult thinker remains *Franz Rosenzweig: His Life and Thought* by Nahum Glatzer (Schocken,

1973). For some simple essays and the critical exchange of letters with Martin Buber on the role of law in Judaism, see *On Jewish Learning* (Schocken, 1965). William Hallo's translation of *The Star of Redemption* (Holt, 1971) is for the intellectually intrepid. A helpful volume on *The Star* as a philosophic work is Stephane Moses' *System and Revelation* (Wayne State, 1992). For the diverse contemporary reception see the essays in *The Philosophy of Franz Rosenzweig*, ed. Paul Mendes-Flohr (University Press of New England, 1987).

7. Religious Existentialism: Martin Buber

The easier introduction remains Malcolm Diamond, *Martin Buber: Jewish Existentialist* (Oxford, 1960), but the more searching, standard work is Maurice Friedman, *Martin Buber: The Life of Dialogue* (Chicago, 1955). Buber's Jewishness is best met in the essays gathered in *Israel and the World* (Schocken, 1965), though it is based on his general theory of existence and religiosity, *I and Thou*. It is available in two translations, one by Walter Kaufmann (Scribners, 1970) and an earlier one by Ronald Gregor Smith (Scribners, 1958). Some insight into his thinking may be gained by consulting the one-volume Buber biography by Maurice Friedman, *Encounter on the Narrow Ridge* (Paragon, 1993).

8. Neo-Traditionalism: Abraham Heschel

The pivotal work remains *God in Search of Man* (Jewish Publication Society, 1956), which is best supplemented by *Man Is Not Alone* (Jewish Publication Society, 1951) and various of his essays, such as those on evil in *The Insecurity of Freedom* (Farrar, Straus, and Giroux, 1966) and on time versus place in Judaism in *The Sabbath* (Farrar, Straus, and Young, 1951; but see subsequent printings where he appended an essay qualifying his views). On the Land of Israel, see *Israel, an Echo of Eternity* (Farrar, Straus, and Giroux, 1969). John C. Merkle's

Genesis of Faith (Collier Macmillan, 1984) is helpful but not yet the critical academic introduction to Heschel's thought we ought to have.

9. *Confronting the Holocaust*

Elie Wiesel's extensive writing on the Holocaust finds caring theological treatment in *The Vision of the Void* by Michael Berenbaum (Wesleyan, 1978). The first edition of *After Auschwitz* by Richard L. Rubenstein (Bobbs Merrill, 1966) has been significantly modified in the work's second edition (Johns Hopkins, 1993). The development of Emil Fackenheim's thought through several decades of writing can most easily be tracked in the reader *The Jewish Thought of Emil Fackenheim*, ed. Michael L. Morgan (Wayne State, 1987), but his culminating statement, *To Mend the World* (Schocken, 1982), deserves attention in full. A second edition, with an additional preface responding to some of his critics, extends Fackenheim's thought somewhat (Indiana University Press, 1994). Irving Greenberg's thinking about the Holocaust has not yet been given book-length exposition but two key statements are "Cloud of Smoke, Pillar of Fire: Judaism, Christianity and Modernity After the Holocaust," in *Auschwitz: Beginning of a New Era*, ed. Eva Fleischner (Ktav, 1977), and the pamphlet "Voluntary Covenant" (National Jewish Resource Center [now CLAL], n.d.). Eliezer Berkovits' most significant work on this topic is *Faith After the Holocaust* (Ktav, 1973). David Blumenthal's *Facing the Abusing God* (Westminster/John Knox, 1993), by linking the Holocaust with various varieties of interpersonal abuse, has given us the first new if debatable insight in a decade into this ever-deepening mystery.

10. A *Theology of Modern Orthodoxy: Joseph B. Soloveitchik*

Three major papers are available, two focusing on his confrontation with rationalism and one ranging more broadly over the dialectical nature of being human and its religious consequences: the early classic (in Hebrew) is translated as *Halakhic Man* (Jewish Publication Society, 5743/1983), while a previously unpublished study appeared as *The Halakhic Mind* (Free Press, 1986); the essay "The Lonely Man of Faith" (*Tradition*, Summer 1965) has been reprinted as a free-standing volume (Doubleday, 1992). His subjective, existential side remains in his untranslated major Hebrew statement "*Uvikashtem Misham*" ("And from there you shall seek" *Adonai*, your God . . . Dt. 4:29). It is in *Hadarom* (Vol. 47, Tishri 5739/1978). Michael Wyschogrod's *The Body of Faith* (Seabury, 1983) and David Hartman's *A Living Covenant* (Free Press, 1985) can be put in context given the fine collection of papers *Orthodoxy Confronts Modernity*, ed. Jonathan Sacks (Ktav, 1991).

11. The Turn to Mysticism

Something of Zalman Schachter-Shalomi's "teaching" may be found in his books (with various disciples) *The First Step* (Bantam, 1983) and *Paradigm Shift* (Aronson, 1993). For similar insight into Lawrence Kushner consult *Honey from the Rock* (Harper, 1977); *The River of Light* (Rossel, 1981); and *God Was in This Place and I, I Did Not Know* (Jewish Lights, 1991). Adin Steinsaltz's view of *kabbalah*, classic Jewish mysticism, is found in *The Thirteen Petaled Rose* (Basic Books, 1980). Aryeh Kaplan's many publications regularly touch on the mystic experience. Two treat it quite directly: *Jewish Meditation* (Schocken, 1985) and the posthumous *Innerspace* (Moznaim, 1990). A rather philosophical approach to *Rav Avraham Itzhak HaCohen Kook* is taken by Benjamin Ish-Shalom (SUNY, 1993). A reader of his many writings, *Abraham Isaac Kook* (Paulist Press, 1978), was compiled and translated by Ben Zion Bokser. Arthur Green's major statement is *Seek My Face, Speak My Name* (Aronson, 1992).

12. Postmodern Judaism: Eugene B. Borowitz

The mature argument is presented in *Renewing the Covenant* (Jewish Publication Society, 5752/1991). Its companion volume, in which the application of the emerging thought became one critical test of its adequacy, is *Exploring Jewish Ethics* (Wayne State, 1990).

13. *Jewish Feminist Theology (by Ellen M. Umansky)*

To date there have been no published volumes of essays by Jewish feminist theologians nor any book-length analysis of Jewish feminist theology (though such volumes would be enormously useful). However, *On Being a Jewish Feminist*, ed. Susasnnah Heschel (Schocken, 1983), and *Weaving the Visions: New Patterns in Feminist Spirituality*, ed. Judith Plaskow and Carol P. Christ (Harper and Row, 1989), include a number of Jewish theological essays, and *Four Centuries of Jewish Women's Spirituality*, ed. Ellen M. Umansky and Dianne Ashton (Beacon, 1992), offers a number of rituals, prayers, religious poems, *midrashim*, sermons, and so on written by Jewish women between 1567 and 1990. The most complete exposition of Judith Plaskow's theology remains *Standing Again at Sinai: Judaism from a Feminist Perspective* (Harper and Row, 1990). Also noteworthy is the more recent "The Problem of Evil" in *The Reconstructionist* (Spring 1992) and "The Ambiguity of God," *Tikkum* (September/October 1991). Among Rachel Adler's many theological works, recommended are "I've Had Nothing Yet So I Can't Take More," *Moment* (September 1983); "Breaking Boundaries," *Tikkun* (May/June 1991); "In Your Blood, Live: Re-visions of a Theology of Purity," *Tikkun* (Vol. 8, No. 1); and "Feminist Folktales of Justice: Robert Cover as a Resource for the Renewal of *Halakha*," *Conservative Judaism* (Spring 1993). Those interested in a clear exposition of Marcia Falk's theological approach should read her "Notes on Composing New Blessings" in *Weaving the Visions*; "What About God?" *Moment* (1985); and "Toward a Feminist Jewish Reconstruction of Monotheism," *Tikkun* (Vol. 4, No. 4), while especially helpful in delineating Drorah Setel's theological visions are "Feminist Reflections on Separation and Unity in Jewish Theology," *Journal of Feminist Studies in Religion* (Vol. 2, No. 1); "Feminist Insights and the Question of Method" in Adela Collins et al., *Feminist*

Perspectives on Biblical Scholarship (Scholar's Press, 1985); and "Prophets and Pornography: Female Sexual Imagery in Hosea," in *Feminist Interpretations of the Bible,* ed. Letty Russell (Westminster Press, 1985). Finally, essays in which Ellen Umansky describes her own theology include "Reimaging the Divine," *Response* (Winter 1981–1982); "Creating a Jewish Feminist Theology" in *Weaving the Visions;* and "Beyond Androcentrism: Feminist Challenges to Judaism," *Journal of Reform Judaism* (Winter 1990).

14. Looking Ahead

Neil Gillman's theology is explicated in *Sacred Fragments* (Jewish Publication Society, 5750/1990) while Elliot Dorff has limited his focus to *Knowing God* (Aronson, 1992). (David Blumenthal also is part of the eclectic school. For his most extensive theological statement, see the listing for Chapter 9.) Louis Jacobs' grand reading of Jewish religious thought is found in *A Jewish Theology* (Behrman House, 1973), which can be supplemented by his intensive study of the Maimonidean "creed," *Principles of the Jewish Faith* (Basic Books, 1964). His defense of his method is found in the opening pages of *God, Torah, Israel* (HUC Press, 1990). David Novak's religious philosophy surfaces in several of his works, most notably *Halakhah in a Theological Dimension* (Scholars Press, 1985); *The Image of the Non-Jew in Judaism* (Mellen Press, 1983); and *Jewish Social Ethics* (Oxford, 1992). (For Schwarzschild's and Seeskin's philosophical papers see the bibliography for Chapter 2; for Moses' philosophical approach to Rosenzweig, see the list for Chapter 6.) An intriguing version of the *Correlations in Rosenzweig and Levinas* (Princeton, 1992) is presented by Robert Gibbs. The Jewish Levinas may be found in *Difficult Freedom,* trans. Sean Hand (Johns Hopkins, 1990), and *Nine Talmudic Readings,* trans. Annette Aronowicz (Indiana University Press, 1990). Perhaps the philosophical density of Emanuel Levinas' style and substance can be overcome by way of *The Levinas Reader,* ed. Sean Hand (Blackwell, 1989).

Index

363